Echoes of Truth:

Christianity in The Lord of the Rings

Michael C. Haldas

Text Copyright © 2018 Michael C. Haldas
Cover Illustration *Lembas and Miruvor* © 2018 Elaina Olga

First published by Luna Press Publishing, Edinburgh, 2018

Echoes of Truth: Christianity in The Lord of the Rings©2018. All rights reserved. No part of this publication may be reproduced, stored in a retrieval system, or transmitted in any form or by any means, electronic, mechanical, photocopy, recording or otherwise, without prior written permission of the copyright owners. Nor can it be circulated in any form of binding or cover other than that in which it is published and without similar condition including this condition being imposed on a subsequent purchaser.

www.lunapresspublishing.com

ISBN-13: 978-1-911143-61-1

This book is dedicated to J.R.R. Tolkien, whose sub-creation,
and example as a Christian, husband, and father,
have been a source of inspiration, comfort and joy to me
for years uncounted.

Contents

Abbreviations	v
Introduction	1

PART ONE: THE CHRISTIAN ETHOS IN *THE LORD OF THE RINGS* — 11

Chapter 1: The Nature of Reality	13
Chapter 2: The Importance of Choice	24
Chapter 3: Life and Death	37
Chapter 4: The Nature and Aspects of Evil	43
Chapter 5: Temptation	59
Chapter 6: The Power of Sacrifice and Friendship	70
Chapter 7: Pity, Mercy, and Judgment	83

PART TWO: THE CHRISTIAN TYPOLOGY IN *THE LORD OF THE RINGS* — 91

Chapter 8: An Explanation of Typology	93
Chapter 9: Frodo as a Type of Christ	98
Chapter 10: Gandalf as a Type of Christ	104
Chapter 11: Aragorn as a Type of Christ	115
Chapter 12: The Christ-like Traits of Tom Bombadil	123
Chapter 13: The Holy Spirit in *The Lord of the Rings*	128
Chapter 14: Holy Communion: Lembas and Miruvor	135
Chapter 15: The Holy Mother, Elbereth, and Galadriel	140
Chapter 16: Other Biblical Types	150
Chapter 17: The Sacraments in *The Lord of the Rings*	158

Author's Note	165
Acknowledgements	166
Bibliography	167

Abbreviations

The Lord of the Rings	*LotR*
The Fellowship of the Ring	*FotR*
The Two Towers	*TT*
The Return of the King	*RotK*
The Hobbit	*TH*
The Silmarillion	*TSil*
Unfinished Tales of Númenor and Middle-earth	*UT*
On Fairy-Stories	*OFS*

Introduction

I have had two seminal and transcendent reading moments in my life. The first was in the early 1970s when I was six years old. My mother had bought me *The Children's Bible* published by Golden Press and I remember flipping through it while alone in my bedroom. Something struck me when I came to pages 362 and 363. It was a picture of Jesus standing atop a mountain with His arms upraised and looking toward heaven. Flying around Him with horns, wings and cloven hooves was the devil who was pointing downwards towards a kingdom on earth. The scene was from Matthew 4, "the temptation in the wilderness." I retrospectively realised that what captivated me in that moment was the Holy Spirit, and I became fascinated with Jesus. This fascination would eventually turn into my Christian faith and devotion to my relationship with Christ.

The second moment came in 1977 when my late cousin started raving about a book called *The Hobbit* and its sequel *The Lord of the Rings*. I grew curious and eventually bought a copy of each. I was hooked immediately and devoured both books that spring and summer. I remember finally finishing *The Lord of the Rings* while visiting my aunt and uncle in Potomac, Maryland. Some people say they remember where they were when Kennedy was shot, the first moon landing, September 11, or other major world events. But I remember my exact locations where I finished *TH* and *LotR*. When I finished *LotR* I felt like someone kicked me hard in the stomach – not only because of its melancholy ending with a broken Frodo going overseas for healing but because I realized that I had just finished the greatest fiction story I had ever read and would ever read. It was all over. There was nothing more to look forward to. Life at that moment temporarily ceased to have purpose now that I was done reading *LotR*. After a serious bout of situational depression, it eventually dawned on me that I could read Tolkien again (and again, and again) and I have done so now almost annually for nearly forty years.

At the time, I finished *TH* and *LotR* (and eventually *The Silmarillion*[1],

---

1. *The Silmarillion* is divided into five parts: 1) *The Ainulindalë*, which is Tolkien's version of the creation story; 2) *The Valaquenta* which is a description of the prominent "God and Goddesses" of his universe; 3) *The Quenta Silmarillion* which is the main story and history of the time before time was counted and the First Age of his universe; 4) *The Akallabêth* which

Unfinished Tales of Númenor and Middle-earth and anything else Tolkien-related that I could get my hands on, I did not see any connections between my love of Christ, the Bible, and Christianity with my love for Tolkien's works. Tolkien's world was simply the most in-depth, complex, and coolest thing ever which moved me like nothing else in reading ever had. I could not get enough of it. It was not until the mid-to-late 1990s that I started to realize just how devout of a Christian Tolkien was and just how much of his faith was deeply embedded in his works, especially in *LotR*. This understanding opened a new world for me and renewed my enthusiasm. It suddenly made so much sense to me why I fell in love with Middle-earth and had consumed any book that I could find dealing with the Christian treatment of Tolkien's works. As I reread *LotR* and his other works I saw them through new eyes and they enriched me even more than they did before.

Facts Versus Truth

Tolkien once wrote "the chief purpose of life, for any one of us, is to increase according to our capacity our knowledge of God by all the means we have, and to be moved by it to praise and thanks."[2] For me personally, I have always found fantasy books such as Tolkien's, C.S. Lewis's, J.K. Rowling's Harry Potter Series, and others that may be interpreted as reflecting a Christian worldview to be a primary vehicle to understand and deepen my relationship with God. Perhaps it is the medium of storytelling that speaks to my heart since Christ Himself chose stories in the form of parables to communicate profound truths. Or perhaps it is because good fantasy grounded in a Christian worldview ultimately deals with truth though not necessarily facts.

People in my life who have told me they dislike the fantasy genre have said so because they prefer books that are "more realistic." With all due respect to them, I think they miss the point of good fantasy. What is more realistic than truth? Further, what fantasy books are grounded more in truth and thus reality than Tolkien's? As his great friend C.S. Lewis once said, "When we journey to Middle-earth, we do not retreat from reality: we rediscover it."[3] And what is the reality we are discovering that moves us so much? What is the gift that Tolkien is giving us through his work? Professor Peter Kreeft answers these questions poetically when he writes "...*The Lord*

---

is a history of the Second Age primarily focused on the rise and fall of the kingdom of men known as Númenor; and 5) *Of the Rings of Power and the Third Age* which is a summary of the Third Age. These parts are important to distinguish because when I refer to *TSil* I am referring to it as a whole.

2. Humphrey Carpenter, *The Letters of J.R.R. Tolkien*, Houghton Mifflin, 2000, Letter 310, p. 400.

3. Devon Brown, *The Christian World of The Hobbit*, Abingdon Press, 2012, E-book.

of the Rings is a gift of divine grace, an opening of the curtain that veils Heaven to earthly eyes, a tiny telepathic contact with the Mind of God."⁴

The "Experience" of Tolkien

Reading and rereading *LotR* and Tolkien's other works helped me through some very tough times when I needed a place of comfort to retreat to in my youth. My experience is not unique. As the late Stratford Caldecott points out, "Many return to *LotR* again and again for refreshment of the soul – perhaps even for the kind of healing the author must have experienced writing it."⁵

Tolkien is able to bring us this comfort through *LotR* because he introduces and draws us closer to both the Person of Christ and the nature of reality as sacramental in a subtle yet extremely powerful way. Middle-earth is "gloriously haunted by the Presence of a Person 'who is never absent and never named.'"⁶ and allows us to experience Christian sacramentality through its beauty and holiness.⁷

Naturally, as evidenced by so many Tolkien biographies, experiencing his work leads to greater curiosity about the man. In addition to being a devout Christian, he was also a committed family man with his priorities in order. He went to Mass every day, loved his wife and four children, performed his professional work and then worked on his great mythology when time permitted. Perhaps if Tolkien had been a self-centred man who put his art before his faith, family, and work, we may have had more works to enjoy than we do. However, I suspect the beauty of his writing, in large part, is due to it coming from a man who loved God and his family first.

The Lord of the Rings and Hints of Christianity

Even as a young reader who first read *The Lord of the Rings* as a great adventure story and who knew some of the basics of Christianity, I found some clear clues that *LotR* had at least some Christian elements. For example, Tolkien writes in the opening chapter that the "long expected party" celebrates both Bilbo's one hundred and eleventh birthday and Frodo's thirty-third. He explains that the thirty-third birthday for all hobbits is significant because it means in hobbit culture that they are coming of age. I remember knowing, even as a youth, that thirty-three was the accepted age

---

4. Peter Kreeft, *The Philosophy of Tolkien*, Ignatius, 2005, p. 143.
5. Stratford Caldecott, *The Power of the Ring: Spiritual Vision Behind the Lord of the Rings and The Hobbit*, Crossroad Publishing Company, 2003, p. 5.
6. Jim Ware, *Finding God in The Hobbit*, SaltRiver, 2006, pp. 167-168.
7. Craig Bernthal, *Tolkien's Sacramental Vision*, Second Spring, 2014, p. 289.

when Christ was crucified.

Of course, this alone is not enough to claim that *LotR* is a Christian work. But there were more clues. I recall perusing the appendices at the end of *The Return of the King* and seeing that the Fellowship started their quest on December 25, Christ's date of birth. I knew from reading *LotR* that the Ring was destroyed on March 25, which is traditionally considered in Christendom to be the date of the first Good Friday, the Fall of Adam and Eve, and also the Annunciation when the Angel Gabriel visited Mary to announce the conception of Christ (see Luke 1:26-38). But all that Tolkien said in the narrative concerning when the Fellowship left Rivendell was that "It was a cold grey day near the end of December."[8] Professor Tom Shippey makes an interesting point that the main action of *LotR* take place between Christmas, December 25, and the Annunciation, March 25. He states that the latter is also the date Adam and Eve fell and the effects it leads to are the purpose for the birth, death, and resurrection of Christ.[9]

There are more allusions, such as Barliman Butterbur having to pay "thirty silver pennies" to Bill Ferny as recompense for the hobbits' stolen ponies. It is hard not to associate Bill Ferny's act of treachery being "rewarded" with thirty pieces of silver with that of Judas's compensation by the Jewish leaders for betraying Christ. An even more overt nod to Christian tradition is Faramir's prayerful looking to the west and offering a form of grace before the meal when he says "we look towards Númenor that was, and beyond to Elvenhome that is, and to that which is beyond Elvenhome and will ever be."[10]

Is Christianity in *The Lord of the Rings* Intentional or Unintentional?

There are many hints of Christianity in *The Lord of the Rings* and it legitimately raises the question of whether this was Tolkien's true intent. Was he, like his friend C.S. Lewis, deliberately trying to insert Christian messages into his work? It would seem not, since in *LotR* (and *TH* and *TSil*) men, elves, dwarves, and hobbits do not have organized religion. God is not even mentioned in *LotR* except for a brief reference to "the One" in the appendices.[11] Fortunately, we have the author's answer to this question:

> "*The Lord of the Rings* is of course a fundamentally religious and Catholic work; unconsciously so at first, but consciously in the revision. That is why I have not put in, or have cut out, practically all references to anything like

---

8. J.R.R. Tolkien, *The Lord of the Rings*, Houghton Mifflin, 1954-5, 1965-6, p. 272.
9. Tom Shippey, *J.R.R. Tolkien: Author of the Century*, Houghton Mifflin, 2000, pp. 208-209.
10. Op. cit. [8], p. 661.
11. Op. cit. [8], p. 1013.

"religion," to cults or practices, in the imaginary world. For the religious element is absorbed into the story and the symbolism. However that is very clumsily put, and sounds more self-important than I feel. For as a matter of fact, I have consciously planned very little; and should chiefly be grateful for having been brought up (since I was eight) in a Faith that has nourished me and taught me all the little that I know."[12]

Tolkien essentially believed that as human beings our creative capacity, especially for writing fantasy, reflects God, our Creator since God created us in His image and likeness (Genesis 1:26).[13]

Tolkien coined the term "subcreation" to describe what we do when we create works of art or anything else. He believed that despite our "fallenness", sin, and sinful choices, we still retain this creative ability in our nature because it is God's nature that He put within us.[14] Further, Tolkien believed that the fairy story or fantasy story was one of the highest forms of subcreation. He did so because he believed that the Gospel was the greatest "story" of all; the ultimate fairy story. I put story in quotes because for him it was a story that is true, or better stated, the ultimate truth, God inserted Himself into human history. God is revealed to us, in part, through story, so good fantasy stories can be an echo of this ultimate revelation.

Christianity naturally flowed into Tolkien's work because of who he was and what he believed. As he himself stated, the religious element in *LotR* is absorbed into the story itself and its symbolism. The transcendent truths of Christianity bubble up throughout this story.[15] But Tolkien was telling a story, not proclaiming a message. Both philosophically and personally he was not comfortable with direct evangelical messages. We see this in a letter he wrote where he explicitly said, commenting on his own personal nature, that he expressed what he feels most deeply in tales and myths.[16]

By his own admission, *LotR* and his related works are stories set in a pre-Christian age so they can pre-figure Christianity and reflect it, but not express it in full. Many find *LotR* and Tolkien's other works to have a pervasive sadness. The author states that this comes from the absence of Christ and thus the absence of a means for redemption and salvation. To be fair, this sadness is also the result of the influence on Tolkien of Norse myths where heroes fought heroically despite the inevitability of Ragnarök.[17] Tolkien imagined *LotR* and his other stories of Middle-earth to take place in our

---

12. Op. cit. [2], Letter 142, p. 172.
13. J.R.R. Tolkien, "On Fairy Stories," *Tales from the Perilous Realm*, HarperCollins, 2008, E-book.
14. Op. cit.
15. Kurt Brunner and Jim Ware, *Finding God in The Lord of the Rings*, Tyndale, 2001, p. x.
16. Op. cit. [2], Letter 340, p.172.
17. Matthew Dickerson, *A Hobbit Journey*, Brazos Press, 2012, E-book.

deep past in time long before Christ as he describes in both the prologue and appendix D of *LotR*. He states in one of his letters that the events of *LotR* take place more than 6,000 years ago.[18] He explored incorporating the idea of God incarnating, though not in *LotR*. Within *Morgoth's Ring*, Volume X of *The History of Middle-earth* series, there is a fascinating tale called *Athrabeth Finrod ah Andreth* (*The Debate of Finrod and Andreth*). Finrod is an immortal elf and Andreth is a mortal woman and they speculate about Ilúvatar, God, eventually incarnating to heal the world.

Tolkien's Christian worldview pushed itself up of its own accord.[19] Because he was a Roman Catholic, his understanding of Christianity was sacramental in nature. With this understanding, some have speculated that he longed to smuggle a vision of goodness and truth into the readers' lives and that he achieved this through sacramental theology, and the understanding that there is holiness that hovers over all things.[20] However this is not apparent at first due to how Tolkien, by his own admission, tells his stories: "I have deliberately written a tale, which is built on or out of certain 'religious' ideas, but is not an allegory of them (or anything else)."[21]

LotR contains many elements of Christianity but does not repeat it.[22] It is permeated with a sense of eternity, of the objective order of good and evil, and of an all-wise providence (the sense that God somehow orders all things, even apparent coincidences). We see in *LotR*, the spirit of courtesy, the respect for women, the determination to protect the weak, the virtues of courage, fortitude, prudence, and justice. These are patterns of goodness present in the Gospels.[23]

Sometimes, both readers and critics misunderstand the Christian aspects of *LotR* and Tolkien's other works. I would argue that this is in part because Tolkien's depth of understanding of Christianity was more profound, his understanding of language as a professor and philologist was unrivalled, and thus he saw deeper than most. Some have written that the Christian understanding of *The Lord of the Rings* by many is forced and misguided to some degree. For example, Ronald Hutton writes in his essay, *The Pagan Tolkien*, "…while I am happy to accept Tolkien as a Christian author with reference to his personal beliefs, and to some of his published work, I do not think this can be done simply and straightforwardly, with reference to his mythology."[24] Some Christians have rejected *LotR* as a Christian work using

---

18. Op. cit. [2], Letter 211, p.283.
19. Op. cit. [15], pp. xiii-xiv.
20. Paul E. Kerry (Editor), *The Ring and the Cross*, Farleigh Dickinson, 2011, p.22, quoted from Kerry Dearborn, "Theology and Morality" 98, 96.
21. Op. cit. [2], Letter 211, pp.283-284.
22. Op. cit. [9], p. 210.
23. Op. cit. [5].
24. Ronald Hutton, *The Pagan Tolkien, The Ring and the Cross: Christianity in the Lord of*

a similar, and even stronger arguments. Ministry leader Eric Barger writes, "I have come to the final conclusion that those wishing to be consistent with scripture should completely abstain from endorsing, reading the books, or watching the motion picture adaptations of *The Lord of the Rings*."[25]

Craig Bernthal argues that critics such as these lack an in-depth sacramental understanding of Christianity and thus mistakenly attribute aspects of Tolkien's work such reverence of the living beauty of the natural world and other aspects as pagan. In his response to Patrick Curry's assertion that "Catholicism desacralizes the world, and so Tolkien looked to paganism for succour," he argues that this "gets everything backwards." He points out that the sacramental understanding of Christianity inherent in Catholicism is what Tolkien drew upon and what made his world "grace-filled."[26] It may be noted that the early Church, and probably Tolkien himself, saw pagan myths as incomplete pointers to the truth of Christ.[27] Professor Matthew Dickerson further points out that what Tolkien did in *LotR* is not too different from what St. Paul did when trying to convince the Athenians about the truth of Christ. Paul used the Athenians' pagan understanding of their "Unknown God" to guide them to a conversation about his "known God" in the Person of Jesus Christ.[28] Perhaps Humphrey Carpenter sums it up best:

> "Some have puzzled over the relation between Tolkien's stories and his Christianity, and have found it difficult to understand how a devout Roman Catholic could write with such conviction about a world where God is not worshipped…Tolkien cast his mythology in this form because he wanted it to be remote and strange, and yet at the same time not to be a lie. He wanted the mythological and legendary stories to express his own moral view of the universe…So while God is present in Tolkien's universe, He remains unseen."[29]

The Contents of this Book

The Christianity in *LotR* is both intentional during the initial writing and subsequent rewriting and drafting; and is unintentional in that it also flowed unconsciously into his work due to who he was. It is embedded, or absorbed, so deeply in the story it is often not consciously recognized, or at least not immediately, but instead unconsciously experienced and felt. Ironically,

---

the Rings, Madison Teaneck Fairleigh Dickinson University Press, 2001, p.68.
25. https://www.ericbarger.com/lotr.c.c.2.htm. [Accessesed 30 May 2018].
26. Op. cit. [7], p.35.
27. Matthew Dickerson & David O'Hara, *From Homer to Harry Potter*, Brazo Press, 2006, pp. 32-33, 50-51.
28. Op. cit. [17]..
29. Op. cit. [3].

this actually makes his work *more* Christian rather than *less* Christian. In my book *Sacramental Living: Understanding Christianity as a Way of Life*, I make the same argument as the late Father Alexander Schmemann, a respected and revered Priest and author, when he wrote that Christianity was meant to be the end of religion because religion is only needed when there is a wall of separation between God and man.[30] *LotR* does not have explicit religion in it because it was written by a man who experienced Christianity as a complete way of life, not something compartmentalized into a service once a week. Because these barriers of separation did not exist in his mind and heart, it comes through in his worldview reflected in his work.

In this book, I highlight much of the Christian element that I believe Tolkien deliberately infused into *LotR* and what I believe he unconsciously poured into the story due to his worldview. I also take the liberty to discuss elements of Christianity that struck me in *LotR* that I cannot claim he intentionally or unintentionally put in the story. Certain things I read simply affected me as Christian. Tolkien acknowledged that *LotR*, once created, was no longer his, in one of his letters: "Of course The L.R. does not belong to me. It has been brought forth and must now go its appointed way in the world, though naturally I take a deep interest in its fortunes, as a parent would of a child. I am comforted to know that it has good friends to defend it against the malice of its enemies."[31]

Professor Craig Bernthal in his book *Tolkien's Sacramental Vision* makes the point that despite many books written on the Christianity in Tolkien's works, it is still not a universally accepted way of approaching Tolkien's writings. He goes on to describe several of the books that do tackle this subject and admits that what he wrote is not completely new but his contribution focuses strongly on the Catholic sacramentality of Tolkien's work.[32] I share the same sentiment. My contribution is a very deep dissection of *The Lord of the Rings* though I do reference Tolkien's other works where needed. Further, I discuss aspects of his work that I have not found in the many wonderful books I have read that Bernthal references. This should not be understood as me being negative toward other works. Rather, since Tolkien was a philologist who understood language more than most and was so deliberate with his words, I take a very exacting approach in this book in the spirit of the Professor. Though I do reference and quote other works, for the most part I use Tolkien's books, the letters he wrote that were compiled by Humphrey Carpenter, and accounts of direct conversations with him as my primary sources.

This book is divided into two parts: 1) Christian Ethos and 2) Christian

---

30. Father Alexander Schmemann, *For the Life of the World*, SVS Press, 1963, pp. 19-20.
31. Op. cit. [2], p. 365.
32. Op. cit. [7], pp. 18-20.

Typology. Ethos is a Greek word meaning character that is used to describe the guiding beliefs or ideals that characterize a community, nation, or ideology. In Part 1 I deal with how *The Lord of the Rings* reflects many of the guiding beliefs within Christianity.

Christian typology, in its formal understanding, is essentially a term that points to the predictive relationship of the Old and New Testaments. In other words, the people, events, or statements of the Old Testament are viewed as types that pre-figure and point to the person, life, and events of Christ and His revelation in the New Testament. For example, Abraham being willing to sacrifice his beloved son, Isaac, the son of the promise made to him by God (see Genesis 15 18, 21 and especially 22) is a "type" pointing to the ultimate sacrifice God will make by sacrificing His beloved son, Jesus Christ. In Part 2, I broaden the definition of typology as I endeavour to demonstrate people and events in Tolkien's work that are types of Christ, the Eucharist, Mary, and others.

My hope is that you will enjoy reading this book as much as I enjoyed writing it

Michael Haldas

PART ONE

THE CHRISTIAN ETHOS IN *THE LORD OF THE RINGS*

Chapter 1: The Nature of Reality

When Frodo first beholds the Noldorin elf, Glorfindel, during his flight from the Nazgûl, he does so with perception altered by the shard of the Morgul-knife working its way toward his heart. He sees the mighty elf as a shining figure of white light. "To Frodo, it appeared that a white light was shining through a form and raiment of the rider, as if through a thin veil."[1] As he lies in bed in Rivendell recovering from his knife wound, Gandalf explains to him that he momentarily saw Glorfindel "as he is upon the other side" and that great elven lords like Glorfindel who once dwelt in the Blessed Realm of Aman have great power over "both the Seen and the Unseen."[2]

Before this we see a glimpse of a reality of some nether world when Frodo is stabbed on Weathertop. Moments before the stabbing, he gives in to the irresistible pull of the Ring generated by the presence of the Nazgûl. Whereas in one reality the Ringwraiths are shadowy figures wrapped in dark cloaks, Frodo, with the Ring on his finger, can gaze "beneath their black wrappings" and see their grey hair, grey robes, "merciless eyes," and silver helms.

What was Tolkien conveying through these descriptions and his explicit mention of the seen and the unseen? Frodo does not question Gandalf's mention of the unseen thus accepting this reality without any need for further discussion. It is possible to infer that, growing up with Bilbo, Frodo already has knowledge of the seen and the unseen but now is able to match it with his experience. Bilbo knew much about the history and nature of both the Eldar and the elder days, as evidenced by his eventual writings that Tolkien attributes to him in the Red Book of Westmarch. Bilbo also had frequent visits to the Shire from Gandalf and likely had many conversations about various topics.

Beyond this, Tolkien seems to expect his readers to know about the reality of the seen and unseen worlds and does not feel the need to explain it in any more detail. But what is this reality that seems to be beyond normal sight and can only be perceived by those who are discerning? What truth of Christianity does this echo and why is it critically important to appreciate and

---
1. J.R.R. Tolkien, *The Lord of the Rings*, Houghton Mifflin, 1954-5, 1965-6, p. 209.
2. Op. cit., pp. 216-217.

better understand *The Lord of the Rings* and Tolkien's universe in general?

The answer to these questions is that Christians see God as the creator of both the material and spiritual dimensions of reality and these two dimensions are closely bound together.³ Tolkien sees his created universe the same way, periodically reminding readers of both the seen and unseen reality of his created world where the unseen and spiritual is just as tangible and real as the seen and material."⁴

Viewing the spiritual and material as two aspects of the same reality that are linked is critical to understanding Christianity. It is also, in my opinion, critical to understanding Tolkien's universe and thus why I address this topic as the first chapter of this book.

As a Roman Catholic, Tolkien's view of reality was sacramental as Professor Craig Bernthal describes:

> "The Catholic vision is that the holy is not located outside of material universe that is corrupt, but within a material universe that is mainly good, though fallen, and this means that holiness can enter through the senses and that the world at large has a sacramental quality. Christianity makes spiritual goods out of the most mundane material: bread, water, wine, oil; everything is meaningful."⁵

For instance, the elf Glorfindel exists on both the spiritual and material planes at once. He is both flesh and blood, and the shining vessel of light that Frodo sees. This type of existence is mirrored in how Tolkien understood Holy Communion (see Chapter 14).

Catholics share the belief with the Orthodox that the Eucharist (Holy Communion) is composed of bread and wine that becomes mystically transformed by the Holy Spirit into the body and blood of Jesus Christ. The reality they see, touch, smell and taste is the bread and wine; the reality they experience is the body and blood of Jesus Christ and communion with Him.

Tolkien, among his many pursuits, was also an editor of the Jerusalem Bible that was published in 1966. Specifically, he translated the Book of Jonah. I offer this as a small bit of evidence of his familiarity with Scripture (see *Letters of J.R.R. Tolkien* by Humphrey Carpenter in which Tolkien frequently references the Bible for a broader view of his Biblical knowledge). He was undoubtedly familiar with the three birth stories of Christ written in the Scriptures.

---

3. Rev. Dr. Stanley S. Harakas, "For the Health of Body and Soul: An Eastern Orthodox Introduction to Bioethics. ", https://www.goarch.org/-/for-the-health-of-body-and-soul-an-eastern-orthodox-introduction-to-bioethics. [Accessed 30/05/2018].
4. Matthew Dickerson, *A Hobbit Journey*, Brazos Press, 2012, E-book.
5. Craig Bernthal, *Tolkien's Sacramental Vision*, Second Spring, 2014, p. 24.

In the Bible, in the books of Matthew and Luke, we are told two versions of the story of Christ's birth. In Matthew, we have the visit of the wise men, the star of Bethlehem, the flight of the Holy family to Egypt, and Herod's slaughter of the innocents. In Luke, we are told about the visit of the Archangel Gabriel to Mary, the visit of the heavenly host of angels to the shepherds in the fields, and the manger. Both stories are told from an earthly, or material, point of view.

In the Book of Revelation, Chapter 12, there is a third version of the birth story. In this version, we get a glimpse of what is going on in Heaven, the spiritual plane, though in a somewhat cryptic fashion and one that is subject to multiple interpretations. We are told of a "woman clothed with the sun, the moon under her feet, and on her head a garland of twelve stars" (Revelation 12:1). She is about to give birth. We are then told of a dragon that stands before her waiting for the birth so that he may "devour her Child as soon as it was born." (Revelation 12:4). The woman flees into the wilderness for protection in a place prepared for her by God. The dragon gathers a third of Heaven's angels and makes war in Heaven but is defeated by the Archangel Michael and his angels and is cast down to earth where he then tries to make war on the woman, her Child, and all followers of Christ.

There are several interpretations to this story but many see the woman as Mary, the Child as Christ, and her flight analogous to her journey to Bethlehem and eventually to Egypt to escape Herod's command to slaughter all male children under two years of age. The dragon is undoubtedly Satan. This story has some similar elements to the story told in Matthew and Luke, the material plane, but it clearly portrays what is going on in the spiritual realm.

This type of dual depiction of events – spiritual and material – is important to *LotR* because Tolkien uses an analogous style. Tolkien, by his own admission, despised allegory; so, in *LotR* he did not try to deliberately create characters, events or places that were meant to be a direct representation of something else.[6]

In C.S. Lewis' *The Chronicles of Narnia*, Aslan is an allegorical representation of Christ and the great lion's death at the stone table and subsequent return to life represent the crucifixion and resurrection. Tolkien employs no such device in *LotR* or any of his works concerning his fictional world. When he created it, this understanding of reality from a Christian perspective crept in by its own accord as opposed to a deliberate approach to represent the teachings of Christianity.

Understanding that both the seen and the unseen planes of existence drive the plot of *LotR* is crucial to gaining a fuller picture of the story.

---

6. Op. cit. [1], p. xvii.

The events taking place in the seen world are overtly described by Tolkien through narrative, dialogue, and action. What is driving these events from the unseen world is hinted at and validated by the occasional glimpse into the unseen world that simply lets the reader know it exists. These hints and glimpses ultimately points to the unseen guiding hand of Providence that is critical to the eventual outcome of *LotR*.

Glimpses of Spiritual Reality in *The Lord of the Rings*

The examples of the stabbing on Weathertop and Glorfindel's appearance are by no means the only glimpses of the unseen world that Tolkien offers. As Gandalf and Frodo conclude their conversation about Glorfindel and other events as Frodo lies recuperating in Rivendell, Gandalf observes Frodo and says to himself that Frodo "may become like a glass filled with a clear light for eyes to see that can."[7]

What I find most important about this scene, other than a hint of what Frodo may become, is Gandalf's reference to "eyes that can see." This speaks to the power of discernment and explains why, as Tolkien's characters either grow throughout the story or have native ability because of who and what they are, some can see into the spiritual realm. For example, during their encounter with a group of riders lead by Éomer in Rohan, Aragorn, Legolas, and Gimli must navigate a difficult encounter. The riders are very suspicious of the Three Hunters. It is unusual to see three members of three different races together. They also seemingly appear out of thin air due to the elven cloaks given to them during their stay in Lothlórien. Additionally, Rohan is at war with Saruman, though not formally due to King Théoden's refusal to deal with reality because of the traitor Gríma Wormtongue's poisoning of his mind and body. In particular, this group of riders led by Éomer, who was not deceived by Wormtongue rebelled against his own King's orders and led the men under his charge to hunt orcs. When the Three Hunters speak to them of Lothlórien and Galadriel, it intensifies hostilities since the riders mistakenly believe her to be a sorceress. At one point in the conversation, Aragorn confronts Éomer. During the confrontation, Legolas has a spiritual vision and sees white flame on Aragorn's brow that resemble a shining crown.[8]

Legolas, unlike Gimli, is discerning and sees a brief glimpse Aragorn as he appears on "the other side." "Gimli and Legolas looked at their companion in amazement, for they had not seen him in this mood before. He seemed to have grown in stature while Éomer had shrunk; and in his living face they caught a brief vision of the power and majesty of the kings

---

7. Op. cit. [1], p. 217.
8. Op. cit., p. 423.

of stone. For a moment it seemed to the eyes of Legolas that a white flame flickered on the brows of Aragorn like a shining crown."[9] However, this episode does not elevate Legolas above Gimli. Tolkien does not necessarily create a hierarchy for his characters based on their discernment or any other abilities. Instead, he repeatedly demonstrates in *LotR* that a person's worth is not based on their abilities and stature but rather on their moral integrity. For example, Gimli has simplicity of faith and integrity that enables him to be the first to see through Saruman's deception though he sees no visions of the unseen world. When Gandalf leads Théoden and his riders, Aragorn, Éomer, Legolas, Gimli, Merry and Pippin to the doorsteps of the tower of Orthanc to confront Saruman, the wizard comes out on a balcony to speak to them. He mesmerizes them with his "fair and fitting" words, and they find Gandalf harsh, "rough and proud." It is Gimli who is not deceived and reminds all present that the Saruman is a liar.[10]

Gimli again later demonstrates his unshakeable, matter-of-fact faith when he and Legolas enter Minas Tirith after the Battle of Pelennor Fields. As both the elf and the dwarf observe the city and the improvement work it needs and what they will do to help Aragorn when he becomes king, they use different language. Legolas, the individual in this duo who is given to spiritual vision, uses the word *if* when talking about Aragorn's potential kingship implying that the outcome is still in question. From this it would seem Legolas harbours some doubt. Gimli, who is not given to spiritual vision or perception, simply says *when* Aragorn becomes king.[11] To him there is no doubt.

There are several other glimpses into the spiritual reality similar to Legolas's visions. For example, Pippin seeing the light shining in Gandalf's face as Gandalf rides up to Isengard[12] (this was the first time Merry and Pippin encountered Gandalf the White having last seen him as Gandalf the Grey falling into the abyss in Moria); and Sam seeing Frodo as a white-robed figure with a wheel of fire on his chest and Gollum as a shadow of lust and rage locked in a struggle for the Ring on the slopes of Mount Doom.[13]

But perhaps the most important glimpse into the spiritual reality that pervades *LotR* is one shown in dialogue rather than discerning vision. As Boromir lies dying, he tells Aragorn that he has failed.[14] He falls to the Ring's temptation and so madly desires it, he attacks Frodo, prompting the hobbit to continue to Mordor alone. Furthermore, Boromir fails to prevent

---

9. Op. cit. [1], p. 423.
10. Op. cit., p. 565.
11. Op. cit., p. 854.
12. Op. cit., p. 555.
13. Op. cit., p. 922.
14. Op. cit., p. 404.

Merry and Pippin from being captured by the Uruk-hai. Boromir's failure thus causes the Fellowship to break. In his mind, he has also let down his people since he cannot return to Minas Tirith to lead them in their fight against Sauron.

Yet Aragorn's last words to Boromir are that he has conquered and gained victory so few have gained.[15] By this time in the story it is clear that Aragorn is a person of utmost integrity and character. It is not plausible to think that he would be saying these words just to comfort a dying man. Later in the book, Ioreth, a woman of Gondor, describes Aragorn as a good man but not too soft of speech.[16] So what is Aragorn saying? Matthew Dickerson describes it as a moral victory and that Boromir's sense of failure is based on the outcome on the material plan where Aragorn speaks of the spiritual one.[17] Aragorn gestures towards a greater and more important reality than the physical world.

The reality of what Aragorn says to Boromir is confirmed later in the book. Before leaving to try and rescue Merry and Pippin from the orcs, Aragorn, Legolas, and Gimli, unable to inter him, lay Boromir in one of the three boats they received in Lothlórien. They send the boat to the Falls of Rauros where Aragorn says the river Anduin "will take care at least that no evil creature will dishonor his bones."[18] They watch as the boat plunges over the falls and then perform a funeral service of sorts before leaving to try to save the hobbits. Tolkien writes: "But in Gondor in after-days it long was said that the elven-boat rode the falls and the foaming pool, and bore him down through Osgiliath, and past the many mouths of Anduin, out into the Great Sea at night under the stars."[19]

This is not language that describes someone in perdition. Further, Tolkien confirms Aragorn's statement of Boromir's victory through the ghostly encounter Faramir has with the elven boat carrying the body of his brother.[20] Later, Faramir comments on this vision stating Boromir "died well, achieving some good thing. His face was more beautiful even in life."[21]

This brief dialogue between Aragorn and Boromir and its implications will be revisited later in this book.

The Guiding Hand of Providence

The chapter "The Shadow of the Past" contains a dialogue between Gandalf

---

15. Op. cit. [1], p. 404.
16. Op. cit., p. 945.
17. Op. cit. [4].
18. Op. cit. [1], p. 405.
19. Op. cit., p. 407.
20. Op. cit., p. 651.
21. Op. cit., p. 654.

and Frodo where the wizard explains the history and nature of the Ring and makes the curious statement about "more than one power at work."[22] He implies that there is a force that ordained that Bilbo and then Frodo should find and possess the Ring.

Context is necessary here. *The Lord of the Rings* was published in 1954 and 1955. *The Hobbit* was published in 1937. For many years, readers had virtually no other knowledge of Tolkien's universe except for these two works. Some books about Tolkien and his works were published but the writers of these books had incomplete knowledge of the Tolkien universe. *The Silmarillion* was not published until 1977, four years after Tolkien's death, and *Unfinished Tales* and the twelve volume *History of Middle-earth* series came out between 1980 and 1996.

Apart from one mention in *LotR* Appendices of "the One" and cursory information about the Valar, the readers of Tolkien's works had no knowledge of the cosmological forces behind the creation of Arda prior to the publication of the Silmarillion. However, that does not equal the absence of the underpinning Power in *LotR* and *The Hobbit*. Tolkien writes in one of his letters to his publisher that his works are about "graced and gifted" or "ordained individuals" who have been "inspired and guided by an Emissary."[23]

This unnamed emissary Tolkien refers to, and the other power Gandalf speaks to Frodo about, though never specifically mentioned, can be read as the Christian God. The word 'ordain' is significant, since it is used in *LotR* to imply the work of this other power. We also see in this quote that Tolkien believed that a more explicit discussion of grace, giftedness, and ordination would have spoiled the story. *LotR* echoes the passage in the Book of Acts where St. Paul states "…for in Him [God] we live and move and have our being" (Acts 17:28). Middle-earth is a world of a loving God and his servants who care for it.

At the Council of Elrond, when Frodo learns of the history of the Ring he turns to Aragorn and tells him that the Ring rightly belongs to him. Aragorn replies that it is ordained that Frodo should have it for the present.[24] This is the only mention of this word "ordained" in *LotR*; however, "ordered", "chance" and "called" are also used in the text. Elrond says at the Council of Elrond that he believed those present have been "called." And it not "chance" that has brought them all together.[25] He clearly indicates his belief that it is no accident that Frodo, the Ring, and the rest of those at the council

---

22. Op. cit. [1], pp. 54-55.
23. Humphrey Carpenter, *The Letters of J.R.R. Tolkien*, Houghton Mifflin, 2000, Letter 281, p. 365.
24. Op. cit. [1], p. 240.
25. Op. cit., p. 236.

are present at that moment in time.

Os Guinness, author of *The Call*, points out that if we are called, there must be a caller.[26] Tolkien, as a Christian, believed that caller to be God. It is possible to presume that Elrond believed the council was the result of Ilúvatar working through his Valar. This is somewhat validated through the prophetic dream Boromir had once and that his brother Faramir had twice (an important point that I will explore in Chapter 2). In his dream, Boromir saw a pale light in "the West" and a voice coming from it that spoke the prophecy that led him to journey to Rivendell. Tolkien capitalized the word "West" in his writing indicating something more than simply a compass point. The West is the direction in which lies the Blessed Realm, the abode of the Valar. This is, perhaps, a hint at the Valar's intervention here and perhaps it can even be attributed it to the Vala Irmo, known as Lórien, who is "the master of visions and dreams."[27]

Earlier in the story Tolkien uses the word "chance" to imply something else at work beyond that character's choices. Gildor Inglorion characterizes his group of elves meeting with Frodo, Sam and Pippin on the road just as the Black Rider was approaching the hobbits as something that may have been more than just chance.[28] At the Council of Elrond, Gandalf expressed a similar sentiment when he notes that the White Council drove Sauron out of Mirkwood the same year that Bilbo found the Ring and says it was "a strange chance, if chance it was."[29] Even the mysterious Tom Bombadil, whom some have characterized as a neutral nature spirit (see Chapter 12), in response to Frodo's asking him if he just happened to come upon the hobbits when they were attacked by Old Man Willow expressed doubt that it was simple chance that has brought him. Tom clearly points to both something more than chance and the possibility of a plan beyond his and the hobbits'.[30]

Providence runs like a strong and constant undercurrent throughout *LotR*. Though God is not mentioned and there is no organized religion in Middle-earth, most of the characters seem to accept that there is a greater power at work. For instance, when Sam foils Frodo's plan to go to Mordor alone, Frodo discerns that he and Sam were meant to go together.[31]

Because of this general acceptance of the reality of Providence, the characters often try to discern it, especially in moments of crisis. As the Fellowship is trying to decide if some or all should go to Mordor or Minas Tirith, Aragorn, as the leader of the company, seemingly is considering the

---

26. Os Guinness, *The Call*, Word Publishing, 1998, pp. 4, 29-31.
27. J.R.R. Tolkien, *The Silmarillion*, Houghton Mifflin, 1977, p. 28.
28. Op. cit. [1], p. 83.
29. Op. cit., p. 244.
30. Op. cit., p. 123.
31. Op. cit., p. 397.

'other powers at work' as he contemplates.³² Even Sam, whom Tolkien described as slow but shrewd,³³ has his own epiphany about Providence in his greatest moment of crisis when he thinks Frodo has been killed by the giant spider Shelob and he is trying to decide if he should take the Ring and continue the quest. He realizes he is being "put forward" by another power beyond his will just as Bilbo and Frodo have been.³⁴

LotR also contains evidence of direct divine intervention. We see it in several examples. Twice for Sam, in moments of major crises, Tolkien hints at direct intervention. The first is when Sam bravely faces Shelob, a creature of such evil that no warrior, man, or elf, has defeated it for millennia. The thought of using the Phial of Galadriel comes to him "as if some remote voice had spoken."³⁵ This suggestion leads Sam to use the phial which becomes the key to his defeat of Shelob. A second and more obvious example is when Sam is on the slopes of Mount Doom and both he and Frodo are nearly spent and he feels a "sudden sense of urgency" which feels to him like a calling and he knows he must take immediate action.³⁶ He does not know it, but his and Frodo's window of opportunity is small. Sauron is momentarily distracted by the Captains of the West and will not sense Sam and Frodo so close to Sammath Naur. Further, Gollum is getting ready to impede the hobbits' progress. If Sam did not rouse Frodo because of the strong sense of urgency that came into his thought seemingly out of nowhere, this window may have been missed.

The most striking example of divine intervention is the return of Gandalf, which Gandalf himself directly states that he has been sent back until his task is done.³⁷ Tolkien in one of his letters makes it clear that it was Eru, not the Valar, who resurrected Gandalf and send him back to Middle-earth. In this letter, he refers to "the Authority" who has taken the prudent plan of the Valar which sent the Istari, or Wizards, to Middle-earth in the first place and enlarged it at the moment of its failure; the failure being that Gandalf, the only one of the five wizards faithful to his mission, perished fighting a Balrog. Though Tolkien does not mention Eru Ilúvatar by name, he capitalized the word "Authority" and only Eru had the power to alter the Valar's plan.³⁸

---

32. Op. cit. [1], p. 394.
33. Op. cit., p. 625.
34. Op. cit., p. 715.
35. Op. cit., p. 713.
36. Op. cit., p. 921.
37. Op. cit. [1], p. 491.
38. Op. cit. [23], Letter 156, p. 203.

Eucatastrophe versus Deus Ex Machina

It is Gandalf's return and the other examples of this undercurrent of Providence, that some negative critics of Tolkien often attack as what they call convenient or simplistic plot devices. For example, Colin Manlove refers to Tolkien's plotting as "mere posturing in a rigged boat."[39] However, these plot devices are much more compelling when read through a Christian lens, which, considering Tolkien's own faith, was undoubtedly present in his writing of *LotR*. According to the Christian worldview, our own will power and our own moral will are not enough to overcome evil. We need what he terms often in *The Hobbit* as "luck" and in *The Lord of the Rings* as "chance." These are not actually mundane luck or chance. At the end of *TH*, Gandalf explains to Bilbo that none of his adventures and escapes were managed by mere luck.[40]

A secular humanist would easily and dismissively see these instances of grace and providence at work as the *deus ex machina*.[41] Critics often apply this term to a sudden and contrived resolution of a narrative conundrum by the author introducing a new character, event, or plot device to ensure a happy ending. However, just as many scholars criticized Tolkien's use of language in *LotR* but failed to realize that as a philologist who understood language far better than most, he was introducing different modes of speech and other language on purpose, they also misunderstood his use of plot devices.[42]

Tolkien was not succumbing to the *deus ex machina*; he was being consistent with what he called *Eucatastrophe*. In his famous lecture "On Fairy Stories" delivered in 1939, Tolkien introduces this word of his own invention to describe the sudden joyous turn in a story that is like a form of grace. He refers to it as a miraculous grace that occurs suddenly and will not recur, and that provides a glimpse of a more permanent joy that exists beyond the world as we see it.[43] Tolkien saw the Gospels as the supreme example of Eucatastrophe. He also believed the Gospels to be the ultimate story from which all other stories derive and is a true story.

---

39. Colin Manlove, *Modern Fantasy: Five Studies*, Cambridge University Press, 1978, p. 182.
40. Joseph Pearce, *Bilbo's Journey: Discovering the Hidden Meaning in "The Hobbit"*, Saint Benedict Press, 2012, E-book.
41. Lat. 'god from the machine'.
42. Allan Turner, in his essay *Style and Intertextual Echoes* found in *A Companion to J.R.R. Tolkien* points out how critics such as Catherine Stimpson and Burton Raffel criticisized Tolkien for not using what they refer to ordinary diction or too simple of a style that warrants *LotR* not to be considered as literature. His essay established Tolkien's deliberate use of style and syntax that these and other critics do not understand.
43. J.R.R. Tolkien, "On Fairy Stories," *Tales from the Perilous Realm*, HarperCollins, 2008, E-book.

"The Gospels contain a fairy story, or a story of a larger kind which embraces all the essence of fairy-stories. They contain many marvels—peculiarly artistic, beautiful, and moving: "mythical" in their perfect, self-contained significance; and among the marvels is the greatest and most complete conceivable Eucatastrophe. But this story has entered History and the primary world [that is, our world]; the desire and aspiration of sub-creation has been raised to the fulfilment of Creation. The Birth of Christ is the Eucatastrophe of Man's history. The Resurrection is the Eucatastrophe of the story of the Incarnation. This story begins and ends in joy. It has pre-eminently the "inner consistency of reality." There is no tale ever told that men would rather find was true, and none which so many skeptical men have accepted as true on its own merits. For the Art of it has the supremely convincing tone of Primary Art, that is, of Creation. To reject it leads either to sadness or to wrath."[44]

Unlike the *deus ex machina*, Tolkien's Eucatastrophe is not artificial. It is his worldview and thus it is part of the fabric of the reality of his sub-created world. Within the events of *The Lord of the Rings*, its occurrences are completely consistent within the story's fundamental structure. In the Gospels, we are introduced to many flawed and fallen persons (e.g., the twelve disciples, Mary Magdalene, Zacchaeus) who encounter Christ and these encounters result in both a change in their character and in the events which they are part of. We have the same elements in *LotR* though Christ is not present because Tolkien set his story in our deep past and in a pre-Christian age. However, despite the constant undercurrent and guiding hand of Providence in the events of *LotR*, the characters retain their free will and the capacity to choose.

---

44. Op. cit. [43].

Chapter 2: The Importance of Choice

While wearing the Ring on Amon Hen, Frodo feels the mental pull between two powers, each urging him to take a course of action. Tolkien describes him as momentarily writhing between the two in torment. Depicted as the Eye and the Voice, the powers represent Sauron urging Frodo to give into temptation on one hand, and Gandalf imploring him to resist on the other. Despite their influence, the hobbit is suddenly 'aware of himself again' and 'free to choose.' This brief scene is the clearest demonstration of Tolkien's view on the importance of free will and personal choice in all of *The Lord of the Rings*.

Tolkien further elaborates on and demonstrates this type of choice-making in *The Choices of Master Samwise*. This is one of the most poignant chapters in the story, when Sam thinks Frodo is dead and is trying to decide what to do. Tolkien, with heartfelt and touching writing, explores the psyche of a character who goes through a range of emotions wrestling for the right course of action. Sam first feels intense anger, followed by despair, grief and even suicidal thoughts.[1] While experiencing the range and intensity of these emotions, he recalls his own words from his encounter with Gildor six months prior, his sense of having "something to do before the end" and that he has to "see it through."[2] He decides he has to go on, has to continue the quest, but wrestles with doubt, telling himself that the Council gave the Ring to Frodo, not to him. The answer to this conundrum is that the Ringbearer was given companions so that the errand would not fail.[3] It feels like what Frodo experienced on Amon Hen, as if another power is behind it. At this point Sam realizes, as Tolkien puts it, that he is being "put forward" and finally decides to take the Ring and go on, though he is still riddled with doubt. Sadly, orcs find Frodo's body and Sam, using the Ring not to be seen, hears with the acute sense of hearing the Ring brings him, that Frodo is alive but incapacitated by Shelob's venom. Sam finally breaks down and condemns himself for leaving Frodo and pleads for forgiveness.[4] It turns out

---

1. J.R.R. Tolkien, *The Lord of the Rings*, Houghton Mifflin,1954-5, 1965-6, p. 715.
2. Op. cit., p. 714.
3. Op. cit., p. 715.
4. Op. cit., p. 724.

later that he, unknowingly, made the right decision or the orcs would have found the Ring and Sauron would have recovered it.

Both Frodo and Sam's struggle to choose rightly in a dire situation is akin to a Christian's movement to reconcile individual fallibility and the Christian ethos in the face of a free choice. For Christians, it is challenging to try to discern God's will and exercise their ability to choose. Fear and doubt can immobilise Christians from action. But choice and free will have always been a difficult thing to reconcile within the Christian ethos. If God knows all and is in control of all, do Christians really have choice and do their choices matter? The answer is 'yes', but how do Christians reconcile this within the limitations of human logic as well as the heart? The answer lies in the understanding and acceptance of mystery, paradox, and absolutes versus relativity.

Understanding Choice Within Christianity and *The Lord of the Rings*

To understand free will and our ability to choose freely, we first need to understand the parameters laid out in Christian doctrine, which are that God loves mankind and gave it *near complete freedom*. It is *near* complete because humans have freedom of choice but not freedom from choice. Only God has freedom from choice. For mankind, even a decision not to choose is a choice.[5] Within Christianity choices are never neutral. There is no moral relativity in Christianity. All thoughts, choices, and actions in this life result in moving either toward God or away from God. Choices always have consequences. But the consequences of choices do not alter God's purpose even though His purpose is not always clear.

Choice within *The Lord of the Rings* functions within the Christian framework of understanding as explained above. However, we understand this best from words Tolkien wrote that are not within *LotR*.

> "Then Ilúvatar spoke, and he said: 'Mighty are the Ainur, and mightiest among them is Melkor; but that he may know, and all the Ainur, that I am Ilúvatar, those things that ye have sung, I will show them forth, that ye may see what ye have done. And thou, Melkor, shalt see that no theme may be played that hath not its uttermost source in me, nor can any alter the music in my despite. For he that attempteth this shall prove but mine instrument in the devising of things more wonderful, which he himself hath not imagined."[6]

In this passage from the creation story *The Ainulindalë* in *The Silmarillion*,

---

5. Michael C. Haldas, *Sacramental Living: Understanding Christianity as a Way of Life*, Eastern Christian Publications, 2013, p. 33.
6. J.R.R. Tolkien, *The Silmarillion*, Houghton Mifflin, 1977, p. 17.

Tolkien summarizes the consistent thread of the nature of choice that runs subtly in *LotR*. Melkor is the mightiest of the Ainur, the character in Tolkien's universe analogous to Lucifer, the angel of light who becomes Satan. Melkor's name means "he who arises in might" and "To Melkor among the Ainur had been given the greatest gifts of power and knowledge, and he had a share in all the gifts of his brethren."[7] Yet Melkor was not content with his gifts and his role. As Ilúvatar revealed his plans for Arda via music, he tried to play his own notes and also increase the "power and glory of the part assigned to himself."[8] Despite the discordance Melkor tried to sow, Ilúvatar tells him that no matter what he does, it will not thwart, but rather advance Ilúvatar's will in a way he cannot conceive of. In Tolkien's universe, acts of free will can cause cataclysmic disasters in the temporal and incarnate world, but Ilúvatar's ultimate purpose remains eternal and inviolable.[9] Of course, Melkor, in his pride and eventual complete corruption, loses sight of reality and regresses into himself and becomes very nihilistic, dispelling himself of his power and finally being cast into the void.

The Choice of Boromir

Perhaps the most illuminating acts of choosing in *The Lord of the Rings* belong to Boromir and Aragorn. As noted in the last chapter, Boromir has a prophetic dream that serves as the catalyst for his journey to Rivendell, his participation in the Council of Elrond, and him being part of the Company of the Ring. Boromir clearly states that he received the dream once yet his brother received it twice.[10] Why would Tolkien make this distinction? The plot is not altered by the fact that Faramir receives the dream, but it is one of several things we see that marks Faramir as the more in-depth, stronger, and more spiritually stable of the two brothers. However, if the dream is removed from Faramir and only Boromir is the one to receive it, nothing in the plot and outcome of events would significantly change. So why did Tolkien do this?

Later in the story, in a lengthy discussion with Frodo and Sam, Faramir, who loved his brother dearly, laments that Boromir ever went to Rivendell and that he should have been chosen by Denethor but that Boromir "put himself forward."[11] Once he received the dream, Boromir insisted that he be the one to go. Gandalf also states later in the story that "Boromir claimed the

---

7. Op. cit. [6], p. 16.
8. Ibid.
9. Michael D.C. Drought, Editor, *J.R.R. Tolkien Encyclopedia – Scholarship and Critical Assessment*, "Free Will" by Daniel Thomas, p. 222
10. Op. cit. [1], p. 239.
11. Op. cit., p. 656.

errand and would not suffer any other to have it."[12] Contrast this with Sam's words quoted earlier when he was trying to decide what to do thinking Shelob has killed Frodo. He uses the passive in stating that he did not put himself forward, but that he *has been put* forward. In these brief words, Tolkien is making a statement about the willfulness in our choices, their grounding in either humility or pride, and the potential for danger therein.

There is a strong sense in *LotR* that timing matters. The pace of the book vacillates from slow yet deliberate (such as the first few chapters as Frodo slowly yet steadily makes his way out of the Shire) to urgent. For example, Aragorn looking into the palantír and revealing himself to Sauron causes the Dark Lord to initiate his attack sooner than he should have due to his fear of Isildur's heir. Aragorn comments to Legolas and Gimli soon after his encounter with Sauron that "the hasty stroke goes oft astray."[13] Had not Aragorn disrupted Sauron's timing, causing him to strike in haste before he had all of his forces amassed, the Battle of the Pelennor Fields may have been lost.

In the beginning of the story, Gandalf urges Frodo not to call too much unnecessary attention to himself, but to leave the Shire with the Ring, no later than Frodo's birthday in late September. We later learn from a letter in Bree that never got to Frodo that the wizard changed his mind and wanted Frodo to leave by the end of July. It seems Frodo left the Shire just in time. The Ringwraiths were nearly at his door when he left, as evidence by Sam's account of the gaffer's encounter. Had Frodo delayed even one day more, they may have found him at Bag End. The scene on Amon Hen described at the beginning of this chapter shows Frodo has only an instant to choose due to the urgency of the situation. Perhaps Faramir captures the sense of time in *LotR* best when he comments prior to the war breaking out that "time draws swiftly to some great conclusion."[14]

Time is important in the context of speculating why Boromir received the dream. Was it because Faramir hesitated about what to do? It is plausible, since we see in Faramir a man who was strong yet tender, resolute about battle but hateful of slaying anybody, and overall very thoughtful and analytical. It is possible that he was spending time trying to discern the meaning of his twice received dream before taking action. In turn, Boromir, whom Faramir describes as "proud and fearless, often rash"[15] was likely ready to act immediately. And it seems that some point action was needed. We learn in the Council of Elrond about Sauron's plans and that the machine of war was moving. Frodo's vision on Amon Hen while wearing the Ring

---

12. Op. cit. [1], p. 738.
13. Op. cit., p. 763.
14. Op. cit., p. 679.
15. Op. cit., p. 656.

confirms this.[16] Sauron is moving toward a position of power and complete military superiority over his enemies, even without the Ring. Elrond himself makes a strong statement about Sauron's might saying that an armored host of elves from the First Age would do nothing more than provoke Mordor's power.[17]

Surely the Valar, the guardians of Middle-earth and the likely senders of the dream, knew the state of Middle-earth at the time they sent the dream. The Valar had a policy of non-direct intervention. At the end of the First Age, they made direct war on Morgoth and the cataclysmic result was that most of the land west of the Blue Mountains – Hithlum, (except for what would become the island Tol Morwen) sank beneath the sea. Previous direct wars against Melkor had also resulted in changes to the lands and seas. Other factors contributed as well, but the Valar decided that their direct intervention, power versus power, was not good for Middle-earth. It is in that spirit that they sent the Istari, or wizards, to Middle-earth. Gandalf and the other wizards were meant to influence and unite, not use their power to fight Sauron directly.[18]

It seems Tolkien shows how the dream is meant to influence Faramir but due to his hesitation and the sense of urgency on the part of the Valar, the dream instead went to Boromir. The older brother, in keeping with his character, then put himself forward. Perhaps had he been less prideful and humbler, he would have seen that having the dream three times was a sign to move forward, but that coming twice to Faramir meant the younger brother going to Imladris was the wiser choice. Their father Denethor, a man revealed also to be mastered by pride, makes the same mistake, and gives the mission to Boromir[19]. The Valar, knowing both brothers' character, likely sent the dreams in this manner on purpose. No doubt they knew that if Boromir went to Imladris he would be at more risk but events had to be put in motion to stop Sauron from devouring the free peoples of Middle-earth.

Despite all this influence, Boromir still had the power to make his own choices. He could have chosen not to give into the temptation the Ring that led him to try and take it from Frodo. But he gave in and he paid a tragic price for his choice. We already explored how his sacrifice to save the hobbits was redemptive to him as an individual. But true to Ilúvatar's statement that his will would not be thwarted, much in terms of the greater good comes out of Boromir's seeming failure. To understand this greater good, it is necessary to first explore the choice of Aragorn.

---

16. Op. cit. [1], p. 391.
17. Op. cit., p. 268.
18. Op. cit., p. 1059.
19. Op. cit., p. 795.

The Choice of Aragorn

Between the breaking of the Fellowship and until his reunion with Gandalf, Aragorn mistakenly believes the choices he makes as the leader of the company are wrong. There is a scene in the book of Genesis in which the Patriarch Jacob cries out: "Joseph is no more; Simeon is no more; and now you want to take Benjamin. All these things are against me." (Genesis 42:36). He believed that his beloved son Joseph had been dead for years, never realizing he has been tricked by his remaining sons who had been jealous of Jacob's favoritism of Joseph. The irony of Jacob's statement that all things were against him is that he did not realize until later, at that very moment he was in despair, events were in motion that would reunite him with his beloved son Joseph who is alive.[20]

Similarly, Aragorn laments the scattering of the Fellowship, believing that an ill fate is on him and that all his choices are amiss.[21] At that point he truly believes everything he does is going wrong and blames himself for the unravelling of the Fellowship. Boromir's death further aggravates this. He struggles in his decision of whether to follow Frodo and Sam or Merry and Pippin. It is then that he feels that his heart is speaking clearly as he puts it, and makes the choice to try to rescue Merry and Pippin.[22]

Aragorn's heart speaks clearly because he made the right choice, though he was unaware at the time. Further, his heart is at peace with his choice because he did not make it with any form of self-interest. Wayne Hammond and Christina Scull point out that Aragorn never even considers going to Minas Tirith as an option once he realized that Merry and Pippin had been captured.[23] Boromir too made the right choice when he repented and tried to save the hobbits. Combined, the choices of these two men set off a chain of events as described above that led to the defeat and destruction of Saruman and, more importantly, Sauron, ridding Middle-earth of great evil. Out of their "failure" comes victory and both men receive redemption of sorts from the resurrected Gandalf, Ilúvatar's agent.[24]

In Fangorn, after the man in white is revealed to Aragorn, Legolas and Gimli to be Gandalf, a lengthy conversation ensues. In this conversation,

---

20. Op. cit. [5], p. 205.
21. Op. cit. [1], p. 403.
22. Op. cit., p. 409.
23. Wayne G. Hammond and Christina Scull, *The Lord of the Rings: A Reader's Companion*. Houghton Mifflin, 2005, p. 362.
24. I refer to Gandalf the White as Ilúvatar's agent based on Letter 156 in *The Letters of J.R.R. Tolkien* where he wrote, "He was sent by a mere prudent plan of the angelic Valar or governors; but Authority had taken up this plan and enlarged it, at the moment of its failure. 'Naked I was sent back – for a brief time, until my task is done'. Sent back by whom, and whence? Not by the 'gods' whose business is only with this embodied world and its time; for he passed 'out of thought and time'."

Gandalf confirms that Boromir perished and that he "escaped in the end."[25] Boromir certainly did not escape physical death so what did he escape? We know from *TSil* that Ilúvatar gave men the "gift of death"[26] though men would have a long history in Middle-earth of not understanding this gift. Reading *TSil* and *LotR* Appendices, as well as all of Tolkien's Middle-earth related works, shows that men, except for those like Aragorn who were enlightened, did not understand this gift and became envious of the elves immortality. Tolkien alludes in *TSil* and other works, such as *Athrabeth Finrod ah Andreth*, that Melkor found men shortly after their awakening and began to corrupt their thinking about death from seeing it as a gift to seeing it as a curse.

This envy often led to tragic events, the most tragic being the fall of Númenor and the changing of the world as told in *The Akallabêth*. Unlike the elves, who live forever unless they are slain or die of grief, men were not bound to the world. Even when elves die, their spirits remain in the world in the Halls of Mandos where all spirits initially go, or they can eventually take bodily form again. Thus Tolkien, though he himself and many others who write about his works, refer to elves as immortal, this is not true in the sense their bodies can be killed or they can die of grief. Tolkien more accurately described it as "serial longevity."[27] But men only go to the Halls for a time (perhaps Tolkien's nod to purgatory) but then can leave the world and seek that what is beyond it. Aragorn echoes this truth is his dying words to his wife Arwen when he tells her "We are not bound for ever to the circles of the world, and beyond them is more than memory."[28] Aragorn says these final words after he has voluntarily chosen to die at his appointed time. It was the tradition of the Kings of Númenor after a long life and while still of sound mind and body to make the choice to pass on the kingship to their heir and then voluntarily die. This was their tradition until their corruption. Aragorn restores this tradition by his choice and shows death as a gift as Eru intended, not a curse, because of what lies beyond.

Though Tolkien never directly says if there is some form of hell for unrepentant men, it seems that Boromir escaped something. Though Aragorn in truth did nothing wrong, nor did he fail, Gandalf eases his heart as well after he discusses Boromir, telling Aragorn not to regret his choice and that his choice was good.[29]

As readers, though it may have already seemed this way to us, we now know for certain that Aragorn chose rightly in a tough situation. This echoes

---

25. Op. cit. [1], p. 485.
26. Op. cit. [6], pp. 41-42.
27. Humphrey Carpenter, *The Letters of J.R.R. Tolkien*, Houghton Mifflin, 2000, Letter 211, p. 284.
28. Op. cit. [1], p.1038.
29. Op. cit., p. 489.

what Aristotle said over 2,000 years ago when he observed "we become what we are as persons by the decisions that we ourselves make."[30] Boromir's choices both revealed his flaws and his nobility; Aragorn's revealed his selflessness and greater nobility by since being both willing to go with Frodo to Mordor and then not choosing Minas Tirith, he is giving up his dream to marry Arwen (we learn in *The Tale of Aragorn and Arwen* that Elrond would not let his daughter marry Aragorn and give up her immortality unless Aragorn becomes the King of both Gondor and Arnor). This struggle to make the right choice over the easy choice, demonstrated by Aragorn, is also echoed throughout *LotR*.

Choosing Rightly

The following passage from the Gospel of Mark illustrates another aspect of choice Tolkien captures in *LotR*, one of choosing the right thing to do in tough circumstances over rules, law, worldly duty and even over your safety and well-being.

> "Now it happened that He went through the grainfields on the Sabbath; and as they went His disciples began to pluck the heads of grain, And the Pharisees said to Him, "Look, why do they do what is not lawful on the Sabbath?"
> But He said to them, 'Have you never read what David did when he was in need and hungry, he and those with him: how he went into the house of God in the days of Abiathar the high priest, and ate the showbread, which is not lawful to eat except for the priests, and also gave some to those who were with him?'
> And He said to them, 'The Sabbath was made for man, and not man for the Sabbath. Therefore the Son of Man is also Lord of the Sabbath.'" (Mark 2:23-28)

Here, Christ points out an instance when the "rules" are broken, and rightfully so, for the sake of a loving action. Christ does not advocate breaking rules and says in other places in the Gospels that we should follow the rules in spirit and truth. And sometimes, we may violate the letter of the law but honor the spirit.[31]

To illustrate this, I recount a story of a man and a woman who died in the attack of 9/11. They were in one of the burning towers and captured on a photograph, the man holding out his hand to the woman, inviting her to jump with him to their deaths and thus die on their own terms, which was the result of evil, rather than burn in the fire that was shortly going to consume

---
30. Op. cit. [5], 243.
31. Op. cit., p. 231.

them. The question is, did they commit suicide or did they make the best decision they could at that time? Although their action broke a moral law, it was the best possible outcome in the circumstance, and thus, the correct choice. Gandalf echoes a similar sentiment in the beginning of *LotR* that sets the tone for choice throughout the rest of the story. The wizard has just confirmed to Frodo that the golden ring left to him by Bilbo is in fact the Ruling Ring and that the Dark Lord Sauron is seeking it. When Frodo wishes "it need not have happened in [his] time", Gandalf reminds him that "all we have to decide is what to do with the time that is given to us."[32]

Pippin the hobbit and Beregond the man of Minas Tirith, make a tough choice between what is right and what is easy. Denethor succumbs to despair due to his older son being dead, arguably by his father's actions, and his younger being on the verge of death. Further, Denethor looks into the palantír and sees what he believes is the destruction of Gondor due to Sauron's deception. He also knows Aragorn is coming to claim his kingship. All of this causes Denethor to lose his mind. He decides rather than give up his rule, which is his duty as steward, and face the destruction of his kingdom by Sauron's forces, that he will commit suicide by burning himself and Faramir to death. He wants death on his own terms. But unlike the man in the 9/11 example, who lovingly reached out to comfort another person and offer her a choice, Denethor takes the choice between life and death away from his son.

Pippin learns what Denethor intends to do and, despite the raging battle going on, runs through the streets of Minas Tirith seeking Gandalf in an attempt to save Faramir's life. He encounters Beregond along the way, who he has forged a friendship with over the last few days, and quickly explains to him what is going on. Beregond hesitates, citing the rule that he must remain at his post unless the Steward himself commands him differently. Pippin appeals to a higher moral cause than rule-following and tells Beregond he must "choose between orders and the life of Faramir."[33] Beregond does choose to act and ends up killing two of the guards that were ordered by Denethor to light the pyre. They were being obedient to their ruler despite the fact it would mean both Denethor's and Faramir's death. Pippin finds Gandalf at the gate facing the Lord of the Nazgûl. Gandalf is now faced with his own choice, knowing that if he aids Pippin to save Faramir then he cannot engage in the Battle of the Pelennor Fields and that others will die as a result. But he knows other than himself, no aid will come to Faramir. They arrive to see two dead guards and the remaining guards fighting Beregond and calling him an outlaw and a traitor. Through Gandalf, Pippin and Beregond's actions Faramir is saved but Denethor manages to

---
32. Op. cit. [1], p. 50.
33. Op. cit., p. 809.

immolate himself.

In the choice of Beregond we see the characterization of choice Aragorn echoed earlier in the story when describing Gandalf whom he believes perished in Moria. He reminds his companions that Gandalf's choices and advice were never based on foreknowledge or personal safety, and that in general, one should choose what is right regardless of personal outcome.[34] Beregond makes a choice out of his love for Faramir even though he knows it would likely cost him his life one way or another. He demonstrates the same courage and love earlier when Faramir is attacked by the Nazgûl; when everyone else nearby, save Gandalf, cowers in terror, Beregond runs toward the battle, his love for Faramir overcoming the effects of the Ringwraiths.

When the horrible scene of Denethor's pyre is over, Gandalf addresses the remaining guards as 'servants of the Lord, blind in your obedience' and reminds them "that but for the treason of Beregond, Faramir ... would now also be burned."[35] Despite Gandalf's validation, Beregond still states that he regrets killing some of the guards (even though he knew he made the right choice to save Faramir) and his end would have been dark if it was not for Aragorn. Beregond leaving his post and spilling blood in the Hallows warranted the death penalty according to the laws of Gondor. As King, Aragorn spares him this fate, though he must banish him from Minas Tirith. But he rewards Beregond by commanding him to serve Faramir in Ithilien as Captain of Faramir's guard. In doing this, Aragorn acknowledges the right choice of Beregond, who chose love and the well-being of an innocent man over self-concern and the safety of making a choice within the letter of the law.

The Wide and Narrow Roads

> "Enter through the narrow gate. For wide is the gate and broad is the road that leads to destruction, and many enter through it. But small is the gate and narrow the road that leads to life, and only a few find it." (Matthew 7:13-14 NIV translation)

Tolkien evokes the Scripture above when it comes to his characters, making easy (wide) versus hard (narrow) choices. The first poem in *The Lord of the Rings*, 'The Road goes ever on and on" is about the road of life. It is recited in first person.[36] Bilbo recites this as he sets out on the road to leave the Shire forever. Frodo repeats the same poem seventeen years later as he too leaves the Shire and wondering if it shall be forever. What

---

34. Op. cit. [1], p. 430.
35. Op. cit., p. 837.
36. Op. cit., p. 35, 72.

is interesting in Bilbo's case is that just prior to reciting this poem, he has voluntarily given up the Ring. Though not without struggle, he manages to do it and thus at that point in history becomes the only person to have given it up of his own free will.

Years later, after the Ring has been destroyed and Bilbo is feeling his age, he recites a different version of the poem,[37] believing he made the right choice long ago. He had given up the Ring, taken the narrow road that Isildur, Déagol, Sméagol, and Frodo himself could not.[38] In reciting this poem, he is inviting others to take the same journey he did, one of doing the right thing and going to a peaceful rest, literally and metaphorically, in his eventual death. Frodo too recites a variation of the poem before sailing to the Undying Lands. The new road he is taking is one where he too can at last find his peaceful rest.[39]

Elrond evokes the metaphor of choosing the easy versus and hard roads as well during his council when he says going west and taking the Ring to the havens to be sent overseas is the easy road but not the right one. The right road, which is hard and even perilous, lies eastward to the mountain of fire.[40] Victory rests in the choice to take the hard road, a choice that is made repeatedly at critical junctures in the story. Frodo reiterates this choice in his confrontation with Boromir when he tells the man that his heart is warning him against delay and the way that seems easier.[41] Frodo yearns to go to Minas Tirith but is wise enough to know that this easy choice would only delay the inevitable and put others at risk of the Ring's temptation. When Boromir reveals his corruption, Frodo firmly makes up his mind to go to Mordor by himself and thus ensures no one else is the Company is further exposed to the Ring's evil.

Frodo is not the only character to choose the hard road. Merry and Pippin, out of love for Frodo, chose to leave the Shire with him. Legolas and Gimli decide to remain with the quest, rather than go back to their homelands. Aragorn is ready to give up all his aspirations and go with Frodo to Mordor. These characters put aside self-interest to make the right choices.

God's Choices

So far, we have explored the choices of individual characters of different races in *The Lord of the Rings* but what about the choices of the One who created them? The unseen and unmentioned power in *LotR* is God, Tolkien's

---

37. Op. cit. [1], p. 965.
38. Frodo presents a unique case, since he has been exposed to the Ring the most and has endured the greatest torment. His "failure" will be explored in more detail in Chapter 9.
39. Op. cit. [1], p. 1005.
40. Op. cit., p. 260.
41. Op. cit., p. 388.

Ilúvatar, working directly or through his Ainur. Ilúvatar's choices seem consistent with how we understand how God chooses, often that which is opposite of the wisdom of the world.

1 Corinthians 1:27-28 reads "… God has chosen the weak things of the world to put to shame the things that are mighty…" For instance, God chose Moses to be His spokesperson and deliverer of his people, yet Moses was not a gifted speaker and he even questioned why God would chose him who was "weak in speech and slow in tongue" (Exodus 4:10). Paul too was not an impressive speaker (2 Corinthians 11:6) or figure in person (2 Corinthians 10:10) yet God called him His chosen vessel to become the greatest evangelist of the New Testament (Acts 9:15). Samson, chosen by God to lead Israel, had superhuman strength but clearly did not appear so since he was tricked into revealing where he got his strength from (Judges 16:5). If Samson was big and muscular like a great bodybuilder (and he is often drawn by artists as such) his source of physical strength would have been obvious. David was the smallest and least impressive of Jesse's sons yet God chose him to be King of Israel (1 Kingdoms 16:7 or 1 Samuel 16:7). A read of the Gospels reveals the disciples to be often slow witted and not particularly impressive. Even Christ Himself was described in a prophecy to have no form or beauty or one that looked like it had honor (Isaiah 53:2-3).

Why did God choose these people to do His will when He could have chosen more gifted individuals? One of my priests gave a sermon on this topic and astutely pointed out that when we see people who look like models, bodybuilders, or polished speakers and have other assets typically valued by all, we attribute their accomplishment to them and their abilities. We revere the created and not the creator in this sense. This reverence for the created over the Creator is the essence of sin as we understand it in that we veer or wander from our appointed vocation[42] to be in a relationship with God (not in relation to His creation) and grow in His image and likeness. Thus, God always reveals Himself to us to bring our attention back to Him out of love and for our own good. One of the ways He does this is to accomplish great things through those who are not great by the world's standards. God says this explicitly to Paul:

> "And lest I should be exalted above measure by the abundance of the revelations, a thorn in the flesh was given to me, a messenger of Satan to buffet me, lest I be exalted above measure. Concerning this thing I pleaded with the Lord three times that it might depart from me. And He said to me,

---

42. This is essentially what most of the Istari (wizards) except for Gandalf did and thus failed in their vocation – even Radagast who became so enamored of nature that he forgot his mission was really about the peoples of Middle-earth (see *The Istari* in *UT*, pages 389-402, especially p. 390.)

"My grace is sufficient for you, for My strength is made perfect in weakness." (2 Corinthians 12:7-9)

This is an excerpt from a longer passage in which Paul warns that he should not boast about his spiritual experiences and visions. He tells his intended audience this story to show that God's strength is made perfect in Paul's, and more generally, humanity's, weakness.

Tolkien's universe operates in the same manner. Ilúvatar, whether working directly or through his Valar and Maiar, chose the weakest people in stature, hobbits, to be the primary catalysts that defeat Sauron. Frodo, after Gandalf tells him that he was meant to have the Ring, questions why it came to him and why he had been chosen. Gandalf explains that it was not due to his merit, wisdom, or strength.[43] Like the great Biblical figures, Frodo was not chosen because of his strengths, but rather despite them.

Elrond affirms Gandalf's earlier words that Frodo was meant to have the Ring but takes it a step further, explaining that the task of taking the Ring to Mount Doom is a task appointed to Frodo and that if he cannot succeed, no one will. Tolkien echoes the Scripture in Elrond's words: "This is the hour of the Shire-folk, when they arise from their quiet fields to shake the towers and counsels of the Great."[44] Elrond perceives that Frodo, among the smallest and weakest of God's creatures, has been chosen and that no one but him has a chance of destroying the Ring.

We see, in this final aspect of exploring choice in *LotR*, the concept in Christianity known as synergy. The word synergy comes from the Greek word *synergoi* which means "fellow-workers" and cooperating and working together. Synergy is interpreted as God always taking the initiative with His followers and providing them with His grace, enabling them to act, whether they respond to it or not. The synergy comes into play when they finally respond to God's initiative and grace.[45] Frodo and others, responding to Ilúvatar's initiative and grace, bring about the destruction of Sauron, which ushers in, for a time, a period of peace, prosperity, and renewal.

---

43. Op. cit. [1], p. 60.
44. Op. cit., p. 264.
45. Op. cit. [5], pp. 18, 63.

Chapter 3: Life and Death

I chose to address nature of reality and the importance of choice as the first two topics relating to the Christian ethos of *The Lord of the Rings* and Tolkien's universe in general, and did so in that order because that is what I find *LotR* is primarily about. However, Professor Tolkien himself would have likely disagreed with me. In a private letter, Professor Tolkien states that *LotR* is about something else: "But I should say if asked, the tale is not really about Power and Dominion: that only sets the wheels going; it is about Death and the desire for deathlessness, which is hardly more than to say it is a tale written by a Man."[1]

Death, Resurrection, and Restoration

Within *LotR* certain characters profess a belief system that points to a restoration and resurrection of life. It is reminiscent of what we see in Book of Revelation where God restores Heaven and Earth but changed as it was meant to be, free of death and evil. But without the benefit of reading other Tolkien works that add more to this belief system, these indicators in *LotR* are cryptic.

One such example happens early in the story. While in Moria, in response to Sam comparing this once greatest of all dwarf kingdoms to "darksome holes," Gimli responds by chanting a lengthy poem that has as its last line "Till Durin wakes again from his sleep."[2] Durin was the first dwarf and the father of dwarves who lived long ago, as is confirmed in the section of Appendix A called *Durin's Folk*. No more is said of what this line of poetry means but the reader is left at that point with the thought that this is either dwarven lore, and Gimli personally believes Durin will wake from his sleep, or this is part of a broader belief system of a type of resurrection. Gandalf's return makes resurrection a part of reality in Middle-earth.

Furthermore, toward the end of the book, after the Ring is destroyed and Aragorn is crowned King and married to Arwen, amidst this great bliss the

---
1. Humphrey Carpenter, *The Letters of J.R.R. Tolkien*, Houghton Mifflin, 2000, Letter 203, p. 262.
2. J.R.R. Tolkien, *The Lord of the Rings*, Houghton Mifflin, 1954-5, 1965-6, p. 309.

characters begin the process of parting and returning to their homes. Two ancient figures, Galadriel, who we know within the context of *LotR* has lived in excess of seven thousand years and Treebeard, who Gandalf calls the oldest of all living things, have an interesting exchange. Treebeard says goodbye to her and Celeborn in a very reverential way lamenting that they will likely never meet again. Galadriel affirms that they will not meet again in Middle-earth but adds, "nor until the lands that lie under the wave are lifted up again. Then in the willow-meads of Tasarinan we may meet in the Spring. Farewell!"[3]

I had no idea what and where the willow-meads of Tasarinan were when I first read *LotR*. I did not see it on the map provided with the books. Treebeard had mentioned it earlier in the story in a song he sang to Merry and Pippin.[4] Galadriel is not present when he does so, but what she says to Treebeard in the quote above is essentially the first line of the poem he chants to the hobbits. I was to learn in reading *The Silmarillion*, which was not yet published when I first read *LotR*, and consulting Tolkien reference books, Tasarinan was a willow-forest in Beleriand. Beleriand was one of the lands west of the Blue Mountains that was broken and sunk beneath the sea at the end of the First Age more than six thousand years before the events of *LotR*. Galadriel clearly believes these lands will at some point be renewed.

We are not given too many more hints like these in the *LotR*, but we can safely assume they are valid pointers to what Tolkien envisioned in his universe. To quote Professor Clyde S. Kilby, a teacher, writer, and someone who personally spent time with Tolkien:

> "But Tolkien was too pronounced a believer in Christ as the Sovereign ruler to leave the matter thus. There is evidence that, had his story continued to its full and concluding end the ubiquitous evil of such as Morgoth and Sauron would have ceased. He intended a final and glorious eventuality similar to the one described in the Book of Revelation with the true Telperion reappearing, the earth remade, the lands lying under the sea lifted up, the Silmarils recovered, Eärendil returned to earth, the Two Trees rekindled in their original light and life-giving power, and the mountains of Pelóri leveled so that the light should go over all of the earth – yes, and the dead be raised and original purpose of Eru executed."[5]

Death and Deathlessness From Mortal and Immortal Points of View

No one in Middle-earth, mortal or immortal, is immune to the effects of

---

3. Op. cit. [2], p. 959.
4. Op. cit., p. 458.
5. Clyde S. Kilby, *Tolkien and the Silmarillion*, Harold Shaw Publishers, 1976, pp. 64-65.

death and the desire for deathlessness whether it be the desire for individual deathlessness as in the case of men, or the desire for deathlessness in creation as in the case of elves. In *LotR* we get occasional glimpses of this desire and the evil and sadness to which it can lead. For example of all the Rings of Power, the nine for the mortal men seemed to work best according to Sauron's ultimate purpose which was to dominate the wills of each race. In their quest for power and immortality, the nine men who took the rings acquired deathlessness of a sort but it ended up being an enslaved half-life, neither dead nor living, and completely under the control of Sauron's will.

Of all of Tolkien's characters, it is Faramir who gives us the greatest glimpse into the theme of mortal man's desire for deathlessness and the grief it leads to. He tells Frodo and Sam how the Númenóreans sought "endless life unchanging" and made their tombs more elaborate than their homes and treated the thought of their lineage and ancestry more reverently than their children.[6] *The Lord of the Rings* appendices and *The Akallabêth* in *TSil* give light to Faramir's reference.

At the end of the First Age, the Edain, as a gift from Ilúvatar and the Valar for their valiant and unselfish fight against Morgoth, were given a star-shaped island kingdom west of Middle-earth between it and Aman. They were also granted a lifespan far greater than common man. Their first King, Elros, Elrond's brother who chose to be a mortal man, lived for five hundred years. They were told they could not travel to the far west or to Aman. Over time, despite their gifts of long life, they hungered for immortality. This hunger became progressive and their society began to decay morally. They went from a benevolent kingdom with great reverence for Ilúvatar and the Valar, to a conquering one that subdued and enslaved a great part of Middle-earth.

Their last king, Ar-Pharazôn, in response to Sauron's claim of being the supreme ruler of Middle-earth, challenged and captured Sauron, bringing him back to Númenor. Sauron knew he could not challenge Númenor militarily at that time so he allowed himself to be captured. Though a prisoner at first, he gained the king's ear and slowly corrupted the Númenorians over a period of years. He inflamed their hunger for deathlessness telling them if they could possess Aman they would possess immortality for the secret to immortality lay in the land itself. He also caused the Númenorians to fall into blasphemy and they changed their reverence from Ilúvatar to outright worship of Melkor. Ar-Pharazôn listened and launched a massive fleet to Aman. Upon setting foot on the Undying Lands, the Valar laid down their guardianship of Arda and called upon Ilúvatar who changed the world. A great chasm opened in the sea along with a cataclysmic wave and Númenor was swallowed and

---

6. Op. cit. [2], pp. 662-3.

destroyed much like the fabled island of Atlantis. Ilúvatar also removed Aman from the circles of the world. A remnant of the faithful of Númenor escaped and found the Kingdoms of Arnor and Gondor in Middle-earth. It is these Kingdoms that Faramir is essentially referencing in his quote above, primarily Gondor. Though they did not commit the grievous sin of Númenor with its outright blasphemy, they continue lamenting their mortality in a similar fashion.

It is interesting that Tolkien chose Faramir to be his character that best expressed his primary theme. By his own admission, Faramir is the character he believed to be most like himself: "As far as any character is 'like me' it is Faramir – except that I lack what all my characters possess (let the psychoanalysts note!) *Courage*."[7] Tolkien even transferred his recurring nightmare of a great wave to Faramir.[8] This wave Faramir refers to is from Tolkien's recurring Atlantis-like nightmare that he used when constructing the story of Númenor.[9]

In contrast to men's desire for deathlessness, Tolkien presents a different view from the immortal elves, and, in particular, Legolas and Galadriel, who lament their immortality that dooms them to witness the decline of the world, a world they deeply love more so than other races in Middle-earth. Having attained immortality themselves, they seek to immortalize the world around them. Legolas captures this sentiment after the Fellowship departs from Lórien and experiences the effects of leaving the land under the Power of Galadriel. He explains how time moves swift and slow for elves since they change little but the world changes rapidly and the combination causes his race grief.[10]

Though elves themselves are deathless unless slain or stricken by grief, they cannot prevent the death and change around them. Tolkien describes that by the Third Age they were creating nothing new; their art became a means of unnatural preservation, "a kind of embalming ... though they retained the old motive of their kind, the adornment of earth, and the healing of its hurts."[11]

The three elven rings did just that as their chief power. Perhaps lesser in degree than the sin of the Númenoreans, it was this type of thinking that made them susceptible to Sauron in disguise when he suggested to their great craftsmen to forge the Rings of Power in the first place. So, it seems whether moral or immortal, no race in Tolkien's universe was impervious to the struggle between life and death, nor are they immune from evil.

---

7. Op. cit. [1], Letter 181, p. 232.
8. Op. cit. [2], p. 941.
9. Op. cit. [1], Letter 257, p. 347.
10. Op. cit. [2], p. 379.
11. Op. cit. [1], Letter 131, p. 151.

Life, Death, and the Body and Soul

Despite this desire for deathlessness and the sins to which it can lead, there are characters who do not succumb to this thinking and are not guided by fear of bodily death or change. For example, in the Finrod and Andreth's debate about life and death in *Morgoth's Ring* Tolkien includes a dialogue on the *hröa* and *fëa*, the rough equivalent of the body and soul. This gives much insight into Tolkien's view of spiritual and physical death as well as God and salvation in Tolkien's universe.

However, I am going to keep the scope of this sub-topic confined to points made in *The Lord of the Rings*. The quest for bodily self-preservation and avoidance of death, whether it concerns the actual self or works of the self, is clearly denounced within the value system of *LotR* (and Tolkien's universe as a whole). It either leads to outright evil, such as in the case of mortal men, or to stagnation, such as in the case of elves. The good characters in *LotR*, those who struggle to do the right thing morally and ethically despite any flaws they might have, do not make protecting themselves from physical death their priority. Even without any formal religious system with codes of behavior, commandments, and laws, these characters seem to have an inherent sense of what is right and are willing to die for it without much thought of what happens to them after physical death. To these characters, there are more important goals than the preservation of their own lives.

The understanding of what is important beyond just physical life and the willingness to die for what is right is linked to friendship.[12] In the context of this chapter it is enough to understand that this hierarchy of values exists among the characters committed to goodness and virtue and not among those committed to evil. This is evident throughout the entire book. For example, when the Three Hunters are pursuing Merry and Pippin, they come to Fangorn, where they believe the two young hobbits have gone after escaping their orc captors. Gimli, daunted by their unfavourable odds, notes that they "cannot pursue them through the whole fastness of Fangorn... if [the hunters] do not find [the hobbits] soon, [they] shall be no use to them, except to ... show [their] friendship by starving together."[13]

But Aragorn leaves no room for argument. He will not allow himself, Legolas, and Gimli to abandon their search for Merry and Pippin even if it means they all must die a slow death of starvation together. Again, he takes no thought for his lifelong dream to reclaim his kingdom and marry Arwen, or for the wider fight against Sauron in general. He simply knows he cannot abandon his friends.

Sam comes to a similar conclusion on the slopes of Mount Doom. He

---
12. The topic of Friendship is discussed at length in Chapter 6.
13. Op. cit. [2], p. 480.

laments how much he would love to see Rosie Cotton and her family, his own father and his home again, and how things went all wrong when Gandalf died in Moria and killed any hope of he and Frodo returning from Mordor. However, as he slips into hopelessness, he finds a new determination and becomes like "some creature of stone and steel", immune to despair or weariness and unable to be subdued.[14]

In this example, Sam leaves no room for any alternative other than to do what he must: to both help and die with Frodo. However, in a very human way, he laments what he will be missing, and expresses a faith in Gandalf and goodness in general. Sam's own goodness comes through as does the goodness that ultimately comes from God when someone does what is right in a selfless way. Sam's resignation to death out of love for his master and his duty to do what is right gives him a new strength to go on. Sam can be read as doing God's will, and becomes strengthened in his moment of need. Ultimately, it is his small act, combined with myriad small acts throughout the narrative, that leads to the defeat of evil.

---

14. Op. cit. [2], p. 913.

Chapter 4: The Nature and Aspects of Evil

The Lord of the Rings is often read as a classic tale of good versus evil. However, to leave it at that undermines the complexity of how good and evil operate in the story. Evil, especially, is portrayed complexly in the narrative.

The Christian Understanding of Evil

Evil within *LotR* can be approached from a Christian perspective which in turn necessitates understanding paradox. Evil in Christianity is both real and unreal. Christians accept evil as real while paradoxically knowing it is unreal. They do not believe in evil as an equal and opposite power to God. This is dualism that is rejected by the Christian doctrine.[1]

The Bible reads in Genesis that when God created the universe, the world and everything in that He affirmed many times His creation was "very good" which means evil did not appear together with the creation of good.[2] Evil is not something the devil or anyone else creates. It is not a power outside of God nor is it a power at all. Rather, as in the devil's case, it takes that which is good and uses it for selfish purposes. Therefore, in reality, the answer to the question "what is evil?" is that evil is a counterfeit power.[3] C.S. Lewis explains evil as a parasite that takes what is good such as intelligence and cleverness and corrupts it.[4] In the words of Father Thomas Hopko, the most evil vice is always the perversion of the most excellent virtue.[5] Evil is real in that it exists because of created beings' choices, but it is unreal in that it has no lasting permanence because it not created by God. According to the Christian doctrine, only God and His goodness are the true and lasting reality. Other circumstances that affect living beings, including death, are temporary circumstances according to the promises of Christianity.

Another way to understand evil from a Christian perspective is to think

---

1. Michael C. Haldas, *Sacramental Living: Understanding Christianity as a Way of Life*, Eastern Christian Publications, 2013, p. 136
2. Protopresbyter Michael Pomazansky, *Orthodox Dogmatic Theology*, St. Herman of Alaska Brotherhood, 2009 (Third Edition), p. 109.
3. Op. cit. [1], pp. 136-137.
4. C.S. Lewis, *Mere Christianity*, Macmillan, 1960, pp. 50-51.
5. Thomas Hopko, *Ecumenical Review 51*, 4, 1999, p. 364.

of it as the absence of good which is from God. Only God is uncreated and good therefore only when people are in communion with God through their thoughts and actions they are participating in His goodness. Anytime they willfully choose to renounce God whether consciously or as evidenced by sinful thoughts that turn into sinful actions, they cease to be in communion with Him and are therefore bringing evil into existence. Evil, therefore, is also the absence of God.[6]

The "Somethingness" and "Nothingness" of Evil

The critic Edwin Muir accuses Tolkien of having good characters that are always consistently good and evil characters that are immovably evil.[7] He, like other critics, understands that *LotR* is largely about a struggle between good and evil but does so in a simplified and uncompromising manner that misses the nuances of many characters. Some scholars (both favorable to Tolkien and critical of him, such as Tom Shippey, Alison Milbank, and Edmund Wilson) have also argued that Tolkien subscribed, in large part, to a Manichaean view of evil. Manichaeism was a gnostic religion founded by a person named Mani who promoted a dualism where good and evil are indeed equal and opposite powers as described above. Where there is no doubt that Tolkien saw evil as real and a force to be dealt with, he clearly did not see it as an equal and opposite power. Elrond's words that nothing is evil in its beginning, not even Sauron can be taken as evidence that Tolkien did not subscribe to strict dualism of good and evil in his book.[8]

The tangible reality of evil surrounds Sam when he lies in the eerie darkness of Mordor, in the worst physical conditions Middle-earth has to offer, starving, thirsty and cold. But he looks up and sees a twinkling white star (which brings to mind the Star of Bethlehem), high above the blackness and in that moment he has an insight into evil that illustrates Tolkien's view on its true nature. He perceives rightly that it is only temporary and that goodness exists "for ever beyond its reach."[9] Despite his surroundings, that would drive most to despair, this sight and insight causes him to drift off into a deep, untroubled sleep.

This is not the only commentary Tolkien's characters express either in thought or speech are in accordance to traditional Christian views on evil. In the very beginning of the book, as Gandalf reveals to Frodo that the gold ring he inherited from his uncle is indeed the One Ring and evil, Frodo is overwhelmed by the feeling of fate stretching out like "a vast hand" and

---

6. Op. cit. [1], pp. 137-138.
7. Edwin Muir, "Strange Epic", *The Observer* [London], 22 August 1954, p.7.
8. J.R.R. Tolkien, *The Lord of the Rings*, Houghton Mifflin,1954-5, 1965-6, p. 261.
9. Op. cit., p. 901.

"dark cloud" to engulf him.[10] Gandalf tells him that despite respite from evil Middle-earth has enjoyed for a while, "the shadow" always reforms and grows again.[11] Later in the book, as he is journeys to Isengard, the wizard laments that "the evil of Sauron cannot be wholly cured, nor made as it had not been."[12]

In these statements, Tolkien shows evil as both something to be feared and something that is difficult to eradicate and undo. Yet, by the end of the book readers encounter thoughts and actions that counter this threatening "somethingness" of evil and show what Sam realized when he saw the star. Evil is doomed to "nothingness" in the end. In a moment of foreshadowing as he confronts the Lord of the Nazgûl, Gandalf tells the Ringwraith to go back to the abyss and "nothingness" that awaits him.[13] The Lord of the Nazgûl is indeed destroyed a few moments later by Éowyn and Merry. Sauron suffers the same fate when the Ring is destroyed at last after nearly five thousand years of existence.

The language Tolkien employs to describe Sauron's final fate echoes Frodo's premonition in Bag End. However, in contrast with the real fear Frodo felt in Bag End as a "vast hand like a dark cloud reaching out to engulf him," this shadow, Sauron, does reach out like a "vast threatening hand" yet it is blown away into nothingness.[14] This same fate awaits Saruman, after his throat is slit by Gríma Wormtongue. His body decays immediately and a "grey mist" rises from it only to have a cold wind from the west blow and have it dissolve into nothing.[15] It is sad, knowing the complete history of Saruman in the context of all of Tolkien's works, to see a once mighty angel, a being who was in the presence of Ilúvatar during the creation of the universe, to fall so low as to have his throat slit by essentially an abuse victim.[16]

Yet this echoes a theme in *LotR* and Tolkien's world in general that shows evil as something that is regressive: something that starts off good in nature but moves by wrong thought, action, and choice toward a state of unredeemable corruption and eventual nothingness. In *The Silmarillion*, the greatest of all created beings, Melkor, empties himself of his power in his desire to control, until he makes himself permanently incarnate and of much lesser stature than he once was when he was the mightiest of all created

---

10. Op. cit. [8], pp. 49-50.
11. Op. cit., p. 50.
12. Op. cit., p. 537.
13. Op. cit., p. 811.
14. Op. cit., p. 928.
15. Op. cit., pp. 996-7.
16. In *The Ainulindalë* in *The Silmarillion*, though not mentioned by name, Tolkien says that the Ainur, of whom Sauron, Saruman, and Gandalf all were, are the offspring of Ilúvatar's thought and were present at the creation and helped to shape it.

beings. Sauron and Saruman, as shown in the scenes of destruction, regress into nothingness, as Tolkien confirms in his letters about the eventual destruction of the Ring that Sauron would essentially be diminished to a near vanishing point and would be reduced to nothing more than a memory of a malicious will.[17]

The regressive nature of evil is shown best in the character of Gollum, of whom the famous author, Christian and psychiatrist, M. Scott Peck writes "The character of Gollum, for instance, in Tolkien's recently popular *The Hobbit* and *The Lord of the Rings* trilogy, is perhaps the finest depiction of evil ever written."[18] Dr. Peck also acknowledges that Tolkien clearly knew as much about human evil as any psychiatrist or psychologist. Professor Verilyn Flieger further comments on Gollum when she writes that his childish whining shows him to be almost infantile. She also contrasts his constant references to himself in the plural "we" with the rare instances of the singular "I" to show the division in his being.[19]

This regressive state of Melkor, Sauron, Saruman, and Gollum is in direct contrast to the progressive state of those who choose to do good. For example, Frodo, who grows from the beginning of the book from a scared and frightened hobbit to one of great spiritual insight. The other hobbits – Sam, Merry, and Pippin – also grow spiritually (each moved to courage and sacrifice through their love and pity of the others) as do many other characters.

A final point that shows evil as a lesser power that has nothing inherent in itself but just bends and twists its own good nature, is its inability to create. As God's first action in the Bible is creating, so it is Ilúvatar's first action in *TSil* as well. A lack of ability to truly create is something that demonstrates someone removed from God and goodness, perhaps to the point of no return. Frodo, in a moment of insight, understands this when he says of the orcs that the evil that made them cannot create anything by itself but can only mock what has been created. He tells Sam that the evil that made orcs did not give them life but only "ruined" and "twisted" them.[20] Treebeard expresses a similar sentiment on a separate occasion when he tells Merry and Pippin that trolls were made in mockery of Ents, as orcs are of elves, and are counterfeits.[21]

In showing evil to be regressive and counterfeit, Tolkien never glamorizes evil or makes it attractive in any way. By showing the nothingness of evil as

---

17. Humphrey Carpenter, *The Letters of J.R.R. Tolkien*, Houghton Mifflin, 2000, Letter 131, p. 153.
18. M. Scott Peck, *People of the Lie*, Simon and Schuster, 1983, p. 45.
19. Verilyn Flieger, *Splintered Light: Logos and Language in Tolkien's World*, Kent State University Press, 2002, p. 7.
20. Op. cit. [8], p. 893.
21. Op. cit., p. 474.

described thus far, Tolkien's writing suggests that evil and its darkness lack true substance. Consider Sauron, who does not appear in the book directly, but only as a presence in the palantir or as a huge shadow that is blown away by the wind after the Ring is destroyed. He remains a shadowy, remote, and intensely threatening figure lurking in the background. The Ringwraiths have no form except raiment to give them shape and Gandalf tells Frodo the robes they wear give shape to their nothingness.[22] The more tangible evil characters, like Gollum, Saruman, and the orcs, are odious. Saruman and the orcs never show mercy, remorse, or kindness. Gollum's actions are prevalently hateful and self-serving.[23]

Author R.J. Reilly sums up evil in *LotR* as follows:

"Darkness, for example, suggests lack of being, or lack of substance, and all the evil beings of the trilogy illustrate this. Sauron has no body, and like the orcs, and Gollum, and Shelob, and Saruman, and the Ringwraiths, he is voracious, literally lusting after substantiality."[24]

Not only is Tolkien not glamorizing evil, he shows that too much curiosity and fascination with evil is dangerous. Elrond warns, "It is perilous to study too deeply the arts of the Enemy, for good or for ill."[25] The consequences are illustrated by the fall of Saruman. Of all the characters in *LotR*, no one knows more of Sauron and the Rings of Power than Saruman who studied everything about them for roughly two thousand years. But as Gandalf points out in the beginning of the story when giving Frodo the history of the Ring, that Saruman's knowledge of the Rings of Power is deep but that his pride has grown proportionally with this knowledge.[26]

Saruman is described to delve progressively deeper into the palantír until he is caught by Sauron whose will and strength are greater than his.[27] In his fascination with the arts of the enemy, and his desperation for knowledge above wisdom, Saruman gave himself over to darkness and never returned to the light. Saruman is mastered by his own pride and inflated sense of self which makes him susceptible to evil. Even after his defeat, he is so consumed with pride and hate, he can no longer see reality, refuses all offers of help, and becomes Gollum-like in his brokenness.

---

22. Op. cit. [8], p. 216.
23. Gollum's rare instances when the small part of his mind, body and soul that remain his own peaks through is discussed later in this chapter.
24. R. J. Reilly, *Romantic Religion*, Lindisfarne Books. 2006, E-book.
25. Op. cit. [8], p. 258.
26. Op. cit., p. 47.
27. Op. cit., p. 584.

Evil Seeks Domination Not Dominion

> "Then God said, "Let Us make man in Our image, according to Our likeness. Let them have dominion over the fish of the sea, over the birds of heaven, over the cattle, and over all the earth, and over every creeping thing that moves on the earth." (Genesis 1:26-27)

In this passage from Genesis, God is described giving human beings dominion over the world. Father Olof Scott, a priest and a physicist, states that the word 'dominion' is a key word in this passage. He points out that God gives *dominion* over the earth, not domination. Father Scott goes on to say that mankind is to be in union with God in taking care of the Earth.[28] Christians are to embrace the calling as stewards of creation and have synergy with Him in the care of His creation.[29] In a tense exchange with Denethor and in his persuasive speech to march on the black gate, Gandalf echoes sentiments similar to the Genesis passage. He tells Denethor that though he rules over no realm, all things that are of worth and in peril are in his care and that he is also a steward.[30] During *The Last Debate* he emphasizes the stewardship he and all the Captains of the West and their people share in that they must deal with the evils of their day so that those in both the present and the future may benefit.[31]

It is in this desire for either dominion or domination that we see a stark contrast of good and evil in *LotR*. The very reason for the story and events of *LotR* are the result of actions from thousands of years prior to the War of the Ring that were rooted in the desire to dominate. In the Second Age, Sauron convinced the Gwaith-i-Mirdain, the elven smiths of Eregion, to forge the Rings of Power, so that he can forge the Ruling Ring of which its primary power is to dominate, rule and enslave the wills of others.[32]

But Sauron's plan did not work as well as he had hoped. Except for the rings for mortal men, the other rings failed. It is in the elven rings failure from Sauron's point of view that we see the starkest contrast between dominion and domination. Sauron never touched these rings and thus they did not have his influence as Elrond explained. Further, the elf-Lord clarified that the makers of these three did not want domination or wealth, but rather wanted to heal and preserve and that was the power that went into the Three.[33]

It is stewardship and seeking dominion and not domination, which evil cannot comprehend, that leads the good characters to ultimately triumph

---

28. Father Olof Scott, *Come Receive the Light,* Orthodox radio program, May 8, 2007.
29. Op. cit. [1], p. 295.
30. Op. cit. [8], pp. 741-2.
31. Op. cit., p. 861.
32. Matthew Dickerson, *A Hobbit Journey*, Brazos Press, 2012, E-book.
33. Op. cit. [8], p. 262.

over Sauron and his ilk. In *LotR* power, as defined by might, does not defeat power. It is a power not rooted in a desire to dominate that defeats Sauron. This power lies in love, mercy, sacrifice and resistance to evil. Tolkien elaborates on this in one of his letters, noting, despite his cordial dislike of allegorical readings, that readers "can make the Ring into an allegory of our own time an allegory of the inevitable fate that waits for all attempts to defeat evil power by power. But that is only because all power magical or mechanical does always so work."[34]

Within the book itself, it is Elrond and Gandalf who express this sentiment. During the council, Elrond explained that if any one of them used the Ring that they would eventually just become another Dark Lord.[35] Gandalf says it more plainly later in the book before they march on the black gate when he simply states, "victory cannot be achieved by arms."[36]

As Matthew Dickerson adroitly points out it is the simple things "that are really important in the tale; this, and not war and battles, is the stuff of life, the stuff that counts. And thus this, even in the midst of a battle scene, is what Tolkien's narrative brings us back to."[37] For example, Dickerson calls to mind Pippin in the battle before the black gate. As the battle rages around him, Pippin thinks of his best friend Merry and "cool sunlight and green grass." His focus on friends, sunlight, nature even as he faces death reveal priorities which are not power but friendship, God's creation, and what we should treasure as stewards of the world seeking dominion.

Evil is Narcissistic

Evil is by its nature self-centered and cannot imagine thinking beyond the limitations that come with self-absorption. This is why it seeks domination and not dominion, and cannot understand the values of friendship, love, and sacrifice. This proves to be the tool of Sauron's undoing because of the inherent narcissism of evil which leads it to oversights. We first get a glimpse of Sauron's figurative blindness when the Fellowship is in Lothlórien and Haldir, their guide points out to Frodo that the light perceives the heart of the darkness but the darkness does not perceive the light.[38] The scene is augmented by the described contrast between the uncorrupted Lothlorien and the ravaged Mirkwood, Sauron's old fortress Dol Guldur at its centre, separated by a river. It is reminiscent of John 1:5, "And the light shines in the darkness, and the darkness did not comprehend it."

---

34. Op. cit. [17], Letter 109, p. 121.
35. Op. cit. [8], p. 261.
36. Op. cit., p. 860.
37. Op. cit. [32].
38. Op. cit. [8], p. 343.

In this case, the specific good is Galadriel, who possesses one of the Elven Rings, Nenya, to protect and preserve Lothlórien. Galadriel herself echoes this later after she allows Frodo to look into her mirror, which can show glimpses of the past, present, and future. She plainly states she knows Sauron's mind and everything the Dark Lord thinks pertaining to the elves, but that he in turn cannot understand her thought.[39] Sauron's choice of a lidless eye as his symbol is ironic, considering that in Professor Louis Markos' words, he is literally and figuratively myopic and is incapable of thinking that anyone would want to destroy the Ring and not use it against him.[40]

It is Gandalf, the wisest of the characters, and the architect of Sauron's destruction, that exploits Sauron's myopathy, and clearly articulates the Dark Lord's one weakness: the wizard acknowledges Sauron wisdom and might in general, but explains because the Dark Lord lusts for power, that is all he can judge and measure by and thus a strategy to destroy the Ring is something that would put the Dark Lord "out of his reckoning."[41] But it is when he returns from the dead as Gandalf the White that he fully articulates Sauron's inherent blindness and stupidity that results from it. According to Gandalf, Sauron assumed his enemies follow the same logical patterns as he does in attempting to overthrow him with strength of numbers. Gandalf further explains that it has not entered the Dark Lord's "darkest dream" that anyone would want to destroy the Ring and that he is now moving in haste, sooner than he planned, to wipe out his enemies. In his similar self-serving shortsightedness, Saruman has helped the forces of good, though not intentionally, by betraying Sauron. Gandalf ultimately refers to Sauron as a "wise fool."[42]

Where Sauron is a shadowy figure who never appears, we see a tangible, though lesser version of Sauron in Saruman. Both in their origin were Maiar of Aulë thus both had minds for substances, rocks, metals, and crafts.[43] Even their names are similar. Both are deceivers and betrayers. But because the readers encounter Saruman close up, it is easier, in some sense, to appreciate the narcissism and stupidity of evil and how it outsmarts itself in its blindness. Gandalf comments "often does hatred hurt itself!"[44] and the beginnings of this can be seen with Saruman at the Council of Elrond. Gandalf explains that even though Saruman used Radagast, and even mocks him, it is because of the brown wizard' involvement by Saruman that Gandalf is able to

---
39. Op. cit. [8], p. 355.
40. Louis Markos, *On the Shoulders of Hobbits*, Moody Publishers, 2012, E-book
41. Op. cit. [8], p. 262.
42. Op. cit., pp. 485-486.
43. Tolkien writes this about Sauron in *The Valaquenta* within *The Silmarillion* and about Saruman in *The Istari* within *Unfinished Tales*.
44. Op. cit. [8], p. 571.

escape Orthanc. In his encounter with Radagast, Gandalf asks him to send out messages to the "bird and beasts" to alert him of the Ringwraith being abroad and to specifically bring messages to him and Saruman at Orthanc.[45] Among those Radagast alerts are the great Eagles and thus Gwaihir is out looking for Gandalf and is able to rescue him.[46]

Saruman's actions led to his own undoing, once more reiterating the general thread of the book. The actions of good which are pity, mercy, sacrifice, and the actions of evil which are hatred, spite, and malice, all lead to the outcomes of good triumphing over evil. For example, King Théoden spares Gríma's life after Gandalf's healing and his realization that Gríma is a traitor. This act of goodness sows the seed of evil's destruction. Because Gríma was spared, he is alive and with Saruman in Orthanc. After Gandalf confronts and defeats Saruman, Gríma hurls the palantír down from the tower in a last spiteful attempt to injure or kill Gandalf or anyone else with him. Pippin retrieves the palantír and though he gives it to Gandalf, the mere touch of it awakens in him a temptation to look into it to which he eventually succumbs. He encounters Sauron who, instead of questioning him on the spot, mistakenly believes the hobbit to be in Orthanc with Saruman, and dispatches a Nazgûl to retrieve Pippin so he can deal with him personally and torture him slowly.[47]

Again, evil's lust and desire for domination caused Sauron to miss a significant opportunity. Further, Pippin's mistake may have saved Gandalf from looking into the seeing-stone himself that may have resulted in a disastrous encounter with Sauron.[48] Realizing that Aragorn is the rightful owner, the wizard presents the palantír to him. Aragorn in turn, in a deliberate attempt to cause Sauron fear, looks into the palantír a few days later and reveals himself to Sauron. As the rightful owner, Aragorn asserts his authority and strength of will and wrestles the stone from Sauron's will. Fearing Aragorn may have the Ring and knowing now the ranger's strength of will, the Dark Lord reacts in haste and attacks Minas Tirith before he is completely ready.

Sauron's first step in his now hasty plan is to send what he thinks is a debilitating darkness from the fumes of Mount Doom. However, this darkness intended to break the spirits of his enemies allows the Rohirrim to come to Minas Tirith undetected. Éomer rejoices that the darkness of Sauron cloaks them and that Sauron's orcs, "lusting to destroy Gondor" and eager to get to Minas Tirith, knocked down an outer wall that would have impeded

---

45. Op. cit. [8], p. 251.
46. Op. cit., pp. 254-255.
47. Op. cit., pp. 579-580.
48. Op. cit., p. 581.

the Rohirrim's charge.[49]

Meanwhile, Aragorn, having glimpsed Sauron's plan through the palantír, decides to take the Paths of the Dead. This ultimately results in his ability to stop the Corsairs of Umbar from attacking Minas Tirith from the south. Retrospectively, Legolas points out how "strange and wonderful" it is that Sauron's gloom made the dead army Aragorn has summoned even stronger and more terrible and thus Sauron's southern army coming up the river was "worsted" with its own weapons.[50] The chain of events that begins with the evil power's attempt at domination results in Sauron's defeat at the Battle of the Pelennor Fields, the destruction of his great Captain, the Lord of the Nazgûl, and time needed for the Ringbearer to fulfill the quest and destroy Sauron completely.

The same dynamic operates in Frodo's plotline. The reader is aware from the dialogues during the Council of Elrond that Gollum had been captured and tortured by Sauron. Further, that the miserable creature, who still lusted for the Ring and would never stop seeking it, was likely set free in the hope that he would lead Sauron's spies to its location. Gollum himself attests to this when referring to Sauron directive, "'He sees. He knows. He heard us make silly promises – against His orders, yes. Must take it. The Wraiths are searching. Must take it.'"[51] In his narcissism and blindness, Sauron never counted on Gollum's own will and his having a mind of his own. Seeing Gollum as a weak tool, he made a fatal error in underestimating the creature. Gollum, remembering his torture at Sauron's hands and how he promised to find the Ring for the Dark Lord, is filled with hatred of Sauron more than fear and begins seeking the Ring for himself. Thus, Sauron's act of using Gollum this way and so letting him live, proves to be his undoing since Gollum ultimately causes the Ring to be destroyed.

Gollum in turn, despite not wanting Sauron to have the Ring, is still evil and, in a strange twist, brings about his own destruction through malice and the need to show his own spiteful domination. Having a chance to kill Sam as Shelob is attacking Frodo, he misses it because of his need to gloat before taking Sam's life.[52] Later, Sam's mercy to Gollum on the slopes of Mount Doom would not have been possible if not for Gollum's own evil backfiring. This allowed Sam to live and thus let Gollum live until it was his time to perish with the Ring, again gloating, as he dances around in triumph having retrieved his "precious."

---

49. Op. cit. [8], p. 816.
50. Op. cit., pp. 856, 858.
51. Op. cit., p. 619.
52. Op. cit., p. 710.

Evil Thrives from Apathy and Relativity

In *Sacramental Living: Understanding Christianity as a Way of Life*, I touched upon the evil of apathy.

> "Apathy is fertile ground for sinful behaviors that start small but can grow over time to cause many harms. An apathetic state is the worst state you can be in spiritually, save despair... The devil loves a state of laziness and apathy. He does not bother with people in those states because they are at a minimum not a threat and typically do His will by perpetuating evil and misery through non-action. Apathy leads to so much evil that could be overcome with simple loving actions."[53]

In Tolkien's creative universe evil can thrive, grow, and reconstitute itself. Gandalf points this out when he tells Frodo the shadow, after a defeat and respite, is able to take shape again.[54] What the wizard does not say at that time is that this is often due to the apathy of the good races of Middle-earth.

When Galadriel briefly recounts the "years uncounted" of her life, she says that "through ages of the world [she has] fought the long defeat."[55]

She is ancient in years, and a large part of her history has involved fighting Morgoth and then Sauron both of whom she saw defeated multiple times only to rise again and again. At the time of this quote of hers, Morgoth has long since been gone but Sauron is at the height of his power militarily as measured against his chief foes.

Tolkien comments in his letters that, as a Christian and Roman Catholic, he expects history to be nothing more than a long defeat with occasional glimpses of the final victory over evil, in reference to *LotR*.[56] In this short statement, he summarizes one of the core beliefs in Christianity of God's final victory over evil and restoration of the earth and universe as it was intended to be free of evil and sin. Christ defeated evil on the cross during the incarnation, yet evil was not wholly eradicated, simply defeated. According

---

53. Op. cit. [1], pp. 61, 125.
54. Op. cit. [8], p. 50.
55. Op. cit., pp. 347-8. Galadriel is perhaps the character Tolkien most ruminated over throughout his life and certainly into his final years. As a result, this quote does not reconcile with her statements in *TSil* nor her history as recounted in *UT*. For example, there is evidence to suggest that perhaps she did not leave Beleriand prior to the fall of Nargothrond or Gondolin. Further, there are conflicting statements about Celeborn as well. Was he a Sindarin elf related to Thingol, Lord of Doriath of was he a Telerin elf from Valinor as Tolkien seemed to think of him later in life? To me, these inconsistencies, common in real life ancient history, added to the air or reality and authenticity so embedded in Tolkien's works that make them feel so real. (See later, *Chapter 15, The Holy Mother, Elbereth and Galadriel*)
56. Op. cit. [17], Letter 195, p. 255.

to Christianity, when Christ comes again as ruler and judge, evil will suffer a final defeat. Until then the world lives in the period of tension between initial and final victory, or between the present and future experience of the Kingdom, one marked by both sufferings and glory.[57] The task of Christians in this state is to constantly grow in Christ and never be complacent. But it is complacency that breeds apathy that permits evil to flare up and thrive on a continual basis.

A short exchange between Legolas and Gimli, just after the Battle of the Pelennor Fields, captures the essence of apathy in Middle-earth though the word itself is not used. As Gimli appraises the stone work of Minas Tirith, he says men start off well-intended in their actions but when they encounter difficulty they often "fail of their promise."[58] A student of men's history in Middle-earth would have trouble arguing that his characterization of men is wrong. Similarly, Elrond explains that the men of Gondor grew complacent in their once staunch watchfulness of Mordor after Sauron's defeat, and evil things crept back in.[59] Fararmir, in his dialogue with Frodo and Sam in Ithilien, describes how his country fell into apathy through a typical misapprehension of the nature of evil, thinking evil destroyed as opposed to banished.

However, it is not only men in Tolkien's world that suffer from apathy, indifference, or insular thinking. The elves too have a history of complacency. Elrond points this out about his own race during his council, referring to 'the Elves [deeming] that evil was ended for ever [after Morgoth's defeat], and it was not so.'[60]

Further, with few exceptions, dwarves, hobbits and Ents seem to focus more on their own existences for much of their history rather than the greater good. They often remain withdrawn into their own affairs.

A cousin to apathy, and that which can lead to evil or inadvertently aid its cause, is relativity, which Tolkien also addresses. Though Tolkien's characters are not wholly good or evil as Edwin Muir suggested, there is no ambiguity in the moral code of his universe. Aragorn makes this clear to a confused Éomer when he says good and evil have not changed, nor are they different among the different races of Middle-earth, and that their job is to discern them in all circumstances.[61]

It is in Saruman that we see, according to Tolkien, relative belief on the true essence of good and evil is the playground of fools. Saruman forsakes his white robe for one of many colors and proudly displays this to Gandalf.

---

57. *Orthodox Study Bible*, Thomas Nelson, 2008, p. 1536.
58. Op. cit. [8], p. 855.
59. Op. cit., p. 238.
60. Op. cit., pp. 236-7.
61. Op. cit., p. 428.

Gandalf express his preference for white and Saruman boasts that white can be easily altered, Gandalf, ever the wise pragmatist, simply points out to the prideful wizard that it simply means that which was white is no longer white.[62] It is interesting that Tolkien had Saruman choose a many-colored robe to symbolize his change. If Mr. Muir were correct in his analysis, Tolkien would certainly have had Saruman choose black. The multi-colored robe he chooses echoes the Biblical story of Joseph who received a "tunic of many colors" (see Genesis 37:3,4) due to Jacob's love and blatant favoritism of Joseph among his sons. There are also indications that Joseph was prideful, the same condition Gandalf observes in Saruman prior to Saruman's open declaration of his desire for the Ring.

The Addictive Nature of Evil

I had the great misfortune and sadness to watch the slow decay of my cousin over time, and at one time my best friend, due to drugs. His addiction started in sixth grade with alcohol which he had stolen from my parents' bar. He drank so much of it at a friend's house that he passed out in the snow on the walk home. My grandmother found him and had to practically drag him back to his house to save him from freezing to death. By seventh grade he began smoking marijuana, which he would do for the rest of his life. By the time he quit high school in tenth grade, he had tried numerous drugs. But it wasn't until his early twenties, when he tried and became addicted to heroin, that he began to crumble beyond the point of return. Extremely intelligent by nature, he turned into a master of lies and deception and deceived all of us (the family) at times and stole from most of us to get money for the drug. Eventually gone was the person I had once known. Every cell in his body was driven to get the drug. All his thoughts, words, and actions were solely to get heroin. Finally, at the age of thirty, after years of addiction, failed attempts to stop using, and extreme trouble with the law, he shot himself in despair in his bedroom, at point blank range in the head, and died. I cleaned up the room and found, covered in blood in the corner, a pot pipe, a pornographic magazine, a small iron cross, and a religious book, symbols of the dichotomy of his soul.

Possession and addition are terrible things. If it were the sole topic of this book, I could tell many more detailed and both sad and horrifying stories of my cousin, of what I saw in the hardcore drug culture, and other tales of people I literally watched fry their brains and regress into shells of who they once were. Addiction, though a physical condition, is a manifestation of evil, in that it destroys the body and shrivels the spirit over time. I saw this

---

62. Op. cit. [8], p. 252.

in my cousin and others, and an awareness of addiction is present in *LotR*. The power of the Ring, thus the Ring itself, is seductive at first, addictive, and ultimately destructive to its owner, as it is illustrated by the character of Gollum. This power of the Ring is introduced early in the narrative, when Gandalf tells Frodo to throw the Ring into his little fire in Bag End. The wizard knows that fire will not destroy it but points to the addictive nature of the Ring when Frodo realizes, instead of casting it into the fireplace, he has put it back in his pocket.[63]

At this point Frodo has had the Ring in his possession for nearly eighteen years though it seems he never used it. Even so, he shows the early signs of addiction to it. Tom Shippey explains Frodo's reaction to the nature of the Ring by summing up Gandalf's argument:

> [...] that the use of the ring is addictive [and] each use tends to strengthen the urge for another, [but] if the addiction has not been contracted in the first place ... then it has no more power than any other temptation.[64]

The key to understand the Ring's addiction is choice. My cousin, despite whatever addictive nature he had in the first place, could have chosen not to do drugs. It may have been harder for him, same as it is hard for an alcoholic not to drink, but it can be done. The characters Shippey mentions – Gandalf, Galadriel, Faramir – all made choices that resisted the inherent urge of the Ring. However, to those who had some inherent character flaws – Saruman, Denethor, Boromir and Sméagol – this urge posed a challenge that proved to be too much for them. Yet, they were still accountable for their choices.

Denethor's downfall is understandable both through his despair, discussed in Chapter 2, and the circumstance of his life. The Appendixes elucidate that Denethor's bitterness is due to his wife's early death shortly after giving birth to Faramir, perhaps explaining his seeming resentment of his second son. His father, Ecthelion, is said to have favoured Aragorn, disguised as Thorongil, over his biological son. Tragically, Denethor revisits on Faramir the attitude he himself experienced in his youth. His pride and the emotional toll from the death of his own favourite son make it impossible for him to withstand temptation.

Sméagol illustrates a different path of corruption. Gandalf describes him as interested in "roots and beginnings" and tunneling and burrowing.[65] Sméagol's orientation to life, is "downward." He ceases to look upwards as Tolkien describes him. He stops caring about the light and beauty above. He wants knowledge and answers to secrets and origins of things. He seems

---

63. Op. cit. [8], p. 59.
64. Tom Shippey, *J.R.R. Tolkien: Author of the Century*, Houghton Mifflin, 2000, p. 119.
65. Op. cit. [8], pp. 51-52.

eerily like Sauron and Saruman and their focus on knowledge, crafts, and their lack of caring for nature and beauty. Sméagol's misdirected focus is already fertile soil for the evil urge of the Ring to blossom into addiction. He falls to it immediately, murders for it, and becomes, over time, the miserable creature Gollum, the outward sign of the decay within. What is fascinating is that Gandalf is telling the tragic story of Sméagol to Frodo, who in many ways is strikingly similar though this is not immediately apparent. In a vision where Sam sees Gollum as a "whining dog" and Frodo as a "mighty lord," he perceives how they are very similar, despite their differences.[66]

Both Frodo and Gollum are hobbits and both are orphans.[67] Frodo lost both his parents in a boating accident when he was roughly twelve years old. Bilbo shortly thereafter adopted him. Though he calls Bilbo 'uncle', Bilbo was in fact his first and second cousin once removed. Sméagol is raised by his grandmother. Sméagol and Frodo both begin ownership of the Ring at age thirty-three. By all accounts from Tolkien's notes, Sméagol was born in 2430 Third Age and is listed in Appendix B of *The Lord of the Rings* as having found the ring in 2463. Frodo is said to be 33 when he receives it in the first chapter of the book. It is in their initial ownership that we see a striking difference. Frodo loves Bilbo and though he knows about the Ring growing up, he clearly does not care about it. He is delighted in his uncle and does not want him to leave. He is surprised Bilbo left him the Ring. Sméagol refers to his cousin Déagol as "my love" but clearly does not love him enough and murdered him when the latter withheld the Ring. Again, their choices define both hobbits and show, despite these striking similarities, how different they are.

Like Gollum, Frodo suffers from addiction. His unwillingness to destroy the Ring in the beginning of the story is made manifest at the end when he cannot. When Sam rescues Frodo from the orcs in the Tower of Cirith Ungol, Frodo laments believing that the quest has failed and the orcs have taken it and have likely carried it to Barad-dûr. Sam then reveals that he has the Ring. Frodo marvels at first, but then the addiction reveals itself and he greedily and harshly demands that Sam returns it.[68] Sam is reluctant to give over the Ring but he is still able to do it because he is not addicted. Frodo reveals the depth of his addiction in his sudden change of tone. Even after its destruction, the Ring's effects remain to a large extent. We see this in both Bilbo, who owns and uses it for sixty years, and Frodo, who is exposed to the full extent of its crushing evil. Knowing Frodo would suffer even though the Ring was no more, Arwen gives him a gift of a white gem to hang around his neck that he can use as an aid to help him when the "memory of fear and

---

66. Op. cit. [8], p. 614.
67. Op. cit. [17], Letter 214, p. 292.
68. Op. cit. [8], p. 890.

darkness" troubles him.[69]

Continuing the analogy of my cousin and his addiction, Arwen's stone reminds me of the drug methadone, used to wean addicts off heroin. I watched my cousin struggle to stop heroin by going to a methadone clinic daily. Though effective for a time, he was never truly free of the urge to do heroin and went back to the awful drug and never received true healing. Frodo suffers very similarly. Between the destruction of the Ring and Frodo leaving Middle-earth, he is plagued by the echo of suffering near or on the anniversaries of his darkest moments. During mid-March of 3020, on the date coinciding with his attack from Shelob, Frodo laments that the Ring is destroyed and that he feels "dark and empty."[70]

By the time Sam, who was on a short journey, returns by March 25, Frodo is well. Even Bilbo, who by the time the Ring is destroyed has been free of it for years, shows signs of a lingering addiction when the hobbits return to Rivendell to visit him before going home to the Shire.[71] He wants to see it still. Though very mild, the desire is still there. That is why both he and Frodo sail to the Blessed Realm to find true healing from the evil they courageously resisted and fought with all their heart and soul.

---

69. Op. cit. [8], p. 953.
70. Op. cit., p. 1001.
71. Op. cit., p. 965.

Chapter 5: Temptation

Within *The Lord of the Rings*, the fight against the addiction of the Ring is a fight often against the temptation to use it. In order to understand how Tolkien depicts temptation, it is necessary to briefly explore two different schools of thought concerning evil and how it relates to temptation.

Shippey in *J.R.R. Tolkien: Author of the Century*, spends several pages discussing two different views of evil. One of the views is the *Boethian* view, named after the 6th century philosopher Boethius, the author of the famous work *The Consolation of Philosophy*. This view is essentially that there is no such thing as evil. It is only the absence of good. Evil is brought about when people use their free will in thoughts and choices that move them away from God. Contrasting this view is the *Manichaean* as described in the last chapter of this book. In this second view, evil does in fact exist and is a real force to be fought. The Boethian view postulates that evil is internal and is the result of sin; whereas the Manichaean view asserts that evil is external.

Christianity shows the reality of both views. In response to a discussion on clean and unclean food Christ said:

> "Are you thus without understanding also? Do you not perceive that whatever enters a man from outside cannot defile him, because it does not enter his heart but his stomach, and is eliminated, *thus* purifying all foods?" And He said, "What comes out of a man, that defiles a man. For from within, out of the heart of men, proceed evil thoughts, adulteries, fornications, murders, thefts, covetousness, wickedness, deceit, lewdness, an evil eye, blasphemy, pride, foolishness. All these evil things come from within and defile a man." (Mark 7:18-23)

The passage demonstrates the possibilities of the darkness and evil inside us and what it gives rise to. However, the Bible also describes evil in the form of Satan and demons. The Lord's Prayer in Greek specifies *the* evil in "deliver us from evil". In other words, it *personifies* evil.[1] Satan is referenced

---

1. Michael C. Haldas, Sacramental Living: Understanding Christianity as a Way of Life, Eastern Christian Publications, 2013, p. 136.

as a real entity and force.

Judas is perhaps the best example of both views of evil. In the famous scene from the Gospels when the young woman washed Jesus' feet with her tears and expensive fragrant oil, Judas complains saying they could have sold the oil for a lot of money and given it to the poor. St. John comments: "This he said, not that he cared for the poor, but because he was a thief, and had the money box; and he used to take what was put in it." (John 12:6). So clearly Judas has a serious character flaw. Not too long after, at His last supper with His disciples, Jesus gives Judas a piece of bread and St. John further comments: "Now after the piece of bread, Satan entered him... Having received the piece of bread, he then went out immediately. And it was night." (John 13:27, 30). So here we have the external evil, Satan, influencing Judas whose heart seemed ripe to receive him.

Both types of evil, *Boethian* and *Manichaean*, are present within *LotR*, especially noticeable in scenes involving temptation. We see scenes where it seems the temptation is coming more from the mind and heart of the person and we read others where it seems to be coming from the Ring itself. One could easily build a case that the internal weakness of certain individuals makes them susceptible to the external forces, as in the case of Judas. Those most susceptible to temptation seem to be those who have character flaws to begin with that are easily exploited. Conversely, internal strength and virtue also become strong barriers to temptation. Professor Tom Shippey believes that the inclusion of both external and internal origins of temptation is one of the book's great strengths.[2]

Temptation from Without – Bilbo's Story

The first glimpses of temptation in *LotR* seem to be impulses from without, though it is hard to argue in each example that both forms of temptation are not present. In the following examples, it seems the more dominant form of impulse is the external form.

This first temptation we encounter is Bilbo's desire not to part with the Ring in the opening chapter of the book. He has played his little trick at the party, used the Ring to vanish before his astonished guests, and is about to leave the Shire forever. Previously he had agreed with Gandalf to leave everything, including the Ring, to Frodo. Yet when it comes time to honor his agreement he is reluctant to part with the Ring. His reluctance turns into outright anger when Gandalf gently urges him to give it up and he even echoes Gollum's sentiment of the Ring being his precious.[3]

We know from *The Hobbit* that Bilbo finds the Ring by "chance" and

---

2. Tom Shippey, J.R.R. Tolkien: Author of the Century, Houghton Mifflin, 2000, p. 142.
3. J.R.R. Tolkien, *The Lord of the Rings*, Houghton Mifflin, 1954-5, 1965-6, p. 33.

that Gollum, who lost the Ring, refers to it as his "precious". At this point in *LotR* we are a chapter away from knowing that Gollum was once a hobbit who gave in to the temptation of the Ring and became enslaved to it causing his regression and what I call his reverse transformation. Just as the Holy Spirit transforms us over time and gives us new life in Christ, evil does the opposite. In Gollum's case, the Ring and its evil do not grant new life. Instead it stretches out old life unnaturally while causing mental and spiritual regression that manifests in an ugly change of physical appearance. In this scene, Gandalf is several years away from learning the truth of the Ring, but he knows evil in general and becomes alarmed when he sees this sudden personality change in Bilbo caused by his desire to possess the Ring.

Additionally, we know from *TH* that Bilbo does not possess too many character flaws, though he does have them at first. At the beginning of the narrative, he is a content fellow quite satisfied with his comfortable mundane life. He is addicted to comfort, although we learn in *Unfinished Tales*[4] that as a young lad he was adventurous and curious, something very unusual for his race, and that Gandalf noticed it when Bilbo was younger. It was one of a few reasons the wizard seeks Bilbo for the quest of the Lonely Mountain. Gandalf, who had not seen Bilbo in many years, is shocked when he finds the middle-aged hobbit in such a state of "contentment."

In the hospital, when doctors tell friends and family that they are doing everything to make a loved one comfortable, it usually means one thing – death.[5] Most of us hate to be uncomfortable and inconvenienced. But it is in this state of comfort that we often fall into apathy and make little progress in anything. We need some sort of friction that forces us out of our comfort zone if we are to accomplish anything and change and grow as individuals. Everything in nature requires friction to bring about change – a caterpillar to a butterfly, a match and surface to bring about fire – the examples are endless. Human beings require friction as well.[6] Bilbo is resistant to friction and change in his addiction to comfort. Like any mortal, he is dying a slow death physically with each passing day, but, more importantly, he is also dying spiritually.

However, Bilbo does leave comfort behind and transforms into quite the swashbuckling adventurer. It is a slow transformation over the year he is gone, but when he returns to the Shire he is permanently changed for the better. Being initially addicted to comfort is his major flaw. We see from his words and actions that once this shackle is shed that he is a kindly soul, noble, truthful, and charitable as evidenced by his adoption of his orphan cousin

---

4. See *Quest for Erebor* pages 322-323.
5. This was pointed out to me in a sermon by Father George Khitri of the Greek Orthodox Church of St. George.
6. Op. cit. [1], p. 202.

Frodo. With this knowledge, the sudden change Gandalf is witnessing is even more impactful. Gandalf, who does not yet know the Ring is the One, sees clearly that Bilbo is influenced by it and urges him to break its hold over him so he can be free.

As the scene moves forward, Bilbo uses language that shows the addictive effects of The Ring. He says it makes him feel "queer" and admits it would be a relief to be rid of it. As foreshadowing, Tolkien has Bilbo describe the Ring like an eye looking at him. He confesses to Gandalf that it is always on his mind and that he cannot rest unless he knows it is in his pocket. Bilbo struggles for a moment, but only for a moment, which is an important point. Others with more strength but less virtue could not overcome the struggle as the book progresses. Finally, he is able to let the Ring go and laughs for heart's ease. Within minutes he is showing signs of quick recovery and the joy of being healed as he quickly expresses enthusiasm about being off on the road again with dwarves and that he is suddenly as energetic as he has ever been.[7] We learn later that Bilbo is the first person in the Ring's history to date to let it go of his own free will. This is a testament to his character and his ability to do so is routed in his virtue which I describe in more detail later when explaining temptation from within.

Temptation from Without – Frodo's Story

Frodo experiences a different and more difficult level of temptation than his older cousin. Unlike Frodo, Bilbo never has to deal with Ring's temptation outside of the comfort of the Shire save the brief time of his adventure. Frodo faces a progressive form of external temptation that grows stronger as he leaves the confines of the Shire, encounters more and more evil, and draws closer to Mordor.

We do not know much about Frodo and the Ring prior to his long conversation with Gandalf in *The Shadow of the Past* chapter, but there is nothing to suggest any personality flaw. Unlike some of the more flawed characters in the book, there is no apparent gateway to temptation in Frodo's character make-up. Further, at the beginning of *LotR*, Frodo does not seem addicted to his comforts like Bilbo. The younger hobbit certainly comes to enjoy being his own master, but he is never quite settled into his life like Bilbo once was. Tolkien describes him as having strange visions and dreams about lands he has never seen and how a restlessness steadily grows within him.[8]

Frodo experiences his first temptation of the Ring in the Shire due to its penetration by the Black Riders. This is metaphorical in a sense because

---

7. Op. cit. [3], pp. 34-5.
8. Op. cit., p. 42.

the Shire was once a safe utopic space unknown to Sauron and protected by the Rangers. But the once safe-haven is now invaded and infested by the presence of evil. Frodo, like the Shire, is comfortable within himself until an external attack. In a conversation just after Bilbo's final disappearance from the Shire, Gandalf warns Frodo to use the Ring seldom if at all. There is no indication prior to Frodo's first use of the Ring in Tom Bombadil's house that he had used it before, or if so, that much.

Frodo's first temptation is on the road in the Shire, as he travels with Sam and Pippin. His first instinct is to 'hide from the view of the rider', but a second impulse is 'struggling with his desire to hide.'[9] Two powers are at work. Yet, as with all children of Ilúvatar, Frodo is free to choose his course of action and at the last minute, just prior to the rider coming into view, he hides. From the tall grass, he peers out and sees a rider on a black horse and covered in a black cloak and hood that hides the rider's face. Frodo hears what he thinks is sniffing coming from the beneath the hood. He feels the desire to put the Ring on and starts ruminating how Gandalf's advice not to use it is "absurd." He starts to justify using the Ring in his mind, reminding himself that he is in the Shire, and Bilbo certainly used the Ring many times.[10] This first temptation is rather mild. Furthermore, it is a good example of how any of us start rationalizing when we feel the urge to make an erroneous choice. The advice of Gandalf, arguably a Christ figure,[11] and certainly one of the personifications of wisdom, seems ridiculous and undesirable. It seems Frodo would have continued in this train of thought and is only saved here by the "good fortune" of the Nazgûl leaving.

As the episode of Christ's temptation in the desert in Matthew 4 shows, temptation comes often when we are isolated. Christ is led into the wilderness to show that the devil tempts us when he sees us alone and without help from others.[12] As Frodo moves further from his home and into the wilderness, he experiences a stronger urge to use the Ring. Firstly, when he and the other three hobbits are captured by a Barrow Wight. He realizes he could use the Ring and escape the barrow even though it would mean leaving his companions to die. He even rationalizes that Gandalf would support his action since there is, seemingly, no alternative.[13] However, this temptation to save himself at the expense of his friends is easily countered by virtue. Frodo's selflessness and love for his friends invokes the courage within him. He does not use the Ring, attacks the hand of the Barrow Wight and is saved moments later by Tom Bombadil.

---

9. Op. cit. [3], p. 73.
10. Op. cit., pp. 73-4.
11. Gandalf as a Christ figure is further discussed in Chapter 10.
12. "Dynamis", St. George Orthodox Christian Cathedral, January 11, 2014.
13. Op. cit. [3], p.138.

The second temptation outside the Shire happens shortly thereafter in the village of Bree. Tolkien's language is explicit in stating that Frodo clearly realizes the suggestion is coming from "someone or something in the room."[14] Frodo firmly resists the temptation. He is in absolute control because he identifies that the temptation is external to him. There is no second guessing or internal debate, though the Ring seemingly gets its revenge a few moments later. Frodo falls off the table while singing and dancing and it slips onto his finger both alarming his audience and alerting the nearby Nazgûl to his presence.

Frodo experiences the most potent temptation to use the Ring, prior to arriving in Rivendell, on the hill of Weathertop. He and his companions are in the wilderness at night, far from any help. He is terrified, and it proves too much for him to resist. With the Ringwraiths so near, his mind and will are dominated with one thought: to put on the Ring.[15] He does so and is stabbed by the Lord of the Nazgûl. Like many of us when we give into temptation, in retrospect it becomes clear what we did and we chastise ourselves for our weakness. Tolkien shows Frodo going through the same emotion and he realizes he foolishly gave into the Ring's power and berates himself for being weak.[16]

In this instance, Frodo can be seen as deserving the readers' sympathy. By this point in the story, his nobility has shone through several times. He is carrying an ancient evil, which is far more than Frodo is built to bear. Yet bear it he does in progressive suffering. Eventually, at the climax of the narrative, the hobbit crumbles under the Ring's power at Mount Doom and at last claims the Ring as his own: "But I do not choose now to do what I came to do. I will not do this deed. The Ring is mine!"[17] Frodo is spent. He has nothing more to give and he is overwhelmed at last. Shippey encourages readers to discern whether Frodo claims the Ring because he is forced too or finally gives in to inner temptation. Shippey suggests that Tolkien's deliberate use of language when Frodo says "I will not...The Ring is mine" points more toward giving in to temptation.[18]

I agree with Shippey's analysis of this scene, but I quibble with his use of language here and his characterization of this being an inner temptation. The temptation originates from without in Frodo's case before it becomes the struggle from within. Shippey seems to indicate this in spite of his use of language. He writes that, because Tolkien clearly states that in Sammath

---

14. Op. cit. [3], p. 154.
15. Op. cit., p. 191.
16. Op. cit., p. 194.
17. Op. cit., p. 924.
18. Op. cit. [2], p. 140.

Naur "all other powers are subdued"[19], Frodo really could not help himself.[20] He accurately points out that Frodo essentially has no choice: the hobbit is conquered by a vastly greater power that he has no chance of defeating. Tolkien confirms this in one of his letters.[21] Shippey dissects Tolkien's language, showing that Frodo indeed had no choice: "Because Frodo does not choose, the choice is made for him."[22]

Shippey states that Tolkien wrote this scene with the Lord's Prayer in mind, basing this on one of Tolkien's letters.[23] Tolkien goes on in this same letter to explain Frodo in the context of these two petitions within the Lord's Prayer: *Lead us not into temptation, but deliver us from evil*. In terms of *Lead us not into temptation*, Tolkien writes that there are certain abnormal situations in life where the good of the world can depend on an individual's behavior in a circumstance demanding suffering and endurance beyond the strength of body and mind that individual may possess. In this scenario, Tolkien explains this person would be doomed to failure, doomed to fall into temptation or be broken against their will. Such is the case of Frodo. Tolkien describes Frodo as being in a sprung trap. Someone of greater power could have never resisted the Ring's lure to power for as long as the hobbit did; but a person of lesser power, like Frodo, could not hope to resist the Ring's power in the final decision as to whether to destroy it or not.[24] But Frodo is indeed *delivered from evil* shortly after he succumbs to the temptation beyond his power. Gollum attacks him, bites off his finger with the Ring, and then falls into the abyss, destroying himself, the Ring, and Sauron.

Temptation versus Testing

Although the testing of Frodo's fortitude is distressing, a deeper tragedy lies in characters who fall to inner flaws rather than outward pressure. Such are Saruman, Gollum, and Boromir, each of whom falls due to their flawed desire for either knowledge or power or both.

The temptation for knowledge and power is an ancient one. In the Bible, we see it in the very beginning with Adam and Eve's temptation to partake of the Tree of Knowledge of Good and Evil. Adam and Eve's sin was not disobedience. Disobedience is too often thought of in this context as simply children disobeying their parent. As the famous theologian, priest, and writer Father Alexander Schmemann puts it, "the 'original' sin is not primarily that

---

19. Op. cit. [3], p. 924.
20. Op. cit. [2], p. 140.
21. Humphrey Carpenter, *The Letters of J.R.R. Tolkien*, Houghton Mifflin, 2000, Letter 191, pp. 251-252.
22. Op. cit. [2], p. 140.
23. Op. cit. [21], Letter 181, p. 233.
24. Ibid.

man has 'disobeyed' God; the sin is that he ceased to be *hungry* for God and God alone."[25] They gave into the hunger of self-will which meant they were essentially trying to seek life apart from God and on their own terms.[26]

In Tolkien's mythology, the Ring initially came into existence due to the quest for knowledge and power. During the Council of Elrond, Elrond himself recounts how the Elven-smiths of Eregion were eager for knowledge and how Sauron, appearing in a fair guise so they did not realize he was the ancient servant of Morgoth, exploited this. [27]Sauron, like the serpent in the Garden, appears in a form that does not show what he really is, and he is able to manipulate these elves to his own ends. Like the devil, who hates God's children, Sauron hates the children of Ilúvatar and seeks their destruction.

In addition to the Genesis account, which demonstrates the first temptation and the root cause of sin, the following biblical passages may be seen as relevant to Tolkien's portrayal of certain characters to include the fallen wizard, hobbit, and mortal man. The Book of James reads: "Let no one say when he is tempted by evil. 'I am tempted by God; for God cannot be tempted by evil, nor does He himself tempt anyone. But each one is tempted by when he is drawn away by his own desires and enticed." (James 1:13-14)

The elves of Eregion were certainly drawn away by their own desires, as were Saruman and Gollum.[28] Because humanity has free will, if individuals give in to temptation, it is because of their choice to do so. God may test us, but He never *tempts* us. He tests us and His loving gift of free will to us to help us grow. It only feels like temptation if we are succumbing to the desire for knowledge and power to live life on our own terms and not seek Him first.

Tolkien demonstrates the difference between testing and tempting when the Fellowship is brought before Galadriel in Lothlórien and she holds each member of the Company with her eyes and "look[s] searchingly" at them. It is not apparent at first what Galadriel achieves by this. It certainly does not seem malevolent as indicated by her smile and kindly words. Immediately after she is done gazing at each, she says, "Do not let your hearts be

---

25. Father Alexander Schmemann, *For the Life of the World*, SVS Press, 1963, p.18.
26. Op. cit. [1], pp. 59-60.
27. Op. cit. [3], p. 236.
28. In *UT* in the chapter *The Istari*, Curumo (i.e., Saruman) shows hints of pride and jealousy of Olórin (i.e., Gandalf) when the five Maiar are given their mission to go to Middle-earth by the Valar. Curumo volunteers to go as does a Maia named Alatar (one of the Blue Wizards whom Tolkien said failed in their mission). This shows the hints of pride because Olórin (Gandalf) states he does not want to go and is afraid of Sauron. Manwë, the chief of the Valar, tells him that is all the more reason he should go as the third one now chosen. Varda remarks "not as the third" and Tolkien writes Curumo remembers the remark, which shows the first hints of jealousy, another character flaw. Gollum's character flaws are discussed previously in Chapter 4 of this book.

troubled."[29] It is difficult not to draw a comparison between this private audience with the Fellowship and Christ's final private moments with His disciples before His trial and crucifixion. Christ uses similar words when He says, "Let not your heart be troubled" (John 14:1). These words directly follow His revelation of a betrayer in their midst, though it is not apparent to any except John who it is.

As Galadriel faces the Fellowship, in retrospect we realize that a betrayer is in their midst as well, in the person of Boromir. Both Galadriel's purpose in holding them with her eyes and the difference between testing and tempting are revealed a few pages later when members of the Fellowship reveal what they thought while she gazed at them. All of them feel *tested* in their own way except Boromir. He is the only one that feels *tempted* and uses the word temptation to describe his experience with Galadriel.[30] He is also the only one to question her intent, whereas the others seemed to intuitively understand there is no evil behind it. Aragorn astutely corrects him with words that foreshadow Boromir's fate. At the Council of Elrond, Boromir expresses a desire to use the Ring against Sauron but eventually, yet grudgingly, submits to the will of the Council and accepts the Ring should be destroyed. This scene in Lothlórien is alarming and a glimpse of what is to come, when we see this noble man finally allow himself, as St. James put it, to be fully enticed and drawn away by his own desires.

When he finally tries to take the Ring from Frodo, he seemingly transforms and becomes almost possessed.[31] Even though the Ring tempts him and exerts its power over him, Boromir ultimately makes the choice. As described previously and shown by Tolkien later in the book after Boromir's death, Boromir is already prideful and vainglorious, and thus does not have the same armour of virtue: humility, love, and selflessness, against the Ring that the other members of the Fellowship possess. Faramir admits this flaw in his brother's character to Frodo and Sam.[32] Faramir also possesses the same qualities as members of the Fellowship, and unlike his older brother, when the Ring is presented to him unwittingly by Sam, he is not tempted.[33]

Sam experiences the same type of temptation to power as Boromir, but defeats it through love and humility. As he crosses the threshold of Mordor, the Ring shows him a vision of himself as a great hero doing great deeds. Tolkien remarks that in his "hour of trial" it is his love for Frodo that plays a vital part of him being able to resist temptation.[34] Because Sam overcomes the temptation with such virtue, by the time he and Frodo reach Mount Doom

---

29. Op. cit. [3], p 348.
30. Op. cit., pp. 348-359.
31. Op. cit., p. 389.
32. Op. cit., p. 656.
33. Op. cit., p. 666.
34. Op. cit., pp. 880-1.

and the Ring is at the height of its power, he has moved beyond temptation to use the Ring and to even feel despair. His will and reason are completely impervious to attack, subject to be broken only by death.[35]

Others of the Fellowship never even seem tempted and those that do: Gandalf and Aragorn, firmly resist it. When Frodo offers Gandalf the Ring in Bag End, Tolkien describes the wizard's face "lit as by a fire within."[36] As he did with Boromir,[37] Tolkien uses the language of fire to communicate the intensity of the temptation. Gandalf twice tells Frodo not to tempt him as if to reinforce it to himself. Unlike Boromir, even though he is a divine being, in his humility he knows that he is not strong enough to resist its evil. When it is revealed that Aragorn is the heir of Isildur, Frodo offers the Ring to him. Aragorn easily resists temptation and refuses the offer of ownership with a humility born of a sense of the divine at play when he tells Frodo it is ordained that the hobbit should carry it for now.[38]

Notably, Galadriel herself is tempted after testing each member of the Company. Again, Frodo offers her the Ring freely. Considering that by the end of the book Frodo cannot part with the Ring, it is a testament to his own virtue and strength that he is able offer up the Ring at all. Galadriel imagines herself momentarily as what she would be if she took the Ring: a queen in place of a dark lord, and Frodo sees a terrible vision of her as such before she rejects the Ring and simply states "I pass the test, ... I will diminish, and go into the West, and remain Galadriel."[39]

Like Gandalf, Galadriel knows what she would become if she were to accept the Ring, even though she admits to desiring it. She resists the temptation to glory, honor, and power, referring to it as a test. It is interesting that Tolkien has her state that she will diminish, perhaps reminiscent of John the Baptist when he states regarding himself and Christ that "He [Christ] must increase, but I must decrease" (John 3:30). Frodo, as I argue later, is a Christ-like figure in *LotR*, and he too must increase in his spiritual understanding where Galadriel's time and purpose in Middle-earth are nearly at an end.

Galadriel can do this because of her humility attained over her many years of exile. Once proud and willful, she participates in the Noldor's rebellion more than seven thousand years before this temptation. Tolkien describes her in *TSil* as the only woman to stand out as valiant among all of her male family and how she wanted to leave Aman so she could start her own realm that she could rule according to her own will."[40] She attains her goal, and

---

35. Op. cit. [3], p. 919.
36. Op. cit., p. 60.
37. Op. cit., p. 390.
38. Op. cit., p. 240.
39. Op. cit., pp. 356-7.
40. J.R.R. Tolkien, *The Silmarillion*, Houghton Mifflin, 1977, pp. 83-84.

rules over Lothlórien for two Ages, but she knows that either the destruction of the Ring, or Sauron's attainment of it spells doom for her realm and she longs to return home. Pride is the driving force of her rebellion, but humility stands behind her resistance to secure her realm through the Ring.

Boromir lacks the same level of virtue of the characters who pass the test of the Ring, but unlike others who fall to temptation, he redeems himself through virtue with his sacrificial choice to die to save Merry and Pippin.

Chapter 6: The Power of Sacrifice and Friendship

Having explored death, evil, temptation, and some of the darker aspects of *The Lord of the Rings*, the next several chapters focus on the positive aspects of the story. Despite the melancholy of *LotR* and Tolkien's view on "the long defeat" coming through on its pages, the beauty and light in the story far outweigh the darker and sadder aspects. It is ultimately the beauty of the story, and the love its good characters express in thought and action, that is its chief appeal.

To understand sacrifice and friendship is to first understand love. The Bible ascribes Christ the following words: "Greater love has no one than this, than to lay down one's life for his friends." (John 15:13). In this statement, He points to the highest form of love, *agape*, which is considered the purest and most ideal love. There is no motive in agape love except complete desire for the well-being of another. This is the love St. Paul refers to in 1 Corinthians 13 in his famous explanation of love.

In philosophy, types of love are divided into the following, taken from Greek: agape (universal love), eros (sexual affection), philia (friendship), and storge (affection).[1] All of these types of love have their place and are important. For example, in John 21:15-17 the resurrected Jesus asks Simon Peter three times if he loved Him. The original Greek version of the Gospel contains both agape and philia in this passage which points to the importance of all types of love.[2] But it is agape that reigns supreme. It is the love Christ showed for us in his life, crucifixion, and resurrection and the type of love He wishes us to attain.

The Relationship of Love and Sacrifice

Understanding agape goes together with understanding sacrifice and love as *a way of being* not an emotion. It is a genuine concern for another's welfare.[3] Christian love is a choice and an act of will. It is a decision to act

---

1. Michael C. Haldas, *Sacramental Living: Understanding Christianity as a Way of Life*, Eastern Christian Publications, 2013, pp. 113-114.
2. Op. cit., p. 115.
3. Op. cit., p. 110.

in the best interests of others whether it feels good or not; it is an attitude that reveals itself in action. It is more than lovely words or warm feelings; it is commitment and conduct. It produced selfless, sacrificial giving and is expressed through self-sacrifice and servanthood.[4]

Love in action and love as sacrifice are embodied throughout *LotR* and manifest primarily in the characters' actions, not their words. However, Tolkien is not shy about having his characters express love to one another verbally. Sam's words of love for Frodo are prime examples. As Frodo is sleeping in Ithilien, Sam gazes at him adoringly and mutters to himself, "I love him."[5] In another example, Sam offers Frodo his own body as a pillow for Frodo to get rest. In today's world these expressions of genuine love between friends are something cynically interpreted by critics (just do a search on Frodo and Sam on the Internet). The love Sam is expressing is agape and philia, not eros as cynics speculate.

Other male characters also express agape and philia. Aragorn, just before he takes the Paths of the Dead, watches as Théoden, Éomer, and Merry depart and remarks aloud "there go three that I love."[6] Gimli expresses a similar love for Pippin, whom he thought dead, after the Ring is destroyed and the Fellowship is reunited in the Field of Cormallen.[7] Éomer expresses unabashed love for Aragorn shortly after Aragorn is crowned king.[8] But true to Tolkien's style, despite verbal expressions, the agape love of the story comes through most clearly in the characters' heroic actions.

The Sacrifice of Frodo

The first hint we see of selfless sacrifice comes from Frodo. His first reaction to realizing his little gold ring, with its convenient invisibility power, is actually the ancient and legendary One Ring is one of disbelief and then, several moments later, fear.[9] Frodo's reaction is not dissimilar to Moses at the Burning Bush when he realizes that God is giving him a mission. Like Frodo, the great prophet, upon learning God wants him to free the Israelites, reacts by questioning the decision: "Who am I to go to Pharaoh, king of Egypt, to bring the children of Israel out of the land of Egypt?" (Exodus 3:11). Moses then tries to get out of the task, saying he is not capable of it because he does not speak well, referring to himself as "slow of tongue." God becomes angry at his excuses and tells him his brother Aaron will speak for him. Moses then comes to a place of resolve, leaves the Bush and goes

---

4. *Life Application Study Bible*, Tyndale, 1996, pp. 2016, 1900, 1656, 1654, 1625.
5. J.R.R. Tolkien, *The Lord of the Rings*, Houghton Mifflin,1954-5, 1965-6, p. 638.
6. Op. cit., p. 762.
7. Op. cit., p. 935.
8. Op. cit., p. 948.
9. Op. cit., pp. 50, 58.

to his father-in-law and says: "I will go and return to my brethren in Egypt and see whether they are still alive." (Exodus 3:18)

Frodo, too, comes to his own place of resolve. It even seems, when comparing this scene in *LotR* to the events of the Burning Bush, that Gandalf, a God-like figure in the story, is guiding Frodo into this free-will choice. Frodo is staring at his little fire but thinking about the legendary Crack of Doom. Gandalf gazes at the hobbit as he is lost in thought and then merely asks Frodo what does he plan to do, leaving the choice completely up to him.[10]

Foreshadowing is prevalent in this scene: by the end of the narrative Frodo will indeed be staring into wells of fire on Mount Doom. We also see the sacrifice and humility of Frodo and why indeed, as Gandalf hints, the hobbit has "been chosen." Frodo admits that it seems he must keep and guard the Ring for the present no matter what it does to him. He accepts responsibility for what is thrust upon him. His fear and astonishment are replaced by humility; Gandalf tells him this right intent of his heart will guard him against the evil he now bears. Frodo then moves to what will become his *first sacrifice*: he chooses to leave his home, his friends, and everything he loves so that his people might be saved.[11] As Moses is a deliverer of his people from slavery and bondage, Frodo, in his initial sacrifice, assumes the role of protector, trying to keep his people from slavery and bondage. Gandalf tells Frodo earlier in their conversation that Sauron would rather see hobbits as slaves than free.[12]

Returning to the previous passages from the book, in what in retrospect we realize are prophetic words, Frodo acknowledges he can bear his burden if he knows the Shire is safe even if he cannot ever stand there again. He makes his *second sacrifice* in Rivendell by choosing to be the Council's Ringbearer despite an intense longing to remain with Bilbo in Rivendell and enjoy peace. In words of extreme humility he says, "I will take the Ring... though I do not know the way."[13]

This sacrifice ensures that he indeed will not stand in the Shire again, at least not whole and for long. Moses, for all his efforts, does not enter the Promised Land and bequeaths his role to Joshua. Frodo, for all his efforts, cannot find rest in the land he loves. At the end of the story he has to leave the Shire forever to find healing. He leaves his cherished land in the care of Sam, who becomes its beloved mayor for the next sixty years.[14]

Frodo says in the first person that he tried to save the Shire, but then

---

10. Op. cit. [5], p. 60.
11. Op. cit., pp. 60-1.
12. Op. cit., p. 48.
13. Op. cit., p. 264.
14. Op. cit., p. 1006.

shifts to passive voice stating it has indeed been saved, acknowledging his efforts, his failure, and the wonderful outcome. His failing of the Quest is inevitable. Therefore, he also succeeds in that he gives everything he has to give of himself to even get the Ring to the Cracks of Doom. He could do nothing more. Just as in the beginning of the story he quickly shifts focus from himself, at the end he does the same thing. The Shire and Middle-earth have been saved and that is ultimately what matters to him.

The Sacrifices of the Fellowship

Frodo's sacrifice would not have been enough to overcome Sauron. Each member of the Fellowship at some point in the story is completely willing to sacrifice their self-interests, and even their lives, for the sake of others, especially Frodo, and for the greater good. Sam on countless occasions is ready to sacrifice everything for his love of Frodo, and Tolkien refers to Sam as the chief hero of the story.[15] But unlike Frodo, Sam's sacrificial nature evolves with the narrative. Sam is at first willing to leave the Shire with Frodo mainly because of his deep love for heroic tales and his desire to see the elves. This desire is fulfilled before he leaves the Shire when he, Frodo, and Pippin encounter Gildor and his company. It is here after this wish fulfillment that we see the first glimpses of Sam's true character. He tells Frodo after his encounter with the elves that he knows he has a long road into darkness but that he something to do, something to see through to the end.[16]

This vague spiritual sense Sam has of his future becomes concrete to him through his journey. When the Fellowship breaks apart he guesses Frodo's mind and does not let him go to Mordor alone. He continually lets Frodo have more shares of their food as the dark quest continues. When he thinks Frodo is dead due to Shelob's attack and experiences true despair, he sacrifices his heart's desire to remain by his master, recalling his own words to Frodo after meeting Gildor, and realizing he must continue the quest for the good of all. He is even reluctant to give the Ring back to Frodo after he finds him alive, not because he desires the Ring at that point, but because he does not want to burden his master and friend and would rather deal with the burden himself.[17] Finally, as they near Mt. Doom, Sam makes up his mind to die with Frodo for the sake of the quest. Even right after the Ring is destroyed and Frodo has lost his finger, in the face of seemingly imminent death, Sam is still being genuinely sacrificial saying he would have offered

---

15. Humphrey Carpenter, *The Letters of J.R.R. Tolkien*, Houghton Mifflin, 2000, Letter 131, p. 161.
16. Op. cit. [5], p. 85.
17. Op. cit., p. 890.

Gollum his whole hand to spare Frodo losing his finger.[18]

Merry and Pippin are also sacrificial out of their love and friendship for Frodo and are willing to leave the Shire and everything they know behind to go to Mordor. Gandalf sacrifices his life to save everyone from the Balrog. Boromir does the same in a redemptive act to try to save Merry and Pippin. Legolas and Gimli continually demonstrate their willingness to sacrifice as well. Before the quest begins and the Company leaves Rivendell, Elrond makes it clear that no charge or oath is required by anyone in support of Frodo. In his first spoken words of the entire book, Gimli remarks that "Faithless is he that says farewell when the road darkens."[19] Gimli's response shows his heart, and both he and Legolas live these words throughout. They are willing to go to Mordor and die, by their free will choice, if necessary. This is demonstrated most when the Fellowship reached the point where they must choose between going to Minas Tirith and going to Mordor. Aragorn has given Frodo his requested time to be alone while the rest of them, save Boromir who they did not notice had left, tried to decide what to do. None of them will forsake Frodo if he chooses to go to Mordor instead of Minas Tirith. Legolas echoes Gimli's earlier sentiment by stating it would be faithless to led Frodo go to Mordor and not go with him.[20]

Perhaps next to Sam, Aragorn is the member of the Fellowship whose willingness to sacrifice himself is the most poignant. But unlike Sam, Aragorn's is a subtle case because Tolkien only gives us vague hints to his relationship with Arwen and what the quest truly means to him. We see glimpses of their relationship a few times through Frodo's eyes, once in Rivendell in the Hall of Fire and once in Lothlórien on the hill of Cerin Amroth. We are not made aware of the full extent of Aragorn's affection for Arwen until the end of the story, when he marries Arwen and we read their tale in full in Appendix A. At the time of the main events of *LotR*, Aragorn and Arwen have been in love for nearly seventy years. Elrond refuses to let his daughter give up her immortality and marry Aragorn, even though he loves him like a son, unless Aragorn becomes King of the reunited Kingdom of Arnor and Gondor. Aragorn knows this, and despite his great love for Arwen, he is willing to give up his dreams of being with her and his life for others and the quest. He reveals his heart when he first encounters hobbits in Bree, when he simply states that if by his life or by his death he can save them that he will.[21]

We see Aragorn prove his words as he fends of the Nazgûl and gets the hobbits safely to Rivendell. Before the Fellowship sets out on the

---

18. Op. cit. [5], p. 926.
19. Op. cit., pp. 273-4.
20. Op. cit., p. 393.
21. Op. cit., p. 168.

quest, we see Aragorn sitting with his head bowed to his knees, on which Tolkien comments that only Elrond knows what the quest means to him.[22] It accentuates the sacrificial statement Aragorn makes as leader of the company, that he will not go to Minas Tirith and follow Frodo into Mordor, all the more profound.[23] He turns his back on his desire to go to Minas Tirith, reveal his identity as the Heir of Isildur and rightful King, and fight the war as he wishes. He is consigning himself to a likely fatal quest to go to Mordor. Echoing back to the chapter on choice, he is choosing what he sees as right over what is easy and abandoning his own heart for both the greater good and love and friendship for the young hobbits he has sworn to protect. Neither Legolas nor Gimli protest doing the same thing, and Merry and Pippin follow suit, choosing Mordor and death over leaving Frodo.

The Sacrifices of Characters Outside of Fellowship

Furthermore, Elrond and Galadriel are willing to sacrifice the power of the Vilya and Nenya, their Rings of Power which have preserved their beloved homes for thousands of years, to rid Middle-earth of Sauron. Éomer sacrifices his position and good graces with his uncle, father figure, and king to do what is right for Rohan by disobeying an order that is damaging for his homeland. Treebeard tells Merry and Pippin that he and the Ents are likely "going to [their] doom"[24] when they go to Isengard to challenge Saruman but they willingly go. Aragorn's friend Halbarad, who was with Aragorn when he challenged Sauron in the palantír, goes willingly to the Paths of the Dead, knowing it will result in his death.[25] He does indeed get killed at the Battle of the Pelennor Fields as we learn later.[26]

Perhaps the ultimate show of sacrifice is the march on the Black Gate by the Captains of the West. Gandalf offers up a strategy to distract Sauron, with hope that the hobbits are still alive and will be able to complete the quest. He characterizes it a suicide mission, but a necessary one to give the Ringbearer as many opportunities as possible. He says that even if Frodo succeeds they will likely not live to see the fruits of victory. All Captains agree without hesitation to follow Gandalf to their probable death.[27]

The Power of Friendship

These sacrifices do not prove in vain as the Ring is destroyed and Sauron is

---
22. Op. cit. [5], p. 273.
23. Op. cit., p. 393.
24. Op. cit., p. 475.
25. Op. cit., p. 769.
26. Op. cit., p. 831.
27. Ibid.

so crippled that he can never rise again. Without the collective sacrifices of many, Sauron would have never been defeated. One of the great motivators for the selfless acts that ultimately brought Sauron down, was simple friendship.

The Christian ethos teaches of the importance and value of friendship. Notably, the Gospel of John 15 verses 13-15 reads:

> You are My friends if you do whatever I command you. No longer do I call you servants, for a servant does not know what his master is doing; but I have called you friends, for all things that I heard from My Father I have made known to you.

Here, friendship, while being philia, is also agape, the highest form of love. This is a powerful statement on how God values friendship and how Christians should. The combination of agape and philia destroys Sauron in the end more surely than power and might.

We know from Scripture the often-overlooked power of friendship that those who do evil seem to always miss. The Disciples, except for Judas Iscariot, filled by the Spirit, go on to change the world.

As we explore friendship in *LotR* and how it contributes to destroying evil, we see, as Stratford Caldecott points out, friendship seems most intense in pairs within the Fellowship: Frodo and Sam, Merry and Pippin, Legolas and Gimli, Aragorn and Gandalf.[28]

Friendship – Merry and Pippin

The most impactful friendships, in terms of the fate of the Ring and Middle-earth in general, are those of the four hobbits. In the pair of Merry and Pippin we first see the value Tolkien places on friendship. Because of their friendship and love for Frodo, Merry and Pippin form a "conspiracy," to watch Frodo, should he ever try to leave the Shire alone like Bilbo. Frodo is surprised, touched and aghast when he tells them in the little house in Crickhollow that he must leave for the sake of the Shire and they should not hinder him. Pippin responds as a true friend, saying that if Frodo must leave the Shire, he and the others must as well.[29] To Pippin, there simply is no choice. He and Merry must go with Frodo on the older hobbit's dark adventure.

Their loyalty to Frodo is so strong that, surprisingly, Gandalf, at the Council of Elrond, supports the hobbits going with the Ringbearer and

---

28. Stratford Caldecott, *The Power of the Ring: Spiritual Vision Behind the Lord of the Rings and The Hobbit*, Crossroad Publishing Company, 2003, p. E-book.
29. Op. cit. [5], p. 102.

tells Elrond to trust to their friendship rather than what would seem to be wisdom.[30] In a rare instance, Elrond's wisdom is misplaced, though mainly out of concern and compassion for the hobbits. Gandalf understands that despite the danger the four hobbits have faced getting the Ring to Rivendell, they still do not understand the gravity of their choice and situation. True to the sentiment that both he and Elrond expressed at the Council, that no form of might will overthrow Sauron, Gandalf rightly perceives they need to continue this train of thought and trust in a power deeper than sheer might.

Gandalf's trust is not initially rewarded but not at first. From this point in the story until the Company of the Ring breaks apart due to Boromir's betrayal, it would seem that Elrond has the greater wisdom than Gandalf. Merry and Pippin do not contribute much to the Company. Further, it is Pippin, whose youthful curiosity leads him to throw a rock down a dark well in Moria, that alerts the enemy to their presence.[31] One could even argue that if it was not for Pippin alerting the enemy through his stupidity, that they may have made it out of Moria without incident. Not only does it seem Gandalf's trust is not rewarded, it seems his wisdom fails him since it is Pippin who indirectly causes the wizard's death due to the encounter with the Balrog. However, no member of the Company ever blames Pippin, and Pippin himself never expresses guilt. To their credit, it seems the emotion they all feel intensely is pure overwhelming grief for the loss of their leader.

The Company escapes Moria due to Gandalf's sacrifice, rests briefly in Lórien, and then continues to quest until their breakup. It is at this point in the story that we again glimpse the steadfast and profound nature of Merry and Pippin's friendship and brotherly love. The quest cannot continue at this point until the Company decides to go to Mordor, Minas Tirith, or break apart and do both. Aragorn believes Frodo, as Ring bearer, must make this decision; Frodo leaves to be apart from the Company for a time. Aragorn then leads the remaining members of the Fellowship in a discussion not knowing that during this hour Boromir has betrayed them and Frodo is trying to set off alone. Like Elrond, Aragorn ultimately decides that he, Sam, Legolas, and Gimli should go with Frodo to Mordor and Merry and Pippin should go with Boromir to Minas Tirith. Merry and Pippin immediately protest, admitting now that had no idea when they said they would follow Frodo what it truly meant, but still refusing to leave him even if it means going to Mordor.[32] It is in this protestation that we see Merry and Pippin now fully understand the danger, and can even safely infer they know going East will lead to their likely death; but their love and friendship for Frodo trumps their own sense of well-being.

---

30. Op. cit. [5], p. 269.
31. Op. cit., p. 305.
32. Op. cit., pp. 393-4.

However, the Company breaks apart and the next time we encounter the hobbits they are captives of the Uruk-hai. We know Frodo and Sam have left for Mordor, and that Boromir is dead. We also know that Aragorn, Legolas and Gimli are pursuing the Uruk-hai to try to save Merry and Pippin. As Aragorn, in his "Jacob moment",[33] believes everything is against him including his inability to make a good choice, Pippin echoes the same sentiment. He is the first to return to consciousness after being captured by the Uruks, and we learn the specifics of Boromir's failed rescue of them from his point of view. He laments that Elrond listened to Gandalf and let them come on the quest: "What good have I been? Just a nuisance: a passenger, a piece of luggage."[34]

The reader is encouraged to challenge both Aragorn's and Pippin's sentiments which are completely wrong as we eventually find out. Further, just as the disciples believe Christ's wisdom has failed Him due to His Crucifixion, it is easy to think the same of Gandalf, a Christ-like figure in *LotR*.[35] However, as with the resurrection and the coming of the Holy Spirit at Pentecost reveals the truth, it becomes clear with Gandalf's return that the wizard's wisdom prevails. He reminds us of this after the Battle of the Pelennor Fields when he and Pippin find the wounded Merry. He tells Pippin that had not Elrond listened, things would have turned out different and not for the better.[36]

Gandalf is not exaggerating: without Merry and Pippin, the Ents would have never attacked Isengard and broken the power of Saruman; the palantír would not have come into Aragorn's hands and Sauron would not have struck Minas Tirith in haste; Faramir would have died at the hands of his father; the Lord of the Nazgûl would not have been destroyed thus perhaps ensuring Sauron's victory at the Battle of the Pelennor Fields and sealing the fate of the Ringbearer. One could credibly argue that without Merry and Pippin and their actions rooted in love and friendship, the War of the Ring would have been lost.

Friendship – Frodo and Sam

Whereas the friendship of Merry and Pippin has a broader effect in terms of the many events it influences, Frodo and Sam's friendship has a much more targeted outcome. From the point in time when the Fellowship breaks apart, their friendship is about sustaining Frodo in his impossible quest to destroy the Ring. Had it not been for this friendship, Sauron would have recovered

---

33. See Chapter 2, 'Aragorn's Choice' passage.
34. Op. cit. [5], pp. 434-5.
35. Discussed further in Chapter 10.
36. Op. cit. [5], p. 841.

the Ring and the deeds of all the other friendships would have meant nothing in the end.

After the breaking of the Fellowship at the end of Book II of *The Fellowship of the Ring*, we do not encounter Frodo and Sam again until Book IV of *The Two Towers*. Prior to this in both Books I and II, we see Sam's loyalty and devotion to Frodo, but it is not until they split from the Fellowship, that we see the friendship blossom and Sam's true character emerge. However, it is suggested that Sam's relentless decision to follow Frodo and Frodo's acceptance of Sam's companionship is crucial to the narrative. Upon learning that Sam went with Frodo after the breaking of the Fellowship, Gandalf's "heart is lightened". Given how grave the situation is at the moment: Saruman is about to crush Rohan, a country that is essentially leaderless, and Sauron is only days away from unleashing an even greater attack on multiple fronts, it is remarkable that Gandalf feels better over such simple news. The wizard perceives something Tolkien puts into words later through Frodo – that "it [friendship] turns evil to great good."[37] In these words Frodo reminds us about friendship's tremendous capacity for healing and redemption of both situations and people. Arguably, this simple statement by Frodo summarizes Tolkien's prevailing thought on friendship as demonstrated throughout *LotR*. We repeatedly see how friendship helps the main characters to cope with fear, despondency, grief and despair.

Friendship even affects Gollum, who is arguably the most tragically wicked of all the *LotR* characters. His inward corruption is so strong, it is manifested outwardly in his decrepit appearance. Yet, the power of friendship nearly heals him. We see the beginnings of this in *The Taming of Sméagol*. After being subdued and shown mercy, when Frodo removes the elvish rope from his ankle, Gollum begins to change and this change lasts for a while.[38] Louis Markos attributes this change to philia, stating how, because of firm but gentle love shown to Gollum, Sméagol emerges for a time.[39] This "firm but gentle love" is from Frodo and is genuine. Frodo, because he bears the Ring, understands Gollum's torment, and pities him and genuinely wants to help him. Sam feels a degree of pity but far less acutely than Frodo.

This leads to "perhaps the most tragic moment of the Tale"[40] for the author himself, which demonstrates the redemptive power of friendship. As Gollum returns from secretly visiting Shelob, he sees Frodo lying with his head in Sam's lap, and Sam's hand resting on Frodo's forehead in loving protection. Gollum is moved and his inner conflict manifests itself outwardly to the point that Tolkien writes that if either Frodo or Sam could have seen

---

37. Op. cit. [5], p. 679.
38. Op. cit., p. 604.
39. Louis Markos, *On the Shoulders of Hobbits*, Moody Publishers, 2012, E-book.
40. Op. cit. [15], Letter 246, p. 246.

him at that moment, they would have seen "an old weary hobbit, shrunken by the years that had carried him far beyond his time, beyond friends and kin, and the fields and streams of youth, an old starved pitiable thing."[41]

Tolkien repeatedly references this scene in his private letters, suggesting it was of great importance to him. It is also Tolkien at his best in terms of writing. He captures so much and so poignantly in this scene. He writes that Gollum is "crawling and creeping down the path out of the gloom."[42] At this moment, Gollum emerges from the gloom symbolically as well, toward the light of repentance. He sees Frodo and Sam at peace, a perfect picture of pure brotherly love, and is moved by the sight. He looks back in pain toward the mountain pass, wrestling internally with his treacherous plan to betray the hobbits and then, it seems, he repents. He reaches out to touch Frodo's knee.[43] Gollum seems to want to touch Frodo to experience the peace and love he sees in both hobbits at that moment. It makes sense that he reaches out to Frodo. Frodo is the one who has demonstrated love to Gollum. Further, as I will explore in chapter 9, Frodo is a Christ-like figure in the book, and Gollum is a type of Judas.

Tolkien, as he does throughout *LotR*, describes a kind of a spiritual vision. For a moment, the readers are invited not to see Gollum as the wretched thing that he has become, but simply an old hobbit who is beyond his time and place. Tragically, the moment is destroyed by Sam who awakens and offers no love or kindness but only suspicion and condemnation. The brief moment in which Gollum could have been redeemed, that he could have experienced what is known in Greek as *metanoia*, which is a transformation of mind and heart and complete repentance, is gone. The power of friendship and that type of love nearly undoes, in a moment, more than five hundred years of corruption (Gollum is 589 years old and held the Ring for 556 years). But in the end, it is an expression opposite of love and friendship that killed what could have been.

Later, Sam realizes the full extent of Gollum's suffering and fall when he himself bears the Ring briefly.[44] It is difficult not to lament what could have been Sméagol's redemption. It is true that without a corrupt Gollum the quest would not have been achieved since Frodo is overwhelmed and unable to destroy the Ring. However, Tolkien's description of Gollum's lost opportunity suggests to the readers a scenario where Gollum is redeemed and Ilúvatar's purpose: the destruction of the Ring is still achieved somehow. Instead, Gollum executes his plan with Shelob. It fails and becomes the

---

41. Op. cit. [5], p. 699.
42. Ibid.
43. The scene may be compared to the passage in the Bible when the woman with the issue of blood reaches out and touches Jesus's robe in the crowd as she sought to be healed by the mere touch (Mark 5:24-34), Church tradition holds this is St. Veronica.
44. Op. cit. [5], p. 923.

springboard for Sam to emerge in full, as his love for Frodo shines brighter from this point until they reach Mount Doom. It is Sam's simple friendship that for all of these chapters is the sustaining force, the very heart of the quest and the main reason for its success in the end.

Friendship – Legolas and Gimli

This can be considered the least likely friendship in *LotR*. Legolas and Gimli represent the very current issue of race and racial discrimination. Romans 2:11 reads, "...there is no partiality with God." In *Sacramental Living* I argue that racism and prejudice are not only morally wrong, but also sacrilegious. Sacrilege means the disrespect or damage of something sacred. Christians believe life comes from God and that human beings are created in "the image and likeness of God." To then disrespect or damage others in thoughts and actions is to profane God's creation. Jesus said the greatest commandments are to love God and love your neighbor as yourself (Matthew 22:36-38, Mark 12:29-31, and Luke 10:26-28). In His farewell discourse to His Disciples before He was crucified He implored them to love one another (John 13:34). Prejudice in any form is in direct opposition of these commands of love from the Lord and it separates the person from Christ.[45] It creates division due to perceived differences. However, as Kyriacos C. Markides writes, "to follow Christ means to have the capacity to coexist with other people who may be radically different from you."[46]

According to the Christian perception of reality, Christ unites and Satan divides. The Dark Lords of Tolkien's works, Morgoth and Sauron, are also the consummate dividers, always seeking to sow discord, distrust and hate among the free peoples of Middle-earth. As a result of this discord, elves and dwarves have a long-standing enmity. Initially, Legolas and Gimli do not get along. Before they enter Moria, Gandalf has to practically beg them to be cordial.[47] Even the tragedy of Gandalf's death does not bring them together. Just a few days later in Lothlórien, Haldir insists that Gimli alone of the Fellowship must be blindfolded before they enter further into Lórien simply because he is a dwarf. Gimli naturally protests and Aragorn intervenes as their leader and, in an expression of solidarity, insists they must all be blindfolded. It is now Legolas's turn to protest the treatment. Both he and Haldir illustrate, through their prejudice, the successful power of divisiveness Sauron wields even among those that oppose the Dark Lord.[48]

What the request of and death of Gandalf could not heal between Legolas

---

45. Op. cit. [1], p. 247.
46. Kyriacos C. Markides, *Inner River*, Image Books, 2012, p.92.
47. Op. cit. [5], p. 295.
48. Op. cit., p. 339.

and Gimli, the love of Galadriel does. Galadriel and Celeborn together may be seen as representing Adam and Eve prior to their Fall. In this paradise, Galadriel wields great powers, not the least of which is her capacity for love. Christ says in the Gospels that we should love our enemies knowing that love expressed in the face of hate and malice could be transformative and bring about healing to all involved. In Galadriel, Gimli meets love where he expected hate. He hears the semi-secret language of dwarves, Khuzdul, from a person he would consider more of an enemy than a friend. Galadriel puts Gimli at ease by speaking to him in his own language, meeting him at a place in his heart he can relate to.[49] Gimli, being the true-hearted person he is, immediately responds with wonder, "Yet more fair is the living land of Lórien, and the Lady Galadriel is above all the jewels that lie beneath the earth!"[50] This begins his lifelong and pure devotion to Galadriel. This Marian devotion[51] eventually leads him in his old age to sailing with Legolas to the Undying Lands, despite the ban on mortals from doing so, to see Galadriel one more time before his passing. Tolkien hints that Gimli receives a special grace due to his being a "servant' of Galadriel."[52]

Soon after this encounter with Galadriel, Gimli's relationship with Legolas changes dramatically. As Legolas goes abroad, while in Lothlorien, he often takes Gimli with him and the other members of the Company "wonder at this change."[53] From this point forward their relationship grows into a bond of brotherhood. Tolkien tells us nothing else of what happens between them. However, I think we can safely say that Gimli's heart changed toward all elves. Legolas' likely does as well, since he and the others are witnesses to the exchange between Galadriel and Gimli.

---

49. Op. cit. [5], p. 347.
50. Ibid.
51. Op. cit. [15], Letter 213, p. 288.
52. Op. cit., Letter 154, p. 198.
53. Op. cit. [5], pp. 349-350.

Chapter 7: Pity, Mercy, and Judgment

Jesus says in Matthew 5:7, "Blessed are the merciful, for they shall obtain mercy," while James writes in his Epistle (James 2:13), "Mercy triumphs over judgment." Mercy, our ability within our limitations to extend a measure of undeserved grace to others, is often driven by pity; and pity, in Tolkien's tale, is just as critical to other virtues in saving Middle-earth. It is so important that the wisest of Tolkien's characters, Gandalf, whose heart is so big that he continually teaches and perpetuates it throughout the book and at one point even states he pities even Sauron's slaves.[1]

The Pity and Mercy of Bilbo

LotR is riddled with acts of pity and I use the word "riddled" on purpose. It is in *The Hobbit* that the seminal event that saves Middle-earth occurs.

> He [Bilbo] must fight. He must stab the foul thing, put its eyes out, kill it. It meant to kill him. No, not a fair fight. He was invisible now. Gollum had no sword. Gollum had not actually threatened to kill him, or tried to yet. And he was miserable, alone, lost. A sudden understanding, a pity mixed with horror, welled up in Bilbo's heart: a glimpse of endless unmarked days without light or hope of betterment, hard stone, cold fish, sneaking and whispering. All these thoughts passed in a flash of a second. He trembled."[2]

In a brief moment, Bilbo goes through a major transition. It is a microcosm, or a reflection, of a larger transition that he is going through throughout *TH*. During his adventure, Bilbo gradually transforms from a self-focused hobbit addicted to his creature comforts to a much more selfless individual with a strong sense of life's purpose beyond just himself. Seeing Gollum, he forgets about himself to the point of risking his own life because of the pity he feels for this miserable person blocking his way to freedom and safety. He perceives just enough of what Gollum has endured, though he has no idea about the Ring, what it is and what it has done to Gollum, or anything

---
1. J.R.R. Tolkien, *The Lord of the Rings*, Houghton Mifflin,1954-5, 1965-6, p. 725.
2. J.R.R. Tolkien, *The Hobbit*, Houghton Mifflin,1937, 1966, 1994, 1996, p. 96.

else about Gollum's background. He feels empathy that leads to pity, which prompts him to risk a giant leap to escape his potential killer rather than kill him with his sword. Bilbo is trembling in fear for his own safety but it does not overcome his strong sense that killing Gollum to save himself would be murder. Devon Brown writes that this moment is the theological foundation of *LotR* and that the War of the Ring is won, long before it occurs, in this brief moment of Bilbo's pity.[3]

The Pity and Mercy of Frodo

In *LotR*, Frodo goes through the same transition as Bilbo, though in a more protracted manner. In a few very curious passages of *LotR* (curious because Tolkien was so detailed and precise with language) we see Frodo's growth and transition. At the beginning of the book, Gandalf relates to Frodo the full history of the Ring including Sméagol's sad story of his immediate fall to the temptation of the Ring, murder of his cousin Déagol, exile from his family, and eventual isolation in the darkness beneath the Misty Mountain for more than five hundred years. Despite this, Frodo feels no pity for Gollum. He wished Bilbo has killed Gollum when he had the chance and that Gollum deserves death and he and Gandalf have a brief but meaningful exchange suffused with foreshadowing and insight.

We learn in this exchange that Bilbo "took so little hurt from the evil, and escaped in the end, because he began the ownership of the Ring so. With Pity." We also see in Frodo, by his own admission, a frightened and overwhelmed hobbit who is very focused on his ill fate of inheriting this Ring and the fear that the Dark Lord knows about the Shire and hobbits because of Gollum. His mind, dominated for the moment by his sense of self-preservation and love for the Shire, immediately asserts that Gollum "deserves death." Gandalf, in turn, gently points out to Frodo that he has not seen Gollum:

> Many that live deserve death. And some that die deserve life. Can you give it to them? Then do not be too eager to deal out death in judgment. For even the very wise cannot see all ends.[4]

Gandalf knows Frodo is speaking out of emotion and that knowing about Gollum is very different than encountering him. Frodo has some sense that he is reacting emotionally because he concedes the correctness of Gandalf's point because he does not refute it but admits he is frightened. Frodo then slips into judgment stating Gollum deserves to die. This time Gandalf openly

---

3. Devon Brown, *The Christian World of The Hobbit*, Abingdon Press, 2012, E-book
4. Op. cit. [1], p. 58.

corrects him telling him specifically not to be so quick to assign death in judgment.

When Frodo finally encounters Gollum, he recounts the conversation in his mind between himself and Gandalf. However, Tolkien uses slightly different words which I believe to be deliberate on his part. In the original passage, Gandalf says "Then do not be too eager to deal out death in *judgment*."[5] However, Frodo recalls it as, "Then *be* not too eager to deal out death *in the name of justice*."[6] Tolkien is doing this deliberately to show Frodo's growth. Judgment in the context Gandalf used it during the conversation at Bag End connotes a rather harsh mindset. In his thought, Frodo had quickly determined Gollum deserves to die. Frodo remembering the conversation as more about justice than judgment shows that he has become wiser since he set foot outside the Shire. In the Bible, and within Christianity more broadly, justice and mercy are not opposites but rather are linked. Micah 6:8 reads:

He has shown you, O man, what is good;
And what does the Lord require of you
But to do justly,
To love mercy,
And to walk humbly with your God?

In its commentary on this verse, the *Orthodox Study Bible* reads: "The classical definition of true religion: Micah in one verse knits together the basic themes of the books of Amos (righteousness—to do justly), Hosea (steadfast love—to love mercy), and Isaiah (humility and faith—to be ready to walk [or "to walk humbly"] with the Lord your God)."[7] The *Life Application Study Bible* offers these questions: "Are you fair in your dealings with people? Do you show mercy to those who wrong you? Are you learning humility?"[8]

True Christianity ought to reflect righteousness or justice, love as expressed in mercy, and the humility that allows us to do this in faith all at once. Christ says in Matthew 7:1, "Judge not, that you be not judged." He does not speak about discernment of a given situation where one makes a judgment or judgments, but about a sweeping judgment of someone's entire person. Frodo is demonstrating in this internal dialogue that he has grown in wisdom enough to know the difference. Further, Tolkien adds another nuance in this regard: Frodo remembers Gandalf's words as "even the *wise*

---
5. Op. cit. [1], p. 58.
6. Op. cit., p. 601.
7. *Orthodox Study Bible*, Thomas Nelson, 2008, p. 1008.
8. *Life Application Study Bible*, Tyndale, 1996, p. 1343.

cannot see all ends," even though what Gandalf actually said was "for even the *very wise* cannot see all ends." Frodo is indeed becoming *wise* but he still has a lot more growth to achieve at this point before he becomes numbered among the *very wise*.

Frodo's transformation echoes Bilbo's. Even though Frodo is not as addicted to his creature comforts as his uncle, is very self-sacrificial in wanting to save the Shire upon learning the truth about the Ring, and again in Rivendell when he volunteers to take the Ring to Mount Doom, he still grows as a person. In addition to changing 'judgment' to 'in the name of justice', Tolkien adds the following words to Frodo's thoughts: "Then be not too eager to deal out death in the name of justice, *fearing for your own safety*." Frodo is sacrificial up to this point regarding his own safety, but as sacrificial as he has been, like anyone who commits to being a Christian, it is a continuing journey of dying to self as Christ commands. Frodo has not yet died to self as much as he would by the end of the story. But it is at this point that he makes the transition, like Bilbo did, of not worrying about his own safety when it comes to the pitiable Gollum. He admits he is afraid but will not hurt Gollum because not that he sees him he does in fact pity him.[9] When Frodo comes out of his thoughts and finally speaks aloud the transition from his self in Bag End is complete. In a moment of authenticity that is a hallmark of Frodo's character, he admits to being afraid, but despite this fear, it is pity that will rule his decision.

The Pity and Mercy of Sam and Others

Sam eventually shows pity to Gollum, but only after he too has borne the Ring for a time. He is reluctant at first to take Gollum on as a third companion and constantly reminds Frodo of Gollum's villainy. Until Sam has his moment of pity for Gollum on the slopes of Mount Doom, he infers on multiple occasions that, had it been up to him, he would have abandoned Gollum or let Gollum be slain. For instance, he wants to tell Faramir to shoot Gollum at the Forbidden Pool.[10] If he had his way, Gollum would have been long dead prior the hobbits' arrival at Orodruin and the quest would have likely failed.

Sam is not the only person to have this attitude to Gollum. At the Council of Elrond, Boromir speaks matter-of-factly about Gollum's deserved fate after he hears how Aragorn has captured the creature and delivered him to Thranduil's kingdom. He assumes Gollum was put to death asking "what doom" did Thranduil's people administer.[11]

---

9. Op. cit. [1], p. 601.
10. Op. cit., pp. 669-670.
11. Op. cit., p. 248.

The tone of the conversation suggests that an assumed death penalty for Gollum would be accepted as just by all at the table. Aragorn's response reminding Boromir of Gollum's suffering and being kept in prison supports this assumption. Legolas then reports Gollum escaped and Aragorn, like Sam, incorrectly assumes a free Gollum is a liability.[12] Aragorn says they all shall rue it but he is wrong. Legolas points out Gollum's escape occurred due to kindness spurred on by Gandalf's pity for Gollum. From Gandalf's perspective, there is wisdom in kindness though this type of wisdom is clearly only perceived through the heart not the logic of the head. Earlier, during their conversation in Bag End, he says as much to Frodo when he tells him Gollum is in prison in Mirkwood but they are treating him with as much kindness as they can.[13] The wizard brings the debate about Gollum and his escape to a close by reminding them something bigger may be going on that neither Sauron nor Gollum can foresee, echoing the same sentiment he shared with Frodo concerning Gollum at Bag End.[14] This kindness and pity, urged by Gandalf, adopted by the Wood Elves, and further perpetuated by Frodo, saves the quest.[15] All of this is a continuation of the pity Bilbo showed Gollum in the cave.

There are other examples of pity that serve to continue and support the quest, though not as directly. For example, pity gives Merry the courage he needs to save Éowyn and destroy the Lord of the Nazgûl, turning the tide of the Battle of Pelennor Fields.

Frodo's Transformation through Pity

We see the culmination of this collective pity in Frodo's words after the death of Gollum. He reminds Sam that Gandalf said Gollum may have something to do before the end and admits without Gollum the Ring would not have been destroyed and that he and Sam should forgive the creature.[16] Frodo's coming to selflessness through suffering is complete and is shown in his forgiveness of Gollum.

With regards to Frodo, Tolkien comments that:

> all the passages dealing with Frodo and the Ring, I think you will see that not only was it quite impossible for him to surrender the Ring, in act or will, especially at its point of maximum power, but that this failure was adumbrated from far back... *He (and the Cause) were saved – by Mercy:*

---

12. Op. cit. [1], pp. 248-9.
13. Op. cit., p. 58.
14. Op. cit., p. 249.
15. Op. cit., p. 923.
16. Op. cit., p. 926.

by the supreme value and efficacy of Pity and forgiveness of injury.[17] [Italics mine]

Tolkien further emphasizes that "at this point the 'salvation' of the world and Frodo's own 'salvation' is achieved by his previous pity and forgiveness of injury."[18]

In the end, pity and mercy save Middle-earth. It is pity that comes from the wisdom of the heart that transcends logic and reason. Sauron, and those that follow him, operated in a logical, myopic manner based on reason; Gandalf, Frodo, Aragorn, Sam, and others, operated from a deep sense of conviction in their hearts as to what was right and what was true, and held to values such as pity that trumped any sense of self-preservation. Thus, as Stratford Caldecott rightly argues, we see God at work in *LotR*, working both within the love and freedom expressed by the good characters as well as within their mistakes, and bringing good out of choices of the evil characters that ultimately result in scenario where providence and mercy triumph and free will and grace are completely vindicated."[19]

---

17. Humphrey Carpenter, *The Letters of J.R.R. Tolkien*, Houghton Mifflin, 2000, Letter 191, pp. 251-252.
18. Op. cit., Letter 181, p. 234.
19. Stratford Caldecott, *The Power of the Ring: Spiritual Vision Behind the Lord of the Rings and The Hobbit*, Crossroad Publishing Company, 2003, p. E-book.

PART TWO

THE CHRISTIAN TYPOLOGY IN *THE LORD OF THE RINGS*

Chapter 8: An Explanation of Typology

Christian Typology, touched upon briefly in the introduction, is more widespread in Eastern Christianity (i.e., Orthodox or Eastern Catholicism) than in Western Christianity (i.e., Roman Catholicism, Protestantism, or non-denomination). Typology was a prevalent way to interpret the Bible from the time of the early church and remained popular in the Middle-Ages after the East-West Schism. In recent years, it seems to have diminished significantly in the west, but not in the east. In the Eastern Church's framework, it is still the primary way the Bible is understood.

What is Christian Typology?

Typology is a way of reading, interpreting, and understanding the Old Testament as something that foreshadows or points to the events presented in the New Testament. In other words, as we read the Old Testament, we may understand many of its events and people as forerunners to the events and people of the New Testament. For example, as described in the introduction, Abraham's near sacrifice of his son Isaac, and God saving Isaac and offering a ram as a substitute, points to the ultimate sacrifice by God of His Son, Jesus Christ, as the substitute for mankind due to its sins. Conversely, within typology, we see the New Testament as something which allows us to look back at the Old Testament and make fuller sense of its events and people. St. Maximus once wrote "the Old and New Testaments together form a single mystery." Often the words "type" and "antitype" are used when discussing typology. The type is the first person or event, and the corresponding future person or event is called the antitype. Strictly speaking, "it is a relationship that begins with a promise and ends with a fulfillment in Christ.[1]

Typology is not allegory, and Tolkien "cordially dislik[es] allegory in all its manifestations, and always have done so since [he] grew old and wary enough to detect its presence."[2] He also makes it clear in a letter of his that *LotR* is built on religious ideas but not an allegory of them.[3] Allegory,

---
1. *Orthodox Study Bible*, Thomas Nelson, 2008, p. 190.
2. J.R.R. Tolkien, *The Lord of the Rings*, Houghton Mifflin, 1954-5, 1965-6, p. xvii.
3. Humphrey Carpenter, *The Letters of J.R.R. Tolkien*, Houghton Mifflin, 2000, Letter 211,

as defined by Webster's dictionary, is "a story in which the characters and events are symbols that stand for ideas about human life or for a political or historical situation." For instance, C.S. Lewis' Aslan is an allegorical Christ. Lewis deliberately developed his character to represent Christ. Tolkien consciously did no such thing with any of his characters. Gandalf, Aragorn, and Frodo have Christ-like aspects and are applicable to Christ but they are not fictional depictions of Christ. Type is more like applicability than allegory.

Understanding and reading Scripture typologically is different from reading it through an allegorical lens. Those who adhere to the typological perspective see it as a faithful way to more clearly see God's revelation of Himself throughout and over time and history, and how he discloses His plan within actual events, versus an allegorical perspective that contains hidden meaning.[4]

Examples of "Types"

St. Paul is the initiator of typology per what he writes in both Romans and First Corinthians:

> "Nevertheless death reigned from Adam to Moses, even over those who had not sinned according to the likeness of the transgression of Adam, who is a type of Him who was to come." (Romans 5:14)

> "And so it is written, "The first man Adam became a living being." The last Adam became a life-giving spirit. However, the spiritual is not first, but the natural, and afterward the spiritual. The first man was of the earth, made of dust; the second Man is the Lord[e] from heaven. As was the man of dust, so also are those who are made of dust; and as is the heavenly Man, so also are those who are heavenly. And as we have borne the image of the man of dust, we shall also bear the image of the heavenly Man." (1 Corinthians 15:45-49)

In the first scripture, St. Paul explicitly uses the word 'type' and in the second does a further comparison. Adam, the prototypical man, falls from his path toward perfection. This perfection is fulfilled in the Second Adam, Christ.

Jonah is another example of a type of Christ. Just as Jonah spends "three days and three nights" in the belly of the whale, Christ spends "three days and three nights" in the belly of the earth. Jonah emerges from symbolic death and Christ emerges from real death. The mysterious figure

---

p. 283.
4. "Dynamis", St. George Orthodox Christian Cathedral, August 1, 2014.

Melchizedek, described briefly in Genesis 14:18-20, is also a type of Christ. After freeing his nephew Lot, who had been captured by enemies during battle, Abraham returns from his mission and is greeted by the King of Jerusalem, who blessed him. We see in this Scripture a type of the Eucharist that Christ would institute during the Last Supper. Melchizedek is never mentioned again in Genesis or in any other Scripture describing a historical event. However, he is mentioned once in Psalms and this is the only other reference to him in the Old Testament, but it shows that this obscure figure was the precursor to an eternal priesthood. The author of the New Testament Book of Hebrews spends chapters 5-7 showing that Melchizedek is a type of Christ, which points to His eternal priesthood.

In addition to being understood as an ultimate priest, Christ is also seen as a prophet and King.[5] King David is often viewed as a type of Christ and his life foreshadows Christ's in that he is anointed, is a "suffering servant" for a time, is persecuted and is king and always relies on God.[6]

Moses is a type of Christ as an ultimate Prophet. Deuteronomy 18:15 contains the following, written from Moses' point of view: "The Lord your God will raise up for you a Prophet like me from your midst, from your brethren. Him you shall hear." In the New Testament, Christ points to Moses as a type of Himself when he says the following: "And as Moses lifted up the serpent in the wilderness, even so must the Son of Man be lifted up, that whoever believes in Him should not perish but have eternal life." (John 3:14-15). The event Christ refers to is in Numbers 21. The Israelites, despite being delivered miraculously from the Egyptians, lose faith in God because food and water is scarce. Venomous serpents then enter their camp and many of them die. They repent and Moses tells them to make a copper serpent, put it on a pole so that it can be lifted up above them, and to look upwards at the copper serpent if they get bitten by any of the live serpents. Those that get bitten and look at the copper serpent live. Here, Christ refers to himself being lifted up on the cross. Just as the ancient Israelites gaze upward at the copper serpent to gain life, those who look to the crucified Christ also find life as the power of sin and death is destroyed in them.[7]

Although typology is primarily about fulfillment in Christ, we do see other examples of type in the Old Testament. Christ himself states that John the Baptist is Elijah come again, so Elijah is a type of the Forerunner (Matthew 17:12-13). Joseph, the son of Jacob, who receives dreams from God that govern his actions is a type of Joseph, the earthly father of Jesus, who also receives dreams sent by the Lord as to what actions he should take.

---

5. Op. cit. [1], p. 190.
6. http://orthodoxwiki.org/David. [Accessed 01/06/2018].
7. Op. cit. [1], p. 1427.

Tolkien and Typology

Tolkien, by his own admission, did not see his fictional world set on another planet or in another universe. In one of his letters he wrote that he saw the events of his mythology as happening in the deep past of our world, about 6,000 before our recorded history.[8] Without Tolkien's letters, admittedly, it is hard to connect the events and geography of Middle-earth to our world. Until his son, Christopher, began publishing the evolution of Tolkien's thought concerning his imaginary world and history in *Unfinished Tales* and the twelve volumes that comprise *The History of Middle Earth*, I did not find it so apparent. *LotR* has a familiarity and historical feel to it, and as a person who loved and read history and studied literature, I connected with it in *LotR* since Tolkien used his vast knowledge of history, language, and literature to inform his creation. A significant moment for me that clearly tied Tolkien's fictional world to our world and to Christianity occurs in *The Debate of Finrod and Andreth* from Volume X of *The History of Middle-earth*. Within it, Galadriel's brother Finrod debates with a mortal woman named Andreth on the nature of hope and potential incarnation of Eru. At first, Andreth is skeptical of Eru entering "into the thing that He has made, and that which He is beyond measure greater." To that, Finrod responds that "he is already in it, as well as outside", referring to him as 'the Author without' and 'the Measureless'. Finrod deems that in order for the world's hurts to be healed utterly, "any medicine for the wounds … must … come from without."[9]

Tolkien wrote this many years after *LotR* was published, which shows how he continued to wrestle with the connection of his imaginary history to the history of our own world. Though there is no direct evidence that Tolkien knew about Eastern Christian typology, it is a plausible assumption. I am not making a case that it was conscious in his thought as he wrote *LotR*. Tolkien considered *LotR* an unconsciously Catholic work in its creation and deliberately Catholic in its revisions. However, given everything presented thus far, his characters and events may well be seen as "types" that point to Biblical history if the narrative is seen through both a Christian and a historical lens.

Christopher Snyder, in *The Making of Middle-earth*, gives a brief treatment of Christian interpretations of *LotR*. He presents arguments from many of the thought leaders of today when it comes to the Christian understanding of Tolkien's works, such as Peter Kreeft, Richard Purtill, and Joseph Pearce. He also provides a typological list while concluding his thoughts on Tolkien's Christian influence and his refuting of allegory. He shows some obvious typological parallels such as Eru being God; Gandalf, Aragorn, and Frodo

---

8. Op. cit. [3], Letter 211, p. 283.
9. J.R.R. Tolkien, *Morgoth's Ring*, Houghton Mifflin, 1993, p. 322.

being types of Christ; Galadriel being like Mary; Morgoth and Sauron being like Satan.[10] I also explore many of them in the next several chapters as well and some not on his list.

---

10. Christopher Synder, *The Making of Middle-earth*, Sterling Publishing, 2013, E-book.

Chapter 9: Frodo as a Type of Christ

Throughout the Old Testament, God raised up prophets, priests, and kings from among His chosen people to serve and lead Israel... many prefigured the coming of Christ our God, the promised Prophet, Priest, and King.[1]

This statement exemplifies a unified thought among Christians that Christ is their ultimate Prophet, Priest, and King. These are the three roles commonly ascribed to Him. There is also a fourth role, that of healer or restorer. Tolkien acknowledged some of his characters reflected these roles, notably in conversation with Clyde Kilby. Kilby's account highlights

> ... a paper called "Kingship, Priesthood, and Prophecy in *The Lord of the Rings*,"...This paper proposed that Tolkien's story was one of the most misunderstood works of modern fiction because critics were so often unacquainted with the Bible. The writer insisted that the story is based on the manner of Christ's redemption of the world. Middle-earth is saved, he argued, through the priestly self-sacrifice of the hobbit Frodo, "the Lamb whose only real strength is his capacity to make an offering of himself." It is saved through Gandalf, "the major prophet figure," as well as the mastery of Aragorn, who begins despised and ends as King....
> Tolkien wrote me of his opinion: "Much of this is true enough – except [the impression] that I had any such "schema" in my conscious mind before or during the writing.[2]

Most books that compare *LotR* characters to Christ focus on Frodo, Gandalf, and Aragorn. These comparisons naturally point to Frodo as the priest, Gandalf as the prophet and Aragorn as the king. Frodo fulfills the role of priest as characterized in both the Old and New Testaments, offering gifts and sacrifices on behalf of the people. Like Christ, Frodo sacrifices himself to save Middle-earth. A prophet is someone who predicts the future but in most Biblical references it refers to both a person of power, but also as a person who edifies and imparts teaching and wisdom. Gandalf is a prophet

---

[1]. *Orthodox Study Bible*, Thomas Nelson, 2008, p. 190.
[2]. Clyde S. Kilby, *Tolkien and the Silmarillion*, Harold Shaw Publishers, 1976, pp. 55-56.

in this respect, being a Maia who occasionally reveals his true nature and power but most often guides others into needed action with teaching and counsel. A king is a leader, warrior, and healer. Aragorn clearly fulfills the role of king by ascending to the throne of Gondor and Arnor near the end of the story, but prior to his enthronement, leading others in battle and healing many as well.

However, these characters cannot be limited to just one role. For example, both Aragorn and Gandalf sacrifice themselves and both are also healers: Aragorn with *athelas* in Houses of Healing and Gandalf with Théoden. Peter Kreeft writes that all three go through a form of death and resurrection and are all saviors.[3] Gandalf dies in Moria only to reappear in Fangorn sometime later. Aragorn symbolically dies when he takes the Paths of the Dead, but reemerges at the Battle of the Pelennor Fields. Frodo's death and resurrection is more complex as it happens multiple times: in the Barrow, after his near succumbing to the wound dealt by the Nazgûl, being thought dead in Moria, and emerging form the Dead Marshes. His most poignant death is when he "dies" as he yields to the Ring only to be unintentionally saved by Gollum and resurrected by Aragorn. Finally, he departs Middle-Earth to find healing and wholeness, to find life again. The fact that none of the characters are clear analogues of Christ suggests Tolkien did not write an allegory nor did he try to represent Christ directly.

The Passion of Frodo the Sacrificial Lamb

Frodo can be read as the sacrificial lamb of *LotR*. He carries the burden of the Ring in a similar fashion to Christ who carries the burden of sin for the world. Further, in many ways, his life ranging from Hobbiton to the Grey Havens, follows a progression like that of Christ as described in the four Gospels. No other Christ-like figure in *LotR* follows such a progression or exemplifies Christ's Passion so clearly. Frodo is the priest who offers himself of his own free will twice as described in Chapter 6 – first to save the Shire when he resolves to "leave Bag End, leave the Shire, leave everything and go away,"[4] and next to save the world when he pledges to take the Ring to Mordor at the Council of Elrond.

It is in these two gestures and the events surrounding them that we first see Frodo as a type of Christ. For example, as he recovers from his wound by the Morgul blade, he is asleep for three days. His sleep and being recalled from "death" is similar to Christ being in the tomb for three days before His resurrection. Not too soon after he wakes from this near-death experience, he attends the Council of Elrond and makes his pledge to take the Ring to

---
3. Peter Kreeft, *The Philosophy of Tolkien*, Ignatius, 2005, pp. 222-223.
4. J.R.R. Tolkien, *The Lord of the Rings*, Houghton Mifflin,1954-5, 1965-6, p. 61.

Mordor though "he does not know the way." This is reminiscent of Christ in the Garden of Gethsemane when he says, "let this cup pass from Me; nevertheless, not as I will, but as You will." (Matthew 26:39). Frodo, like Christ, does not want to commit to a quest of pain and likely death, yet does so anyway. Christ does so to do the will of his Father; Frodo does so out of a sense of something providential beyond himself guiding him. Tolkien writes, "An overwhelming longing to rest and remain at peace by Bilbo's side in Rivendell filled all his heart. At last with an effort he spoke, and wondered to hear his own words, as if some other will was using his small voice."[5] Understood within the full scope of Tolkien's work, this is Eru Ilúvatar. Shortly after his decision, Christ is tortured and crucified. Frodo, in a much more drawn out fashion, embarks upon a quest of torture and excruciating suffering.

Though both sacrificial gestures in Bag End and in Rivendell are Christ-like, Kreeft also points out a comparison to the Virgin Mary. He describes Frodo as a "Marian figure", comparing the hobbit's statement that he will take to Ring to Mordor though he does not know the way to her statement to Gabriel, "Let it be done according to your word" (Luke 1:38). He writes that "they are opposite sides of the same coin" in that Mary agrees to carry Christ, the savior, to save the world, whereas Frodo agrees to carry the Ring, the destroyer, to its death to save the world. Tolkien loved the Blessed Mother. It is not surprising to see something of Mary in the central hero of his book though he certainly also has more a direct and discernable Marian aspects to characters such as Galadriel and Elbereth (see Chapter 15).

However, before Frodo embarks on his quest and leaves Rivendell, Elrond tells him he believes this is the hour of the Shire-folk to arise out of their quiet fields to shake the towers and counsels of the great.[6] This calls to mind Micah 5:1 where the prophet declares that out of Bethlehem, the smallest and least significant of towns, will come the savior of mankind: "…And you, O Bethlehem, House of Ephrathah, though you are fewest in number among the thousands of Judah, yet out of you shall come forth to me the One to be ruler of Israel."

Preparation, Suffering and Crucifixion

Like Christ, Frodo spends many years in a quiet town in a form of preparation for his mission. Unlike Christ, Frodo's mission is not one where he heals people or performs miracles, but it is more like Christ's Passion and he suffers in a Christ-like manner. His life, from his departure from Rivendell after his pledge, to his final crumbling under the weight of the Ring at Mount

---
5. Op. cit. [4], p. 263.
6. Explored in Chapter 2.

Doom, serves as his march to Golgotha, with the trek up the slopes of Mount Doom as his *Via Dolorosa* (the street in Jerusalem that led to Golgotha where Christ was crucified).[7]

In Mordor, Frodo is struck hard with a whip, pierced with thorns, suffers under the weight and burden of the Ring, hungers and thirsts greatly, and is pushed beyond his endurance as he crosses the plains of Gorgoroth and nears Mount Doom. When he gets to the mountain and starts the ascent to Sammath Naur, he is too spent to go on. Sam plays the role of Simon of Cyrene, who carries Christ's cross, and carries Frodo.[8] Together, they make their way up the path to the chambers of fire like Simon and Christ made their way along the *Via Dolorosa*.

Frodo's "crucifixion" comes in Sammath Naur, the chamber of Fire. It is in this scene clearly demonstrates that Frodo is not an allegorical representation of Christ. Whereas Christ succeeds in His mission, remained sin free, and achieves victory; Frodo fails and, by succumbing to the Ring, falls into sin. Christ is in complete control of His choices as He is crucified. His last words are recorded as "It is finished!" (John 19:30). The Scripture goes on to read "And bowing His head, He gave up His spirit." St. John Chrysostom, one the of the three great Hierarchs of the Eastern Orthodox Church, points out on his writings that Christ does not die before bowing his head which would be the natural result of death. Instead, He bowed his head first and then gave up His spirit.[9] Tolkien makes it clear that Frodo does not choose. He is not Christ who can save Himself and offer all the means of salvation in the process. Instead, Frodo requires saving, as he reaches the end of his endurance and fails; ultimately, it is divine intervention that saves him.

Like Christ, Frodo expresses forgiveness despite his suffering, but again, there are differences. In the famous passage, "Forgive them for they know not what they do" (Luke 23:34), Christ petitions for forgiveness to all who have wronged Him while he is on the cross. Frodo asks Sam for forgiveness of Gollum shortly after the Ring is destroyed.[10] Unlike Christ, his crucifixion is over when he offers forgiveness. Further, his petition is focused only on one person, Gollum, though we see later, he has been forever transformed into a person of peace.

Reminiscent of his healing sleep in Rivendell, Frodo is rescued by Gandalf and the eagles and then healed by Aragorn through a deep sleep. When we see Frodo again it is through Sam's eyes once more. Sam, who was also healed and put into a deep sleep by Aragorn, awakens to the sweet fragrance of Ithilien and thinks for a moment much of his recent weeks were a dream until he sees Frodo lying beside him and notices his wounded hand with the third finger missing.[11]

---

7. Richard Purtill, *J.R.R Tolkien: Myth, Morality, and Religion*, Ignatius Press, 1984, p. 74.
8. Op. cit. [3], p. 222.
9. Op. cit. [1], p. 2463.
10. Op. cit. [4], p. 926.
11. Op. cit., p. 930.

This scene echoes that of Disbelieving Thomas in the Gospel of John, when Thomas finally believes the reality of the risen Christ for himself after he sees Jesus with His wounds. In a complementary passage from Luke 24, we also see that the Disciples were scared when they first encountered the resurrected Jesus, thinking Him a ghost or a spirit, until He showed them His wounds and asked for something to eat. Like the Disciples, Sam momentarily doubts his reality, thinking it all a bad dream, until he sees the wounded Frodo.

Frodo's "Resurrection"

Frodo is resurrected symbolically, but, unlike Christ, he is not yet transformed and whole. He does not experience permanent healing. He is still wounded and broken to an extent, and his life from this point forward is more reflective of the pre-resurrected Christ. For example, when the hobbits finally return home and find the Shire being run by ruffian men, they organize a rebellion, win a decisive battle and set things right. Afterwards, they go back to a familiar way of life, but Sam observes that Frodo "dropped quietly out of all the doings of the Shire, and Sam was pained to notice how little honor he had in his own country."[12] Calling to mind the Scriptures in all three synoptic Gospels: "no prophet is accepted in his own country" (Luke 4:24), "A prophet is not without honor except in his own country and in his own house" (Matthew 13:57), and "A prophet is not without honor except in his own country, among his own relatives, and in his own house" (Mark 6:4); we see Frodo suffering the same fate among his own that Christ did.

In another pre-resurrected Christ comparison, we see that Frodo is transformed into a pacifist. Christ is considered the "Prince of Peace" both before and after His resurrection. Just before the Battle of Bywater to cleanse the Shire of Saruman's ruffians, the hobbits are discussing their plan. Merry and Pippin, who have now become warriors, and Sam to an extent, want to fight, but Frodo is reluctant. In Mordor, he gives his sword to Sam, saying that he will not "strike a blow again."[13] He carries this conviction with him all these months later and briefly lectures fellow hobbits as they prepare for the battle about restraint urging them to manage their tempers and only kill if absolutely necessary.

> "... remember: there is to be no slaying of hobbits, not even if they have gone over to the other side. Really gone over, I mean; not just obeying ruffians' orders because they are frightened ... And nobody is to be killed at all, if it can be helped. Keep your tempers and hold your hands to the last possible

---

12. Op. cit. [4], p. 1002.
13. Op. cit., p. 905.

moment!"[14]

As the battle ends and the hobbits are victorious, Frodo takes this sentiment one step further by protecting both the lives of the ruffians and the hobbits by not letting them become murderers.[15] He does not fight or bear a weapon, making good on oath made in Mordor.[16] Here Frodo is Christ-like in his actions, protecting both the ruffians physically and the hobbits spiritually. In the Garden of Gethsemane (See John 18:1-11, Luke 22:47-52 and Matthew 26:47-52) when the soldiers come to arrest Jesus, Peter attacks and cuts off the ear of one of them named Malchus. Jesus heals the man and then tells Peter to put away his sword and reminds everyone that "...for all who take the sword will perish by the sword" (Matthew 26:52).

Frodo's "Ascension"

Once the Shire is restored, Frodo tries to resume his former life but is unable to do so. His wounds are too deep and he cannot find healing and peace. Just as Christ has to leave the earth and ascend to complete His mission, Frodo also must leave Middle-earth. In the latter's case, it is to find permanent healing and peace. Tolkien explains that "Frodo was sent or allowed to pass over Sea to heal him—if that could be done, before he died. He would have eventually to 'pass away': no mortal could, or can, abide forever on earth, or within time. So he went both to a purgatory and to a reward, for a while: a period of reflection and peace and a gaining of a truer understanding of his position in littleness and in greatness."[17]

Frodo may be envisioned as finding peace and healing in the West, being ministered to in his remaining years by Gandalf and even being reunited with Sam who, after Rosie's death and in accordance with the privilege of being a Ring-bearer, was rumored to have sailed West at the end of his life.[18]

---

14. Op. cit. [4], p. 983.
15. Op. cit., p. 993.
16. Op. cit., p. 916.
17. Humphrey Carpenter, *The Letters of J.R.R. Tolkien*, Houghton Mifflin, 2000, Letter 246, p. 328.
18. Op. cit. [4], p. 1072.

Chapter 10: Gandalf as a Type of Christ

Where Frodo exemplifies Christ's Passion and His role as the ultimate Priest, Gandalf is often described in terms of Christ's role as the Prophet. However, Gandalf is more than just a prophet or a wise teacher, but also a healer who works on behalf of many for their salvation.

Frodo's life, from his time of preparation to his quest and everything that happens to him on it, comes close to following the same pattern of Christ's life. Gandalf's life, both prior and during *The Lord of the Rings*, does not follow an identifiable pattern. Instead, certain events and actions in his life bear similarity to those in Christ's life. Further, as a divine being in human form, certain aspects of his nature are similar to Christ's divine and human nature, though with a difference that Tolkien stresses. He writes that Gandalf is a created person, though a divine one.[1] Christ is uncreated; He is God, the Second Person of the Trinity, and there has never been a time that He never was. He has two complete natures as defined by the Seven Ecumenical Councils: entirely human and entirely divine. These two natures function without confusion, are not divided or separate.

Gandalf's Incarnation, Death, and "Resurrection"

The most obvious parallel to Christ in Gandalf's life is his resurrection after the battle with the Balrog. One notable difference is that Christ, as God, lays down His own life of His own power and accord. Gandalf, according to Tolkien,[2] has no such power, nor do the Valar. He was resurrected directly by Ilúvatar. However, before discussing this resurrection in *LotR*, it is important to look back to Gandalf's origin, to paint a more complete picture of him as a type of Christ. Little is known about the wizard from *LotR* itself, and the reader gleans most through Pippin's observation. As the young hobbit listens to the dialogue and tension between Gandalf and Denethor, he thinks that it is the steward who looks more like a great wizard, but perceives Gandalf has greater wisdom and power. The reader is perhaps encouraged

---

1. Humphrey Carpenter, *The Letters of J.R.R. Tolkien*, Houghton Mifflin, 2000, Letter 181, p. 237.
2. Op. cit., Letter 156, p. 203.

to echo Pippin's questions: "What was Gandalf? In what far time and place did he come into the world, and when would he leave it?"[3]

That is all the speculation we get in *LotR* except for Faramir recounting that Gandalf referred to himself as Olórin when he was in "the West".[4] Most of what we know about Gandalf comes from Tolkien's enigmatic chapter in *Unfinished Tales* called *The Istari*. Though I have focused on *LotR* in this book, it is important to go beyond it to fully understand Gandalf as a typological Christ. Philippians 2:5-7 reads:

> Christ Jesus, who, being in the form of God, did not consider it robbery to be equal with God, but made Himself of no reputation, taking the form of a bondservant, and coming in the likeness of men.

A corresponding note to this scripture in the Life Application Study Bible reads:

> Without ceasing to be God, he became a human being, the man called Jesus. He did not give up his deity ... but he set aside the right to his glory and power. In submission to the Father's will, Christ limited his power and knowledge.[5]

The Scriptures accentuates that Christ as a human was subject to the same fears, hurts, trials, and temptations as all of us except that He, as the perfect and sinless human, did not fall and overcame them all. Gandalf's experience is similar, as he incarnates in human form and limits his knowledge and power. However, Gandalf is not sinless: he makes mistakes, though he readily admits to them. Tolkien writes, "that being embodied, the Istari had need to learn much anew by slow experience, and though they knew whence they came the memory of the Blessed Realm was to them a vision from afar off."[6]

One striking difference between Christ and Gandalf, that again shows the absence of allegory, is that Gandalf incarnates at the request of powers greater than himself. According to *The Istari*, Manwë convenes a council with the purpose of sending emissaries to Middle-earth to combat Sauron. However, the last time the Valar fought evil directly with power the result was so devastating that all the lands west of the Blue Mountains sank beneath the sea.

---

3. J.R.R. Tolkien, *The Lord of the Rings*, Houghton Mifflin, 1954-5, 1965-6, p. 740.
4. Op. cit., p. 655.
5. *Life Application Study Bible*, Tyndale, 1996, p. 1889.
6. J.R.R. Tolkien, *Unfinished Tales of Númenor and Middle-earth*, Houghton Mifflin, 1980, p. 390.

Sauron is a fallen Maia, though a very powerful one, and the Valar decided to send Maia in kind but with a mission that is informed by their past mistakes. As described above, the Valar want to correct their earlier errors where they tried to guard Middle-earth by their own might and thus revealed their glory. The Istari, conversely, are forbidden to reveal their divinity or seek to rule any of the free peoples. Rather, their mission is to love and persuade, and to unite people against Sauron. Tolkien describes that "with the consent of Eru they [the Valar] sent members of their own high order…"[7] and that Istari are "clad in the bodies of men" and come in "weak and humble" shapes to Middle-earth. They do not die of age or disease but can be killed and are subject to the suffering of men.[8]

Olórin, as one of the chosen Maia, has to be commanded to go by Manwë. He protests at first, saying he is "too weak for such a task and fear[s] Sauron."[9] Manwë acknowledges this as the exact reason why Olórin should go. Of the five Maiar who become the five wizards of Middle-earth, Olórin/Gandalf is the last to arrive.[10] This echoes the teaching of Christ: "If anyone desires to be first, he shall be last of all and servant of all" (Mark 9:35). Christ utters this shortly after the Disciples dispute who among them is the greatest.

The dynamic of pride and humility, of seeking greatness and power and rejecting them, which is most striking between Saruman and Gandalf, appears subtly in *The Istari*. It begins when Manwë asks who would go on the mission. Only two Maia come forward. "Curumo [Saruman] … chosen by Aulë, and Alatar… sent by Oromë.[11] By volunteering, though Manwë is asking for volunteers, Curumo is "putting himself forward." Olórin, by contrast to Curumo, is put forward.[12] Manwë has him in mind specifically and shortly thereafter commands him to go, making him the third of the five chosen. When it is acknowledged formally that he is the third, Varda says, "not as the third" and Curumo remembers it.[13] Here, Curumo shows the seeds of pride that lead him, as Saruman, to seek the power and greatness that are his eventual downfall.

Olórin becomes Gandalf, a pilgrim both in the sense of following a spiritual quest and in the sense of lacking a permanent abode,

> the last-comer was named among the Elves Mithrandir, the Grey Pilgrim, for he dwelt in no place, and gathered to himself neither wealth nor followers,

---

7. Op. cit. [6], p. 389.
8. Op. cit., pp. 389, 393.
9. Op. cit., p. 393.
10. Op. cit., p. 390.
11. Op. cit., p. 393.
12. Ibid.
13. Ibid.

but ever went to and fro… befriending all folk in times of need. Warm and eager was his spirit.[14]

Here, Tolkien evokes the memory of another Scripture where Christ describes himself as homeless in a sense. "And Jesus said, "Foxes have holes and birds of the air have nests, but the Son of Man has nowhere to lay His head" (Matthew 8:20, Luke 9:58). Like Christ, Gandalf wanders from place to place, addressing the needs of those he encounters and becomes beloved by them, but never loses focus of his mission to defeat Sauron.

Christ never seeks praise or the approval of men and is the essence of humility. Loving, yet stern when needed, He reminds His Disciples to "love one another as I have loved you." (John 15:12). He is beloved to them and the common people but not the prideful scribes, Pharisees, and Sadducees. Christ's joy is to do the will of God the Father. Similarly, Gandalf faithfully does his "father's", Eru's, will. Tolkien writes:

> when Sauron rose again, [Gandalf] also arose and partly revealed his power, and becoming the chief mover of the resistance to Sauron, … brought all by vigilance and labour to that end which the Valar under the One that is above them had designed.[15]

By Ilúvatar's direct intervention Gandalf is "sent back" to fulfil the mission given to him by the Valar at the "consent of Eru."

However, Gandalf also experiences intense Christ-like suffering, as "in the ending of the task for which he came he suffered greatly, and was slain, and being sent back from death for a brief while was clothed then in white, and became a radiant flame (yet veiled still save in great need)."[16] Though Gandalf's return is similar to the resurrection, Tolkien stresses in his letters that it is not the same event that happens in the Gospels and that, although Gandalf suffers death and is sent back to Middle-earth with enhanced power, God's incarnation in Christ is an infinitely greater occurence than anything he would dare to write.[17]

Despite Tolkien's own humility, he infuses the scene of Gandalf's return with allusions to three other significant events of Christ's life: the Transfiguration, "The Road to Emmaus," and His appearance to Mary Magdalene. The Transfiguration as described in Matthew 17:1-8 is strikingly similar in language to Gandalf's return in *The White Rider*. Like Christ, Gandalf's very being shines with a dazzling light:

---

14. Op. cit. [6], p. 390.
15. Op. cit., p. 391.
16. Op. cit., p. 391.
17. Op. cit. [1], Letter 181, p. 237.

His hair was white as snow in the sunshine; and gleaming white was his robe; the eyes under his deep brows were bright, piercing as the rays of the sun; power was in his hand.[18]

Aragorn, Legolas and Gimli are the Peter, James, and John in that they are stunned at what they see. Peter, the leader of the Disciples, is the first to speak, at a loss what to say. Aragorn, the leader of the Three Hunters, is also the first to speak after the old man is revealed to be their lost friend and guide. As Christ veils his light and touches His Disciples to assure and comfort them, we see Gandalf veil his light and touch Gimli in a comforting and redeeming way.

Among the dissimilarities to the Transfiguration of Christ is that the Disciples recognize Christ who has not yet been crucified whereas the Three Hunters think Gandalf long dead and do not recognize him. However, Christ is not recognizable in all his post-Resurrection appearances. For example, He is not known by Luke and Cleopas on the Road to Emmaus[19] until He breaks bread with them, Gandalf is also not recognizable until he engages in a confrontation with the Three Hunters. In the Gospel of John, there are two instances where the resurrected Christ is not immediately recognizable. The first is when He appears to Mary Magdalene outside of His tomb and she mistakes Him for a gardener until He speaks her name. He also is not immediately recognizable to His Disciples on the shores of Galilee until He commands them to cast their nets into the sea and they fill with more fish than they can handle. Again, it is Peter, the leader, who declares they are seeing the Lord.

Similarities to the Life of Christ

Furthermore, Gandalf's life echoes the Temptation in the Wilderness and the Raising of Lazarus. Matthew 4 gives the most detailed account of Christ's temptation by the devil. Christ journeys into the desert and fasts in solitude for forty days. During that time of physical exhaustion, the devil offers Him power, riches, and glory and in doing so takes Him to "the pinnacle of the temple" (Matthew 4:5) and to "an exceedingly high mountain" (Matthew 4:8). Christ rejects Satan who leaves Him and He is then ministered to by angels (Matthew 4:11).

We see something analogous in Gandalf's imprisonment by Saruman. The wizard journeys far to visit Saruman in Isengard. Upon arriving,

---

18. Op. cit. [3], pp. 483-4.
19. See Luke 24:13-35. Cleopas is named in verse 18 but the second man is this story is not. Many traditions hold that it is Luke, author of the Gospel, since it was a literary device at the time for an author not to give his name.

fatigued, he is led by his tempter to a high a chamber within Orthanc where his temptation begins.[20] Gandalf recounts Saruman's speech where he tries to persuade Gandalf that the free peoples are too weak to resist Sauron and that the prudent action is to join the Dark Lord, accept Sauron's evil for a while and bide their time until they can overthrow him and establish a new order.[21] Saruman plays the role of Satan, offering Gandalf power, in hope of getting the Ring. Gandalf rejects Saruman who then takes the Grey Wizard to an even higher place and imprisons him there. Gandalf is not ministered to by angels but rescued by Gwaihir, Lord of Eagles. Tolkien describes the mighty eagles in *The Silmarillion*, whom Gwaihir descends from, as "spirits in the shape of hawks and eagles",[22] messengers and agents, initially of Manwë, but of goodness in general.

In addition to being like Satan, Saruman is also like Judas, a traitor. Yet Gandalf, now as the resurrected Gandalf the White, plays the role of Christ toward his former tempter, and actively works for Saruman's salvation on several occasions. This is a consistent element of Gandalf as both the Grey and the White. Just as he once expressed hope for Sméagol's redemption, and rejoiced regarding Boromir's salvation – echoing the joy Christ talks about when He said there will be great joy in Heaven of the repentance of one sinner (Luke 15:7) – he likewise tries to redeem Saruman. When Gandalf confronts Saruman, the words he uses to summon his betrayer are "Saruman, come forth!"[23] These are alike to Christ's words at Lazarus's tomb: "He cried with a loud voice, "Lazarus, come forth!" (John 11:43). Lazarus is physically dead and Christ restores him to life. Saruman is spiritually dead and Gandalf is offering him redemption. Gandalf is also like Moses in this scene. In his farewell discourse, Moses tells the Israelites: "I have set before you life and death, blessing and cursing; therefore choose life…" (Deuteronomy 30:19). Gandalf pleads with Saruman to come down from his tower and offers him undeserved freedom and life, yet Saruman rejects the offer, mastered by his pride and hate.[24] In his rejection Saruman rejects his own salvation. Gandalf points this out to him before he breaks his staff and casts him out of the order of the Istari.[25]

Despite Gandalf's words, this is not Saruman's final opportunity to be redeemed. He becomes the withered fig tree from the Bible that Christ cursed because it was blooming with leaves yet offered no figs. Instead of yielding fruit of profound spiritual growth, the tree only sprouts leaves, a superficial display of repentance that will soon shrivel up. The next time

---

20. Op. cit. [3], p. 251.
21. Op. cit., p. 253.
22. J.R.R. Tolkien, *The Silmarillion*, Houghton Mifflin, 1977, p. 40.
23. Op. cit [3], p. 564.
24. Op. cit., pp. 568-9.
25. Op. cit., p. 569.

we encounter Saruman is after the Ring has been destroyed and the hobbits and their companions meet him on their way back to the Shire. He has now become barren on the inside and outside. His voice no longer mesmerizes but is "cracked and hideous."[26] Gandalf reaches out to him yet one more time and Galadriel correctly perceives this is the former great wizard's last chance and reminds him of this. Yet he rejects it again and Gandalf recognizes he is beyond redemption and is "withered altogether."[27] We see proof of this subsequently, when Saruman is killed by Wormtongue, the victim of his abuse. His spirit rises from his rapidly decaying body and looks west towards his former home before a cold wind from the West dissolves it into nothing. Saruman, the once noble and divine Curumo of the Maiar, becomes nothingness. He ends life as a dirty homeless man whose throat is slit. Tolkien conveys the full ugliness of his ending with great effect.

In some respects, Saruman is like Judas, and again we see Gandalf's similarity to Christ in the way he deals with him. Judas, a one-time disciple of God-incarnate, ends life in despair hanging from a tree and rotting to the point where is he disemboweled (See Matthew 27:3-10 and Acts 1:18). Yet, even knowing Judas's heart and mind, Jesus reaches out to him until the end. In all the Gospel accounts where The Last Supper is described, Judas is present and, at Christ's direction, receives His body and blood in the bread and wine.[28] Gandalf offers Saruman the same but Saruman, like Judas, makes a wrong choice and takes himself beyond redemption.

Gandalf the Healer

A final aspect of Gandalf that is Christ-like is his role as a healer from both sickness and sin. We see him at the start of the narrative, guiding Bilbo to give up the Ring of his own accord. The Ring, though not allegorically, is symbolic of sin. As was discussed earlier, it is evil and addictive. The owner clings to it, wanting it and hating it at the same time. Through Gandalf's love and patience, Bilbo gives up the Ring and is healed from its bondage to a great degree. Appropriate to Gandalf's character, Bilbo is not completely healed, because Gandalf is not Christ, whose healing in the Gospels is complete. The wizard's healing of Bilbo is commensurate to the power given to him. Bilbo is unable to receive permanent healing until he comes to the Blessed Realm. We see evidence of this on two occasions. In Rivendell, he asks Frodo to see the Ring one more time and his ugly latent desire is revealed, through briefly. Frodo sees spiritually for a moment, beholding Bilbo as a "wrinkled creature with a hungry face and bony groping hands"

---

26. Op. cit. [3], pp. 960-1.
27. Op. cit., p. 965.
28. *Orthodox Study Bible*, Thomas Nelson, 2008, p. 1409.

– the sinful part of Bilbo that still survives made manifest.[29] However, to Bilbo's credit and to Gandalf's as a healer, Bilbo tells Frodo to put it away and does not touch it.[30]

Bilbo is easily able to renounce his desire and even has insight into the reasons behind it. He feels for his nephew but then turns to happier topics. The next time we witness this desire, it is much more benign. The Ring has been destroyed and the four hobbits return to Rivendell to visit Bilbo before they return home to the Shire. Bilbo inquires of the Ring one more time though not with the same greedy desire he had during Frodo's first visit to Rivendell.[31] Bilbo is nearly wholly cured but not quite.

Subsequently, in a dialogue between Frodo and Gandalf, we see both Gandalf's healing power and its limitations. Frodo is in pain as they ride by Weathertop on the anniversary of his stabbing there by the Ringwraith and Gandalf notices it. In a private moment between the two, Frodo confesses his pain. Gandalf tells him that "there are some wounds that cannot be wholly cured."[32] The Ring and its effect on Frodo are much deeper than just physical wounds. Gandalf cannot heal them despite his divinity. Frodo must symbolically pass from life to death in sailing to the West and receive greater healing in the Blessed Realm. But even that healing will not be complete. Only Christ can fully heal and Tolkien states as much in his letters:

> "'Alas! there are some wounds that cannot be wholly cured', said Gandalf (III 268) – not in Middle-earth. Frodo was sent or allowed to pass over Sea to heal him – if that could be done, before he died. He would have eventually to 'pass away': no mortal could, or can, abide for ever on earth, or within Time. So he went both to a purgatory and to a reward, for a while: a period of reflection and peace and a gaining of a truer understanding of his position in littleness and in greatness, spent still in Time amid the natural beauty of 'Arda Unmarred', the Earth unspoiled by evil.
> Bilbo went too...He bore still the mark of the Ring that needed to be finally erased: a trace of pride and personal possessiveness."[33]

Frodo still must die a mortal death at some point. Until then, he receives a much greater measure of healing and peace as he continues to grow and become refined in a place "unspoiled by evil" until it is his time to die.

By contrast, Gandalf, commensurate to his ability, can heal much more easily issues that are not as deeply rooted in the same evil and sin as the

---

29. Op. cit. [3], pp. 225-6.
30. Op. cit., p. 226.
31. Op. cit., p. 965.
32. Op. cit., p. 967.
33. Op. cit. [1], Letter 246, p. 328.

Ring. In Rohan, King Théoden is aged prematurely by the poison of body and mind at the hands of Gríma Wormtongue. Gandalf heals him completely, but in a way reminiscent of a certain type of Christ's healings in the Gospels. Christ healed in many ways in the Gospel: through word or touch, by being present during the healing or from afar. Still yet, some healings are instantaneous and others are gradual. Each healing seemed unique to the person He heals and Christ knows exactly what process to use based on His intimate knowledge of the person He is ministering to.

Théoden's healing is most like the gradual healing we see in the Gospels. The one most similar to Théoden occurs in Mark 8:22-26:

> "Then [Christ] came to Bethsaida; and they brought a blind man to Him, and begged Him to touch him. So He took the blind man by the hand and led him out of the town. And when He had spit on his eyes and put His hands on him, He asked him if he saw anything.
> And he looked up and said, "I see men like trees, walking."
> Then He put His hands on his eyes again and made him look up. And he was restored and saw everyone clearly."

This man is healed in stages. First Christ leads him out of town. Bethsaida's people are unbelieving, and Christ heals outside of town to spare the people who would scoff at the miracle and bring further condemnation on themselves. The man himself has little faith and the healing occurs gradually according to his faith.[34] Many times in the Gospel Christ states that "your faith has made you well" or "let it be done according to your faith." In other words, Christ is not limited by a person's faith, but He works within it.

Similarly, Théoden is in a sinful environment. Many know that Wormtongue is evil yet feel they are unable to do anything. Éomer openly rebels and is exiled. Éowyn feels powerless and sinks further and further into despair. Háma, Théoden's door warden, seems to be aware of the situation and he permits Gandalf to keep his staff even though all visitors are told to leave their weapons outside the throne chamber. Nevertheless, Edoras is suffering under Wormtongue's evil control of Théoden. Gandalf is aware of this and alludes symbolically to Wormtongue's satanic influence over Théoden, comparing him to a serpent and calling him a "witless worm" and tells him to keep his "forked tongue" behind his teeth.[35] Wormtongue is a very appropriate name for Gríma based on what he is doing. The word worm, Old English "wyrm," is a medieval reference to a dragon and Tolkien uses the word as such in his writings.[36] The dragon is often used as a symbol

---

34. Op. cit. [28], p. 1342.
35. Op. cit. [3], p. 503.
36. Michael D.C. Drought, Editor, *J.R.R. Tolkien Encyclopedia – Scholarship and Critical*

of Satan, the liar and deceiver. Wormtongue is using lies to break Théoden's spirit and turn him into an aged puppet of Saruman. Though there is no definitive evidence that Tolkien intended this meaning, it is likely.

Gandalf's first healing act is to cast down the evil itself. Having neutralized Wormtongue, he turns to Théoden. The King's spirit is broken by the death of his only child and heir, Théodred. His body is poisoned and he is losing his humanity as he himself points out when, after he is healed, he tells Wormtongue, "Your leechcraft ere long would have soon had me walking on all fours like a beast."[37] Gandalf then performs the equivalent of Christ leading the man out of town. Gandalf has the King look through his window through the gloom to a patch of shining sky and points to the light amidst the darkness. He asks Théoden if he is willing to hear,[38] like Christ who teaches that "he [who] has ears to hear, let him hear." Christ only preaches to those who are *willing* to hear. Théoden is willing, as he "slowly [leaves] his chair. A faint light [grows] in the hall again,"[39] as the king's returning lucidity lifts the darkness he unwittingly inflicted on his court and land as king.

Next, Gandalf indicates the presence of the Spirit as he leads Théoden out of his hall onto the porch overlooking his lands. Tolkien writes that the wind was blowing on the hill and then Gandalf tells Théoden to breathe the free air.[40] Though not as clear here as in subsequent chapters, Tolkien uses wind liberally to indicate the presence of the Spirit. Numerous examples of Tolkien using wind to indicate imminent change and good fortune and the implied presence of a greater power at work are discussed in Chapter 13. I also show in that chapter that Tolkien explicitly acknowledges the presence of the Holy Spirit in his created world. For now, in this scene, Gandalf further advances Théoden's healing by the power or the Spirit. Théoden is not yet fully healed but he is coming out of his darkness even more as he himself acknowledges.

Judging the time is ready for his complete healing, Gandalf tells him to abandon his cane, which the king does. After the physical healing is complete, Théoden shows lucidity of mind as well as haleness of body, as he acknowledges the difference between his healed state and the 'dark dreams'[41] he had experienced. Although Théoden is healed physically, he is not whole in spirit. As he hears of the plights that plague his land from Gandalf, Théoden almost returns to his state of despair, thinking of his dead son and lamenting about Boromir's death. Recognizing he is wilting,

---

Assessment, "Free Will" by Daniel Thomas, p. 390.
37. Op. cit. [3], p. 508.
38. Op. cit., p. 503.
39. Ibid.
40. Op. cit., pp. 503-4.
41. Op. cit., p. 504.

Gandalf urges him to recover his strength but grasping his sword.[42] Théoden does so and it is then that Gandalf heals him completely by appealing to his fighting spirit. The king is suddenly filled with vigor and lifts his sword and cries out a call to arms.[43] From this point forward except for one brief moment of doubt due to "agony of Minas Tirith he witnesses before quickly recovering and charging into the Battle of the Pelennor Fields, Théoden is renewed. In Appendix A, Tolkien even writes that he became known as Théoden Ednew because he fell into decline but was healed by Gandalf.[44] Gandalf's role as a healer, though limited to characters such as Bilbo and Théoden, is important in the defeat of both Saruman and Sauron.

Gandalf's "Ascension"

"A little while, and you will not see Me; and again a little while, and you will see Me, because I go to the Father," are Christ's words to His Disciples in John 16:16 as He prepares for His crucifixion, resurrection, and eventual ascension. Gandalf's penultimate speech to the hobbits is notably similar:

> "'I am with you at present,' said Gandalf, 'but soon I shall not be. I am not coming to the Shire. You must settle its affairs yourselves; that is what you have been trained for. Do you not yet understand? My time is over: it is no longer my task to set things to rights, nor to help folk to do so. And as for you, my dear friends, you will need no help. You are grown up now. Grown indeed very high; among the great you are, and I have no longer any fear at all for any of you."[45]

Similarly to Christ, who educates his disciples for three years, Gandalf reminds the hobbits of their 'training'. Both the disciples and the hobbits are expected to be ready to face obstacles without their tutor's guidance.

Here, Gandalf anticipates returning to Valinor, his homeland. Unlike Christ, who still had final trials to go through, Gandalf has completed his task. Like Christ, he has trained those closest to him and now empowers them like Christ did when he says: "You will be my witnesses in Jerusalem, and in all Judea and Samaria, and to the ends of the earth" (Acts 1:8-9). The next time we see Gandalf is in the Grey Havens. There, he boards the ship into the West leaving Middle-earth forever. Just like Christ who returns to heaven through His ascension, Gandalf is returning to the Blessed Realm, leaving behind those he had guided and trained to order and grow a renewed kingdom.

---

42. Op. cit. [3], pp. 505-6.
43. Op. cit., p. 506.
44. Op. cit., p. 1044.
45. Op. cit., p. 974.

Chapter 11: Aragorn as a Type of Christ

Aragorn is introduced as Strider the Ranger before becoming known to us as Aragorn son of Arathorn, rightful heir to the throne of both Gondor and Arnor. It is a minor transformation when compared to his major transformation when he becomes King Elessar, the Elfstone, and Evinyatar, the Renewer.[1] Though not included in the main narrative of *The Lord of the Rings*, *The Tale of Aragorn and Arwen* informs us that for the first twenty years of his life he is called Estel, which means "hope."[2] Aragorn becoming King Elessar is hope fulfilled. Though he shares the ability to heal, like Gandalf, when it comes to being Christ-like, he alone in *LotR* assumes the Christ-like role of King. His healing is greater in number than Gandalf's, and arguably in scope, because he heals more people than the wizard and he also heals a land by restoring a kingdom.

Aragorn the Willing Exile

Chapter 6, *The Sacrifices of the Fellowship*, discusses Aragorn's relationship with Arwen and the sacrifices he is willing to make, including dying and giving up his aspirations for the sake of defeating evil. A further comparison contributes to that discussion. Christ commands his followers to die to themselves and to lose their life to find it (Matthew 10:39, 16:24, Mark 8:35, Luke 9:25, 17:33, John 12:23-25). This does not necessarily mean a physical death, but the death to selfish ambitions and desires. Aragorn is not selfish in his ambitions or his love for Arwen. In his willingness to sacrifice a life of fulfilled love for the greater good, he is Christ-like in the sense that he is willing to give up his life in terms of his deepest desire. But Aragorn's similarity to Christ goes deeper than this. Christ, the Second Person of the Holy Trinity, willingly condescends to earth when He incarnated in the flesh. He leaves paradise for a time to live in exile and suffers and dies to establish the Kingdom of God. While on earth, He also lives in exile for a time in Egypt before He returns to Israel after the death of Herod. In all His wanderings, He stays aware of his ultimate mission – the redemption of

---

1. J.R.R. Tolkien, *The Lord of the Rings*, Houghton Mifflin, 1954-5, 1965-6, p. 845.
2. Op. cit., p. 1032.

humanity.

Aragorn is raised in the Edenic, protected Rivendell. Though he leaves it to journey with the sons of Elrond during the first twenty years of his life,[3] he does not learn his identity and lineage until he is twenty when Elrond reveals it to him. The next day, he meets Arwen and falls in love with her. Learning from Elrond he is unable to wed her unless he becomes King of both Arnor and Gondor, he begins a life of willing exile from Rivendell. Aragorn's entire life is one of exile since he is king without his rightful kingdom. Though he would return from time to time to Rivendell to rest, his goal from that point forward is defeating Sauron. Primarily driven by romantic love, it is not his only motivation. During the quest of the Ring, though he focuses on Minas Tirith, he abandons that focus for a time for the sake of the nobler goal: rescuing Merry and Pippin. Like Christ, he confronts evil and struggles with it and heals people affected by it. He goes through a symbolic death and resurrection before completing his mission. The rest of this chapter will address all these facets of Aragorn's life.

Aragorn's "Temptation in the Wilderness"

Aragorn's life is loosely similar to Christ's as it is laid out in the beginning of the Gospel of Matthew. In Matthew 3 Christ is baptized by John, accompanied by a manifestation of the Holy Trinity. A voice from Heaven, the Father, affirms the Son and the Holy Spirit descends upon Christ like a dove. Soon after, Christ goes into the desert, led by the Holy Spirit to face and defeat Satan. Christ begins His mission of salvation upon His return from the desert.

Aragorn has an "anointing" moment, similar to a baptism, before he sets out with the Company of the Ring from Rivendell, as Narsil is reforged into Andúril, signifying at last his mission has formally begun. Either the Ring will be destroyed and he will realize his hopes, or Sauron will reclaim it extinguishing his hopes forever. Like Christ, he must come face to face with the ultimate manifestation of evil – Sauron. He does not go into the desert but into a high chamber in Helm's Deep and looks into the palantír with the specific purpose of challenging Sauron. He defeats Sauron by wrenching the seeing-stone to his will and away from the Dark Lord's. He learns of Sauron's plot to destroy Minas Tirith and comes away from the encounter with a sense of mission. He realizes his only hope is to take The Paths of the Dead. Like Christ, who goes to Jerusalem to offer salvation through His death, Aragorn, to save all in Gondor from death and slavery, must take the path of death.

---

3. Op. cit. [1], p. 1032.

Aragorn the Messianic King of Prophecy

Aragorn's actions surrounding the Paths of the Dead and then later the Houses of Healing present the most obvious parallels to Christ. Like Christ, Aragorn is a messianic King of prophecy. The first hint of this comes early in the book when Frodo reads a letter penned by Gandalf during his first encounter with Aragorn in Bree. Within that letter is a short poem.

> "All that is gold does not glitter,
> Not all those who wander are lost;
> The old that is strong does not wither,
> Deep roots are not reached by the frost.
> From the ashes a fire shall be woken,
> A light from the shadows shall spring;
> Renewed shall be blade that was broken,
> The crownless again shall be king."[4]

Frodo does not know at the time that this poem is composed by Bilbo. We learn later that Bilbo, who has lived in Rivendell for the seventeen years since he disappeared from the Shire, has become friends with Aragorn. Clearly, he learned enough about him and his history to make up these prophetic verses. The meaning of the poem is not elaborated until *The Council of Elrond*, where it is revealed Aragorn is heir of Isildur. Still, we also learn throughout the millennia there have been many heirs, so what is it that makes Aragorn special? Bilbo's poem gives us a hint that he is finally the heir that will become king again. But what does Bilbo know about Aragorn that we, as first time readers, still do not completely know at this point? Galadriel also alludes to the fact that Aragorn is set apart from his brethren as special and the heir that will finally reclaim the throne. When she presents him with the green elfstone in Lórien she tells him to take the name foretold to him, "Elessar, the Elfstone of the House of Elendil!"[5]

This is the first mention in the main body of the book of the name Elessar. In this brief sentence it is clear someone gave a prophecy concerning Aragorn. Aragorn refers to himself as Elessar briefly after this, but the next time we encounter the name is in a similar enigmatic way from Galadriel when Gandalf relays her message to Aragorn that he must consider the Paths of the Dead. The message, set to verse, begins, *"Where now are the Dúnedain, Elessar, Elessar"* and talks about "the grey company" riding from the north and accompany him on a dark path watched by the dead.[6] Later in the story

---
4. Op. cit. [1], p. 167.
5. Op. cit., p. 366.
6. Op. cit., p. 491.

when we are reminded of her words when the "Grey Company" and the sons of Elrond share the message from their father, "Bid Aragorn remember the words of the seer, and the Paths of the Dead."[7] Aragorn reveals that the seer is a man named Malbeth who lived more than one thousand years prior during the days King Arvedui. Aragorn then shares the words of the seer that predict the events we read about when Aragorn and the Grey Company take the Paths of the Dead.[8]

This is the only mention of Malbeth the Seer in the main body of LotR. Appendix A contains another prophecy by him, concerning Arvedui, the last king of Arnor, and tangentially referring to Aragorn as the King who will reunite his people.

> Arvedui was indeed the last king, as his name signifies. It is said that this name was given to him at his birth by Malbeth the Seer, who said to his father: "Arvedui you shall call him, for he will be the last in Arthedain. Though a choice will come to the Dúnedain, and if they take the one that seems less hopeful, then your son will change his name and become king of a great realm. If not, then much sorrow and many lives of men shall pass, until the Dúnedain arise and are united again.[9]

Arvedui attempts to claim the throne of both Gondor and Arnor but is rejected. The Dúnedain of Gondor and their current King at the time refused to accept him despite Arvedui's more direct lineage to Elendil. Arvedui perishes in an icy shipwreck, thus ending the line of Kings in Arnor and within less than a hundred years, Gondor's last King perishes childless thus ushering in the thousand-year rule of the Stewards. The Dúnedain's choice of the 'less hopeful' variant, that is choosing Arvedui over their current King Eärnil, proves to be the choice they should have made. Eärnil's son Eärnur accepts a challenge from the Lord of the Nazgûl and is slain, leaving the throne of Gondor heirless.

The circumstance of Aragorn's family is also evocative of Christ's. Aragorn's mother, Gilraen, is young when she marries and is not at the age when her people typically do so, while Aragorn's father is older. This is vaguely reminiscent of Joseph and Mary. *The Protoevangelium of James*, a book likely written in the middle of the second century, reflects a previously established tradition about Joseph and Mary. According to it, Mary is a thirteen-year old virgin, who by Jewish law, must leave the Temple where she lives after her aged parents die. Joseph is an older widower who agrees to take her as his betrothed to care for her. Further, Joseph dies early in

---

7. Op. cit. [1], p. 764.
8. Ibid.
9. Op. cit., p. 1025.

Christ's life, and, similarly, Arathorn is killed when Aragorn is two years old.

According to *The Tale…*, Gilraen's father, Dirhael, is opposed to the marriage and believes that Arathorn will die young. His premonition is correct since Arathorn is killed when he is sixty-two, which is young by Dúnedain standards. Gilraen's mother, Ivorwen, however, urges her husband to let the couple marry, because "the days are darkening before the storm, and great things are to come. If these two wed now, hope may be born for our people; but if they delay, it will not come while this age lasts."[10] Aragorn is the child of hope as his grandmother predicts. This dialogue between his grandparents, an elderly man and woman who offer prophecies concerning Aragorn, is reminiscent of the aged Simeon and Anna's declarations and prophecies concerning the Christ child (see Luke 2:25-38). When he beholds the child, Simeon declares that he has seen salvation and Anna speaks of Christ as the Savior. Aragorn's name for his first twenty years, Estel, means "hope" in Sindarin and Quenya, and the elves and the Dúnedain revere the star known as Gil-Estel, the "Star of High Hope." It is the ship Vingilot, steered by Elrond's father Eärendil who wears one of the three Silmarils on his brow.[11] Eärendil is the savior figure in *The Silmarillion*. Similar to how Christ is linked to the Star of Bethlehem which shines above the place of His birth; Aragorn too is associated with a star and the hope it signifies.

Aragorn's "Death and Resurrection"

Unlike the other two Christ types discussed earlier, Aragorn never comes near death physically. His "death and resurrection" are much more symbolic than that of Gandalf and Frodo. As prophesied, Aragorn takes the Path of the Dead and for a while is "lost to mortal sight."[12] Tolkien uses ellipsis to take Aragorn and his companions out of the readers' sight for some time. We only discover what transpired after the Battle of the Pelennor Fields, when Legolas and Gimli tell their tale in the Houses of Healing. We learn that beneath the mountain spirits of men have lurked since the end of the Second Age. They had sworn an oath to Isildur to fight against Sauron but they broke it. Isildur cursed them and issued a prophecy that the conflict with Sauron would continue "through years uncounted" and that they would remain in unrest until they are summoned at its end.[13] The traitors flee and upon their deaths haunt the mountains for more than three thousand years, until summoned by a fearless Aragorn who commands them with authority,

---

10. Op. cit. [1], p. 1032.
11. J.R.R. Tolkien, *The Silmarillion*, Houghton Mifflin, 1977, p. 247.
12. Op. cit. [1], p. 773.
13. Op. cit., p. 765.

much to the admiration of Legolas, who recounts the tale for Merry and Pippin.[14]

Aragorn uses his company and the dead army to attack the Corsairs of Umbar, who sail up the Anduin River to make a surprise assault on Minas Tirith, and takes over their ships. After the battle, Aragorn releases the dead so they can at last be at peace.[15] This sequence of events is similar to the "Harrowing of Hell" or "Descent into Hades." Many Christians hold to a tradition that Christ's spirit descends into Hades, which is commonly thought of as the bowels of the earth, between His death and resurrection and frees the righteous spirits who had died since the beginning of the world. Two Scriptures from the First Epistle of Peter are a basis for this tradition. The first reads:

> For Christ also suffered once for sins, the just for the unjust, that He might bring us[a] to God, being put to death in the flesh but made alive by the Spirit, by whom also He went and preached to the spirits in prison, who formerly were disobedient, when once the Divine longsuffering waited (1 Peter 3 18-20).

A second scripture, also from 1 Peter, reads, "For this reason the gospel was preached also to those who are dead, that they might be judged according to men in the flesh, but live according to God in the spirit" (1 Peter 4:6). The *Life Application Study Bible* offers the following commentary on the first passage above. "The traditional interpretation is that between His death and resurrection, Christ announced salvation to God's faithful followers who had been waiting for their salvation during the whole Old Testament era."[16]

Like Christ, Aragorn descends into the earth and frees the dead. When we next see the future king, he is no longer among the dead but is back with the living. He reveals himself as king in a symbolic resurrection by displaying the royal standard of the white tree and seven stars. Aragorn's appearance at the Battle of the Pelennor Fields, told from Éomer's point of view, changes the whole course of the conflict in favour of the armies of Gondor and the Rohirrim. Further, Tolkien writes the future king is "borne upon the wind" which can be read as symbolic of the Holy Spirit.[17] Aragorn's "resurrection" spells doom for the forces of Mordor who are then defeated. Reminiscent of Christ, the King of Kings, defeating the devil through his death and resurrection, Aragorn, the King, defeats Sauron through might of arms, though this is only a temporary victory until the Ring is destroyed ten

---

14. Op. cit. [1], p. 857.
15. Op. cit., pp. 858-9.
16. *Life Application Study Bible*, Tyndale, 1996, p. 2003.
17. See Chapter 13 for a detailed exploration.

days later.

Aragorn the Healer and Restorer

Upon achieving victory on the field of battle, Aragorn does not claim the kingship immediately. Instead, exuding Christ-like humility, he wraps himself in his grey elven cloak and goes to the Houses of Healing to help the sick and wounded. While there, he declares himself as Envinyatar, the Renewer after hearing Prince Imrahil discussing with Éomer his surprise at hearing Merry and Pippin refer to Aragorn, their future King, as Strider.[18]

In the Gospels, Christ performs multiple acts of healing during His three-year ministry. Though His mission was the cross, He takes opportunities to restore and renew people, healing their bodies and feeding the hungry. Aragorn acknowledges that he too is a renewer and is beseeched by men to heal their friends and relatives. Aragorn does so, laboring well into the night with the Sons of Elrond.[19] Tolkien notably uses the word "prayed" to describe the men's actions, possibly to evoke Christ and His Disciples healing. The scene is particularly close to the following passage: "At evening, when the sun had set, they brought to Him [Christ] all who were sick and those who were demon-possessed. And the whole city was gathered together at the door. Then He healed many who were sick with various diseases, and cast out many demons" (Mark 1:32-34).

Tolkien evokes more Christian imagery when he describes Aragorn's healing of Faramir, Éowyn and Merry using *kingsfoil* and his latent skills and power. Aragorn breathes on the kingsfoil leaves and crushes them, releasing a "living freshness" into the room, followed by a sweet fragrance.[20] Aragorn's breathing on the leaves is similar to Christ breathing on His Disciples and telling them to receive the Holy Spirit (see John 20:22). Further, in Christian tradition, a sweet aroma or sweet fragrance is often associated with the presence of God or with the Holy Spirit, and the detailed description of the fragrance associated with the healing of Faramir, Éowyn and Merry can be seen as alluding to it.

In more Gospel healing imagery, Aragorn, prior to the healing, offers words of comfort to Bergil and others who are witnesses. After the healing, he commands Faramir, who he just brought back from the brink of death, to take food. This is very like Christ when He raises the daughter of the synagogue ruler, Jarius, from the dead and then commands that she is given something to eat (Luke 8:49-56).

---

18. Op. cit. [1], p. 845.
19. Op. cit., p. 853.
20. Op. cit., pp. 847-8.

Final Thoughts on Aragorn's Similarity to Christ

Aragorn has other moments in the trilogy that evoke his likeness to Christ. The episode when the Fellowship approaches the Argonath utilizes features from two distinctive episodes from the New Testament: Jesus walking on water and calming the rough seas that threatened to swallow the Disciple's boat. In both cases, He tells them to not be afraid and exerts His power and majesty by controlling the elements. As the Fellowship sails down Anduin, the narrative is given from a terrified Frodo's perspective. The hobbit is cowering and listening to Sam begging to get out of this "horrible place." He hears a strange but authoritative voice say "fear not" and is surprised to see it coming from Aragorn. To Frodo, he briefly no longer looks like Strider the Ranger but like a "king returning from exile to his own land", and he guides them through the dark chasm and into the bright sunlight.[21] Although he does not possess Christ's power over the elements, Aragorn calms fears through his authority and then guides them out of the darkness into light.

Upon ascending the throne, Aragorn exhibits Christ's command to love your enemies. Among his first acts is the issue of pardons to "the Easterlings who had given themselves up, [and] the peoples of Harad; and the slaves of Mordor he released and gave to them all the lands about Lake Nurnen."[22]

Lastly, we see Aragorn's similarity to Christ at the end of his life. The Kings of Númenor are given the authority the choose the time of their death. Gandalf refers to this when he is trying to prevent Denethor from suicide and tells him that he, as a steward and unlike the kings, does not have the authority to order the hour of his own passing.[23] Aragorn, the restorer, has this given authority of old and he tells Arwen that he is "the last of the Númenóreans and the latest King of the Elder Days; and to [him] has been given not only a span thrice that of Men of Middle-earth, but also the grace to go at [his] will, and give back the gift."[24] Though the circumstance of his death are different, Christ also gives up His life by His own power and authority.

---

21. Op. cit. [1], pp. 383-4.
22. Op. cit., p. 947.
23. Op. cit., p. 835.
24. Op. cit., p.1037.

Chapter 12: The Christ-like Traits of Tom Bombadil

Though not often associated with Christ, Tom Bombadil also exhibits Christ-like traits. This chapter demonstrates these after first exploring this enigmatic character's mysterious identity.

The Identity of Tom Bombadil

The identity of Tom Bombadil is a vigorously discussed topic. Some have speculated he is Ilúvatar incarnate, based on his seeming mastery over the Ring and control over nature and the supernatural creatures such as Old Man Willow and the Barrow-wights. One of the most often cited passages in support of this is a brief dialogue between Frodo and Goldberry where Frodo asks who Tom Bombadil is and Goldberry replies that "he is."[1] The "he is" sounds very much like the name God gives of Himself when He speaks through the burning bush: "I am who I am" and instructs Moses to tell the Egyptians that "I am" is who is sending him (Exodus 3:13-14).

The foremost problem with this comparison lies in Goldberry's very next statement that the lands do not belong to Tom.[2] As God, Tom would be both creator and owner. Tom is the Master but he is a steward rather than an owner. In this respect, Tom is more like Adam, or at least Adam as he should have been before he sinned. Tom has dominion over the Old Forest, but not domination.

Later, Frodo asks Tom directly who he is, and Tom gives an enigmatic answer that also seems Adam-like. He says, "eldest that is what I am," and goes on to list all things in the world he precedes.[3] Tom is the first to be created, it seems, just as Adam was the first. Even though discussions and entries in popular internet forums such as *The Tolkien Gateway* and *The Encyclopedia of Arda* raise the issue of Tom as being God-like in this passage, it seems to speak of Tom as a created being, not uncreated. He says he was there before the Dark Lord came from "Outside", possibly referencing Melkor entering Eä with the other Valar. This statement also implies another

---

1. J.R.R. Tolkien, *The Lord of the Rings*, Houghton Mifflin,1954-5, 1965-6, p. 122.
2. Op. cit., p. 122.
3. Op. cit., p. 129.

reality Tom is not part of since his words suggest he is "Inside." It seems Tom is the embodiment of the created earthly reality. In this respect, again, Tom is more Adam-like, than Christ-like or God-like. Furthermore, Genesis 2:19-20 reads: "Out of the ground the Lord God formed every beast of the field and every bird of the air, and brought them to Adam to see what he would call them. And whatever Adam called each living creature, that was its name. So Adam gave names to all cattle, to the birds of the air, and to every beast of the field." Professor Jane Chance points out that Tom is Adam-like in that he too is a "namer."[4]

The most powerful argument that Tom is not God in a human form comes from Tolkien himself when he wrote he would never have attempted to write about the incarnation of God. He speculated about Eru becoming incarnate in Arda in the dialogue between Finrod and Andreth but that seems to be as far as he was willing to go. This rules out Tom or any other character being a direct representation of the Second Person of the Trinity made flesh. Others have speculated that Tom is a Vala, saying that together, Tom and Goldberry are the Valar, Aulë and Yavanna, or they are both unnamed Maiar. The possibility of Tom and Goldberry being either Valar or Maiar is refuted by Tolkien's statement that "…even in a mythical Age there must be some enigmas, as there always are. Tom Bombadil is one (intentionally)."[5] Gandalf, a similarly enigmatic figure, is revealed to be the incarnated Maia Olórin through hints in *LotR* and *TSil*, and direct statements in *UT* and in his many letters, so Tom's lack of identity is likely a deliberate authorial choice. Tolkien does not ever define Tom except for one brief hint in his letters where he refers to Tom as "the spirit of the (vanishing) Oxford and Berkshire countryside."[6]

However, context is crucial in this case. He wrote this statement in a letter to his publisher in 1937, the year *TH* was published. He was informing his publisher, Stanley Unwin, about his other works in manuscript form. Tom was not yet, in Tolkien's mind, a part of *LotR* at that time, as the book would not be officially started until a month later. The letter where he referred to Tom as an enigma was written in 1954.[7] *LotR* was complete and a few months away from being published. Tolkien clearly had moved away from calling Tom Bombadil any type of specific being, though of all the speculations - God, Vala, Maia or some sort of nature spirit - Tom retains more of the characteristic of the latter.

This had led some readers and fans to characterize Tom as a neutral

---

4. Jane Chance, *The Lord of the Rings: The Mythology of Power* (Revised Edition), The University Press of Kentucky, 2011, E-book.
5. Humphrey Carpenter, *The Letters of J.R.R. Tolkien*, Houghton Mifflin, 2000, Letter 144, p. 174.
6. Op. cit., Letter 19, p. 26.
7. Op. cit., Letter 144, p. 174.

being, neither good nor evil. Many draw this from a lengthy dialogue about him that takes place during *The Council of Elrond*. Further, in support of his seeming neutrality, Tom is not concerned too much with the events of the world outside of the Old Forest despite his vast knowledge of history and events. Gandalf says that it would be a mistake to give him the Ring because he would be careless with it. Galdor hints at him being a "nature spirit" when he says the power is not in Tom to defy Sauron unless it is in the earth itself.[8] As we see in Mordor, Sauron can choke and destroy nature thus, as Glorfindel states at the Council of Elrond, "I think that in the end, if all else is conquered, Bombadil will fall. Last as he was First; and then Night will come."[9] However, it seems Tom was not neutral as evidenced by his actions. Though he was not directly involved in the fight against Sauron; but on the continuum of good and evil he was not in the middle and most certainly was good as evidenced by his benevolent actions and his Christ-like attributes.

Tom Bombadil's similarity to Christ

Appropriate to his connection to the earth, Tom, like Christ, demonstrates control over nature. In the scene in the Gospel where Christ and the Disciples are in a wind and storm tossed boat (Mark 4:35-41), Christ pacifies the storm. Tom exhibits a similar power over nature when he frees Merry and Pippin from Old Man Willow. In another scene, Tom is outside in the rain and as he comes toward the house he is waving his arms as if warding off the rain. When he comes inside he is completely dry.[10]

Similarly to Christ, and other Christ-like characters in *LotR*, Tom has the power to heal. When the hobbits are in peril on the Barrow Downs, he rescues them by, in his foresight, teaching them a song they can use to summon him. It amounts to a petitionary prayer, to which Tom responds in his inherent goodness.[11]

In the Gospels, we do not see the event where the stone is rolled away and daylight streams into Christ's tomb as He arises but the event is inferred. We get a similar perspective from Tolkien in this scene. Frodo, a Christ-like figure, is in a tomb and in a symbolic state of death. Frodo prays and Tom appears with a "loud rumbling sound, as of stones rolling and falling." The light that streams into the tomb through the door opened by Tom is "real light, the plain light of day."[12]

With this light comes healing, as it seems to call Merry, Pippin and Sam

---

8. Op. cit. [1], pp. 258-9.
9. Op. cit., p. 259.
10. Op. cit., p. 127.
11. Op. cit., pp. 138-9.
12. Op. cit., p. 139.

from a near death sickness to a deep sleep. Next, in a penitent way, Tom removes his hat, and "casts out the demon", telling the Barrow-wight to get out and vanish and go to the outer darkness where gates stand shut.[13] The gates in question are the Doors of Night, which stand between the created world and the Void. "Till the world in mended" echoes the post-apocalypse restoration described in the Book of Revelation. Tolkien also had his own version of the apocalypse in his imaginary world since his world is an imagined history of our world.[14] Tom's apocalyptic hints are similar to Christ since in the Gospels, Christ also made apocalyptic references.

Tom carries the hobbits outside "on to the clean grass" and into the light. He then goes back into the barrow and brings out "a great load of treasure" and lays it alongside the hobbits in the sunshine. He then heals the hobbits:

> Raising his right hand he said in a clear and commanding voice:
> *Wake now my merry lads! Wake and hear me calling!*
> *Warm now be heart and limb! The cold stone is fallen;*
> *Dark door is standing wide; dead hand is broken.*
> *Night under Night is flown, and the Gate is open!*
> To Frodo's great joy the hobbits stirred, stretched their arms, rubbed their eyes, and then suddenly sprang up.[15]

Tom's words to them echo several of Christ's statements from the Gospels. Christ says that he who is willing to lose his life for Christ's sake will find it (Matthew 10:39). Tom tells the hobbits they have found themselves again after nearly losing their lives.[16] Though not a direct parallel, since Christ talks about forsaking all to be His disciple, the principle of dying to self applies. This is the hobbits' first true encounter with evil and darkness. This encounter with the Barrow-wight is the first of many encounters that result in their dying to self and becoming transformed.

Christ also reiterates on several occasions in the Gospels to take little thought for the material needs when it comes to God and to focus on God first. "Therefore do not worry, saying, 'What shall we eat?' or 'What shall we drink?' or 'What shall we wear?' For after all these things the Gentiles seek. For your heavenly Father knows that you need all these things. But seek first the kingdom of God and His righteousness, and all these things shall be added to you." (Matthew 6:31-33) and "For where your treasure is, there your heart will be also." (Matthew 6:21) and "For what profit is it to a man if he gains the whole world, and loses his own soul." (Matthew 16:26,

---

13. Op. cit. [1], p. 139.
14. Op. cit. [5], Letter 165, p. 220.
15. Op. cit. [1], pp. 139-140.
16. Op. cit., p. 140.

Mark 8:36, Luke 9:25)

In order for the hobbits to be fully healed, Tom has them shed their materiality and run naked.

> The hobbits ran about for a while on the grass, as he told them. Then they lay basking in the sun with the delight of those that have been wafted suddenly from bitter winter to a friendly clime, or of people that, after being long ill and bedridden, wake one day to find that they are unexpectedly well and the day is again full of promise."[17]

Like the baptized infants, the hobbits shed their old clothes, are baptized naked, and emerge from the water anew, in brand new clothes. Sam, Merry, and Pippin never find their old clothes again and must put on new ones. This newness marks the start of their journey of personal growth throughout the rest of the book. Also, like many acts of healing in the Bible in general where those that are healed are immediately fed, the hobbits feel their hunger and share a meal with Tom.

The time with Tom Bombadil seems ill at ease with the overall tone of *LotR*. Yet, Frodo has the prophetic dream of his ending come while in the house of this strange character. He dreams of sweet singing, and a "grey rain-curtain like a veil of glass and silver that rolls back into a far green country that open before him under a swift sunrise."[18] This is reminiscent of St. Paul's transcendent experience in 2 Corinthians 12 when either "in the body or out of the body" he is "caught up to the third heaven" and had an experience of Paradise. Frodo, not knowing whether he is awake or asleep, has his own vision of paradise as he sees a glimpse of what he will experience after his "death." It seems fitting that Frodo has this type of dream in Bombadil's house. Bombadil's Christ-likeness manifests itself in his willingness and ability to rescue and heal. Frodo will need rescuing and healing that he will eventually only find in Aman and his first glimpse of his fate comes to him in the safe home of the Christ-like Tom Bombadil.

---

17. Op. cit. [1], p. 141.
18. Op. cit., p. 132.

Chapter 13: The Holy Spirit in *The Lord of the Rings*

A parallel can be drawn between God the Father and Ilúvatar, and God the Son and Gandalf/Frodo/Aragorn. This notion predisposes to include the Holy Spirit, although not aligned with any one character, but rather represented by the Flame Imperishable, which manifests itself in different ways in *The Lord of the Rings*.

The Flame Imperishable

The "flame imperishable", a sort of inspiration or energy, is mentioned three times, all in the cosmogony portion of *The Silmarillion*, called *The Ainulindalë*. The first mention has Ilúvatar "kindle" the Ainur with it.[1] We can infer from this passage that this flame is something Ilúvatar, God, has given to his angels, the Ainur, that is their source of existence or power. The next mention is shortly thereafter and this time it is something Melkor seeks but is unable to find. The Flame is something Melkor covets. Though he, too, has been kindled by it, he seeks it outside of himself yet finds it not "for it is with Ilúvatar."[2]

It is not until Ilúvatar speaks about the flame again does it start to seem clear what it is. Ilúvatar sends forth the Flame into the very void where Melkor was looking.[3] The Flame comes from him and it is the "heart of the world,"[4] the kindling agent of creation, that is now coming into existence. The Ainur see it manifested as a flame for the first time. Nowhere is it stated that Ilúvatar created the Flame. Rather it seems that it is something that comes from, or *proceeds* from him.

This recalls what Christianity teaches about the Holy Spirit who, as the third Person of God, is also uncreated. The Nicene Creed, a declaration of the Christian faith, states that "the Holy Spirit, the Lord, the Creator of life ... *proceeds* from the Father." A basis for this are Christ's words when He tells His Disciples He will be sending them the Helper who is the Holy

---

1. J.R.R. Tolkien, *The Silmarillion*, Houghton Mifflin, 1977, p. 15.
2. Op. cit., p. 16.
3. Op. cit., p. 20.
4. Ibid.

Spirit: "But when the Helper comes, whom I shall send to you from the Father, the Spirit of truth who *proceeds* from the Father, He will testify of Me." (John 15:26).

There are both tremendous similarities and distinct differences between the Biblical Genesis and Tolkien's cosmogony. However, in reading about the Flame Imperishable and the Void, it is easy to see a parallel to the opening of Genesis:

> In the beginning God created the heavens and the earth. The earth was without form, and void; and darkness was on the face of the deep. And the Spirit of God was hovering over the face of the waters. (Genesis 1:1-2)

The Flame Imperishable is never mentioned in *LotR* by name but it can be inferred in Gandalf's reference to "the Secret Fire... the flame of Anor."[5] That is the only mention of this "Secret Fire", of which Gandalf is the servant. This Secret Fire is the Flame Imperishable which is the Holy Spirit. Gandalf is a servant of the Holy Spirit and wielder of its power as given to him and willed by Ilúvatar. Furthermore, Gandalf is the keeper and wielder of Narya, one of the three elven Rings of Power, and the one known as the Ring of Fire. Gandalf was ever the motivator who "kindled" the hearts of the free peoples of Middle-earth to fight evil.

The correspondence of the Secret Fire to the Holy Spirit can be deduced from a conversation between Tolkien and Clyde Kilby, who in the summer of 1966 attempted to help Tolkien get *TSil* in order for publication. During one of their conversations, regarding Gandalf's words to the Balrog, Kilby reports "Very specifically, he [Tolkien] told me that "the Secret Fire sent to burn at the heart of the world" in the beginning was the Holy Spirit."[6] Tolkien links the Secret Fire mentioned by Gandalf to the Flame Imperishable sent into the heart or world as described in *The Ainulindalë*. Regrettably, the two men did not carry the conversation further. It is not surprising that Tolkien chose fire and flame for the symbol analogous to the Holy Spirit. One of the most famous passages showing the manifestation of the Holy Spirit recounts how during Pentecost the Disciples experience the Holy Spirit by seeing tongues of fire upon each other (Acts 2:1-4). This fulfills Christ's promise from the Gospel of John that the Holy Spirit comes at Pentecost and, filled with holiness, the Disciples speak in strange tongues.

Tolkien draws upon this imagery when describing characters inspired by what is holy. For example, Galadriel's phial contains light from Eärendil's star, Gil-Estel, the Star of High Hope, which is holy. Sam, facing Shelob, clutches the Phial, and becomes empowered by it and speaks in Quenya, a

---

5. J.R.R. Tolkien, *The Lord of the Rings*, Houghton Mifflin,1954-5, 1965-6, p. 322.
6. Clyde S. Kilby, *Tolkien and the Silmarillion*, Harold Shaw Publishers, 1976, pp. 59.

language he does not know.[7] He and Frodo experience the same phenomenon later when escaping from the Tower of Cirith Ungol.[8] In both of these instances, the Phial "blazed" with sudden flames of light and radiance that drove away the darkness. In John 14:17, the Holy Spirit is referred to by Christ as dwelling with us and in us, and responds to us. The Phial and its light within seems to respond each time to Sam's "indomitable" spirit and "hardihood."

Pneuma

Though the Flame Imperishable is the Holy Spirit, Tolkien does not use flame and fire as his predominant metaphor for the Spirit's manifestation in *LotR*. Instead, he turns to something subtler: the flow of air. In a passage quoted from Acts 2:1-4, before the Disciples see the tongues of flame above each other's head, they experience the Holy Spirit as a "rushing mighty wind." Christ says that "the wind blows where it wishes, and you hear the sound of it, but cannot tell where it comes from and where it goes. So is everyone who is born of the Spirit" (John 3:8). The original Greek word used to describe the wind is *pneuma*. It means "wind", "spirit" and "breath." Verilyn Flieger, describing the thoughts of Tolkien's friend Owen Barfield, writes the following concerning *pneuma*:

> the Greek word *pneuma* and the Latin word *spiritus* originally each expressed a concept in which "wind," "breath," and "spirit" were all perceived as one and the same phenomenon. [Barfield] notes that in the King James translation of the third chapter of the Gospel According to Saint John, the word *pneuma* is rendered into English as 'spirit' in verse five and as 'wind' in verse eight. Apparently, for John and his audience, *pneuma* had an undivided meaning that later perception could no longer grasp entirely and for which a later mentality must find different words.[9]

It is *pneuma*, or wind, that Tolkien uses in *LotR*, primarily in *RotK*, as his means of showing the grace of the Holy Spirit. Whereas the Secret Fire is mentioned only once, wind is so prevalent it is easy to miss because of its frequency. Furthermore, he often blends wind and light together, the light perhaps dimly echoing the fire.

---

7. Op. cit. [5], p. 712.
8. Op. cit., p. 894.
9. Verilyn Flieger, *Splintered Light: Logos and Language in Tolkien's World*, Kent State University Press, 2002, p. 38.

Winds of Change

Tolkien seems to deliberately juxtapose wind and darkness. The prevalent mentions of wind begin when things seem their darkest. Mount Doom belches forth a gloom that covers Minas Tirith and the surrounding area. The Rohirrim, who are riding in aid of Minas Tirith, find all ways to the great stone city blocked and seek the aid of the Wild Men who live in Drúadan forest near Minas Tirith. Their chieftain, Ghân-buri-Ghân, says he can guide them to the city undetected by Sauron's forces. Théoden thanks Ghân-buri-Ghân who implores the King to kill the orcs and drive away the darkness. Théoden says he intends to but only the next day will show what he will accomplish. Ghân-buri-Ghân then sniffs the air and with a light in his eyes he cries "wind is changing."[10] This is the first mention of wind that herald's some sort of positive change. The Wild Man senses something that he cannot really express beyond something is changing. Tolkien uses light too here to hint that something good is coming.

The scouts report that Minas Tirith is 'all set about with flame', alerting both the Rohirrim and the readers of the drastic situation. However, Theoden is reminded of the Wild Man's words and the custom that breath out of the South brings the dawn. Here, breath can be interpreted as a reference to pneuma, its connection to the Holy Spirit bolstered by its association with light.

Yet, victory is still uncertain, even when the Rohirrim come to the city. We see through Merry's eyes that the King falters, "motionless, gazing upon the agony of Minas Tirith, as if stricken suddenly by anguish, or by dread." Theoden's wavering hope is echoed by Merry who,

> felt as if a great weight of horror and doubt had settled on him… They were too late! Too late was worse than never! Perhaps Théoden would quail, bow his old head, turn, slink away to hide in the hills.[11]

Tolkien does not leave the characters in this state of despair. In the next paragraph, he explicitly states that the wind is "beyond doubt: a change."[12] With the first light of morning, Merry hears a loud sound, which we learn later is the battering ram Grond destroying the gates of the first level of Minas Tirith, and then in beautiful scene blending wind and light, sees his adopted father, King Théoden, transform before his eyes, and lead his people into the battle.[13] In this wonderful scene, Tolkien uses light and wind to

---
10. Op. cit. [5], pp. 816-7.
11. Op. cit., p. 819.
12. Ibid.
13. Op. cit., pp. 819-820.

show Théoden's glorious transformation and ultimate impotence of evil, this counterfeit power, in the face of the true might of the goodness. Théoden is reminiscent of the scared and trapped Disciples before their glorious transformation. Preceding Pentecost and the coming of the Holy Spirit, they were hiding fearfully in one place in Jerusalem. Once the Spirit came they took boldly to the city streets preaching (see Acts chapter 2). Tolkien returns to the motif of a king empowered by the wind when Aragorn makes his surprising but glorious appearance in the Battle of the Pelennor fields "borne upon a wind" in what tips the scales for the forces of good and enables them to finally rout Sauron's armies.[14]

Characters appear to recall their own experience by its connection to wind and light. Gimli uses languages such as "change coming with a fresh wind from the Sea" and "we came in the third hour of the morning with a fair wind and the Sun unveiled."[15] In another example, as the Witch-king is destroyed, Frodo and Sam sense "wind out of the living world" driving back the darkness of Mordor, allowing dim light to come through. Sam's exclaims that the wind is changing and that Sauron's darkness is breaking up.[16] Wind out of the "living world" brings to mind "the Spirit who gives life" (John 6:63). Here the wind of life sweeps into the land of the dead bringing the light that breaks up the darkness and gives Frodo and Sam hope and reminding us of the power of the Spirit to drive away darkness and evil.

Tolkien reflects the change in the power balance between good and evil in the shifting of the climes. As the two hobbits approach Mount Doom he writes, "The wind had fallen the day before as it shifted from the West, and now it came from the North and began to rise; and slowly the light of the unseen Sun filtered down into the shadows where the hobbits lay."[17] He also reminds us that no matter how powerful darkness seems, it too ultimately fears a power far greater than it. Tolkien deliberately uses the wind as a cause of Sauron's fear and anxiety. Even having almost completed his devilish scheme, he is described "fearing the winds of the world that had turned against him, tearing aside his veils, and troubled with tidings of bold spies that had passed through his fences."[18] Finally, let us be reminded that in their final scenes, both Sauron and Saruman are blown away by the wind, the symbol of the Spirit and goodness, into nothingness. This shows the ultimate power of good in Tolkien's universe and reminds readers of Sam's revelation in Mordor when he realized that evil, the shadow, is nothing more than a "small and passing thing."

---

14. Op. cit. [5], p. 829.
15. Op. cit., p. 859.
16. Op. cit., p. 898.
17. Op. cit., p. 919.
18. Op. cit., p. 913-4.

Winds of Blessing and Healing

My father died suddenly in late May 2004. He died in his bedroom on the third floor of his eighty-year old row house he had grown up in. There was an uncharacteristic heat wave that began that week and temperatures were reaching the mid to high nineties. Shortly after his death and funeral my brother and I began the labor-intensive task of cleaning out a house that had eighty years of stuff and memories. I remember finally finishing after days of intense labor and sitting on the stoop at the bottom of the stairs between the main floor and upstairs. It was still intensely hot and I was exhausted. I looked around at the now near empty house and a wave of sadness passed over me. Suddenly, a cool refreshing breeze blew through the windows filling the room and house and I heard the familiar rustle of the bushes and trees that had grown against the house over the years. I was instantly transported in my memory to the times in autumn where my dad, brother and I would sit around in the family room with the windows open (there was no central air in this old house so we either had window units or open windows). I felt a refreshment of spirit I remember to this day. There was no reason for such a cool breeze on a ninety plus degree day. The words of Julian of Norwich came to mind: "all shall be well and all manner of thing shall be well."[19] I also thought of Elijah in his despair and the comfort he felt in the "sound of a gentle breeze." (3 Kingdoms (1 Kings) 19:9-12). I felt such a sense of comfort my spirit was immediately lifted. I left the house, never looked back, and treasure that memory to this day.

I share this example because in addition to change, Tolkien also uses the wind in *LotR* as an agent of blessing and of healing. The end of the Battle on the Pelennor Fields is punctuated by a wind that quenches flames of destruction and brings a cleansing baptismal rain. Not too long after we get an even greater manifestation of the wind's blessing when Aragorn heals Éowyn while "a keen wind [blows] through the window, and it [bears] no scent, but [is] an air wholly fresh and clean and young, as if it had not before been breathed by any living thing."[20]

Lastly, after the readers witness Sauron's destruction, they are presented with an alternative perspective on the event. Faramir and Éowyn, standing on the ramparts of Minas Tirith, feel that

> ...a great wind rose and blew, and their hair, raven and golden, streamed out mingling in the air. And the Shadow departed, and the Sun was unveiled, and light leaped forth; ... and in all the houses of the City men sang for the joy

---

19. Julian of Norwich, *The Revelations of Divine Love*, Wyatt North Publishing, 2014, E-Book.
20. Op. cit., pp. 849-850.

that welled up in their hearts from what source they could not tell.[21]

Tolkien returns to language reminiscent of the books of Acts and Joel by calling the wind a great wind and coupling it with sunlight that leaps forth and a sense of joy so deep it is numinous. The news of Sauron's demise is fittingly announced by an eagle, a type of angelic messenger, and with this comes the final sense that Sauron's destruction is utter and complete and that light and joy will now reign in Gondor and beyond.

---

21. Op. cit. [5], pp. 941-2.

Chapter 14: Holy Communion: Lembas and Miruvor

Tolkien had a sacramental view of reality, which provides a convenient lens through which to interpret his writing. In addition to his devotion to Christ and his belief in the working of the Holy Spirit which we have explored at length, he particularly revered the Eucharist and the Holy Mother. In a letter written a few years after the publication of *The Lord of the Rings*, he provided facts about himself. He wrote the following:

> "...I am a Christian (which can be deduced from my stories), and in fact a Roman Catholic. The latter 'fact' perhaps cannot be deduced; though one critic (by letter) asserted that the invocations of Elbereth, and the character of Galadriel as directly described (or through the words of Gimli and Sam) were clearly related to Catholic devotion to Mary. Another saw in waybread (lembas) the viaticum and the reference to its feeding the will (vol. III, p. 213) and being more potent when fasting, a derivation from the Eucharist."[1]

Choosing to mention he is a Christian, Tolkien immediately cites Holy Communion and Mary as elements readers have identified in *LotR*. In this chapter and the next, we will explore these two elements which serve as vehicles of grace for Tolkien's characters when they seem to need it most.

Tolkien and the Blessed Sacrament

In a letter to his son Michael, Tolkien concludes with the following:

> I put before you the one great thing to love on earth: the Blessed Sacrament... There you will find romance, glory, honor, fidelity, and the true way of all your loves on earth, and more than that: Death: by the divine paradox, that which ends life, and demands the surrender of all, and yet by the taste (or foretaste) of which alone can what you seek in your earthly relationship (love, faithfulness, joy) be maintained, or take on that complexion of reality,

---

1. Humphrey Carpenter, *The Letters of J.R.R. Tolkien*, Houghton Mifflin, 2000, Letter 213, p. 288.

of eternal endurance, which every man's heart desires.[2]

The Eucharist held a special place in Tolkien's heart and it is possible to see it within the effects of *lembas* and *miruvor*. I use the word effects because Tolkien, as a Roman Catholic, believed that in receiving the Eucharist, he, and others, receive the body and blood of Christ that is Christ Himself in a mysterious way. His imagined history pre-dates Christ and although there are types of Christ, Christ Himself is never present in his pre-history thus anything that is a type of a Eucharist can only be so in terms of its effects and perhaps in divine virtue. The effects are spiritual nourishment and an experience of grace. Of the two, *lembas*, the waybread of the elves, sustains, while *miruvor*, a tasteless liquid used by Glorfindel and Gandalf, reinvigorates.

The Eucharistic Aspects of Lembas

We first encounter *lembas* in Lothlórien. The elves give the Company of the Ring supplies and they hand Gimli, what he thinks is *cram*, a travelling bread made by the men of Dale that is mentioned in *The Hobbit*. Though not particularly tasty, *cram* does not spoil easily and is a good travelling food. Gimli is pleasantly surprised at how savory *lembas* is and begins to devour more pieces until the elves stop him and explain it is unlike *cram*, "more strengthening than any food made by Men."[3] The first interpretation of its virtue is its ability to nourish the body. The Three Hunters rely on it solely as they journey across the fields of Rohan to try and save Merry and Pippin. Tolkien writes that as the third day of their chase begins, that they thank Galadriel in their hearts for the gift of *lembas* as they can eat of it and find new strength as they run.[4]

There are several other references past this to *lembas* doing more than sustaining someone physically, but for the most part they are vague references at best. However, it is not until Frodo and Sam encounter Gollum that the Eucharistic aspects of *lembas* become clear. Gollum is starving and the hobbits only have *lembas* to offer him, which they do. Gollum rejects it, claiming it tastes of ashes and dust and being unable to stand the smell or thought of it. Frodo tells him this food would be good for him but acknowledges that Gollum is not yet ready for it.[5] This is the first time we learn that *lembas* is a food that does not have the same effect or experience for everyone. St. Paul's epistles can be used to elucidate the matter.

---

2. Op. cit. [1], Letter 43, p. 53-54.
3. J.R.R. Tolkien, *The Lord of the Rings*, Houghton Mifflin,1954-5, 1965-6, p. 360.
4. Op. cit., p. 417.
5. Op. cit., p. 608.

Paul writes at length about receiving the Eucharist in either a worthy or unworthy manner, explaining that Christians are both unworthy in an of themselves and worthy through Christ, to receive Holy Communion. The only thing that truly makes Christians unworthy, paradoxically, is their belief they are worthy based on their own merits as opposed to Christ.

St. Paul addresses in 1 Corinthians 11:27-32 the dangers of receiving when someone is truly unworthy:

> whoever eats this bread or drinks this cup of the Lord in an unworthy manner will be guilty of the body and blood[d] of the Lord. But let a man examine himself, and so let him eat of the bread and drink of the cup. For he who eats and drinks in an unworthy manner[e] eats and drinks judgment to himself, not discerning the Lord's body. ... if we would judge ourselves, we would not be judged. But when we are judged, we are chastened by the Lord, that we may not be condemned with the world.

The Orthodox Study Bible comments on this passage explaining that to approach the Communion chalice unworthily is to come to Christ "with hidden immorality (6:18–20), disunity (v. 18), doctrinal heresy (v. 19), or disorder (vv. 21, 22), failing to see the gifts of God as holy things for holy people."[6]

When Christians partake and receive unworthily, they invite judgment and condemnation unto themselves. This is because the Eucharist is more than just bread and wine. It is mystically the body and blood of Christ – Christ Himself – and He cannot come into anyone and dwell in their hearts if by their own free will they will not receive Him. Gollum inability to receive *lembas* is reminiscent of this.

Before Gollum, we do not encounter anyone who truly cannot receive *lembas*. Boromir may eventually have lost his taste for it as he became more corrupted by desire for the Ring, but Tolkien does not describe this. In the scene between Frodo and Gollum it is clear, just like it was with the elven rope that seemed to burn and freeze his ankle, Gollum is so corrupt that anything made and endowed with virtue harms rather than helps him. It would be tempting to leave the analysis here and just assume Gollum is bad, and what the elves make is too good for him or anyone else so corrupted by Sauron. However, Tolkien explicitly tells us more about *lembas* that encourages further discussion. Though much later in the book, he expands on the properties of *lembas* as Frodo and Sam approach Mount Doom:

> The *lembas* had a virtue without which they would long ago have lain down

---

6. *Orthodox Study Bible*, Thomas Nelson, 2008, p. 1565.

to die. It did not satisfy desire, and at times Sam's mind was filled with the memories of food, and the longing for simple bread and meats. And yet this waybread of the Elves had a potency that increased as travelers relied on it alone and did not mingle it with other foods. It fed the will, and it gave strength to endure, and to master sinew and limb beyond the measure of mortal kind.[7]

The Eucharistic overtones are heavily implied. The reliance on *lembas* and no other foodstuff can be read as a metaphor for the Christians sole focus on God and no other worldly ways or philosophies that compete for their attention (Colossians 2:8-12). Furthermore, it speaks to fasting before receiving. Though not as prevalent in most Churches today, the tradition of fasting before receiving Holy Communion is an ancient one. In Orthodox Christian churches today, as part of both their preparation to receive and thankfulness for having received, the worshipers are supposed to abstain from meat and dairy on Wednesday and Friday and let nothing pass their lips on Sunday prior to receiving Holy Communion. This is not a rigid *requirement* in the Orthodox Church. It is a *means* to help people prepare their hearts to receive God's grace through Holy Communion. Fasting is a means to draw people closer to God, because when they choose to fast they are willingly choosing to focus their hearts and minds on God. They fast on Wednesday to commemorate Jesus' betrayal by Judas, and Friday to commemorate His crucifixion.

Lastly, the passage echoes the mystical nature of Holy Communion in that *lembas* feeds the will beyond measure of what mortals typically experience. It is particularly Eucharistic when we consider *lembas* provided a type of sustaining grace to Frodo and Sam, especially Frodo the Ring-bearer. The Ring is evil and the grace conferred by *lembas* helps Frodo resist the evil of it as long as he is able.

In addition to the evidence presented in this chapter, Tolkien's letter, penned three years after *LotR* was published, claims the function of *lembas* is two-fold: "It is a 'machine' or device for making credible the long marches with little provision, in a world in which as I have said 'miles are miles' … It also has a much larger significance, of what one might hesitatingly call a 'religious' kind. This becomes later apparent, especially in the chapter 'Mount Doom' (III 213 and subsequently)."[8] He also writes: "No analysis in any laboratory would discover chemical properties of *lembas* that made it superior to other cakes of wheat-meal."[9] This ineffable nature of the waybread is reminiscent of the mystery of transubstantiation, the change of

---

7. Op. cit. [3], p. 915.
8. Op. cit. [1], Letter 210, p. 274.
9. Op. cit., Letter 210, p. 275.

bread and wine to the body and blood of Christ. Tolkien therefore hints at the Eucharistic nature of *lembas* when he writes that no analysis would ever discover its workings.

The Eucharistic Aspects of Miruvor

Miruvor is not nearly as prevalent as *lembas*. It is only explicitly mentioned three times. All three instances occur in the Fellowship's journey to and through Moria. Gandalf is the drink's distributor and it is probably lost during his fight with the Balrog. Though not named, it also seems to be used by Glorfindel when he, Aragorn, and the hobbits approach the ford leading to Rivendell. He gives them a liquor from a flask that gives them immediate strength.[10] It is not clear what Glorfindel gives them until later when the Company is battling the great mountain Caradhras. Gandalf gives them a liquor that has the same effect as Tolkien describes in the Glorfindel scene and the wizard names it *miruvor*.[11]

Like *lembas*, *miruvor* has an invigorating effect on mind, heart, and body and it seems to work quicker. In addition to its effects, its Eucharistic overtones come from the fact that it is Gandalf, a Christ-type, who is the one to distribute it. He is the only one to even have it. Elrond seems to only have entrusted it to him among the Fellowship. Further, Gandalf refers to it as precious – clearly not something to be given lightly. The wizard also distributes it a total of three times – the time just quoted, a time before they enter the darkness of Moria, and a final time in Moria.[12] Similarly, the Three Hunters experience the full effects of *lembas* on the third day of their pursuit.[13] Three is a number often associated with that which is holy so Tolkien may well be hinting at the holy aspects of *miruvor* and *lembas* by associating them with three.

Lastly, perhaps the most potent evidence of Tolkien's thoughts of *miruvor* as Eucharistic-like is the name itself. According to notes from *The War of the Jewels*, *miruvor* derives from the Quenya word *miruvórë* which means "precious juice" and "a special wine or cordial."[14] It is indeed wine that is used in masses and liturgies that becomes transformed into the blood of Christ. Though not essential to the plot, both *lembas* and *miruvor* add elements of sacramental grace to the story that enriches it and reflect Tolkien's sacramental worldview.

---

10. Op. cit. [3], p. 206.
11. Op. cit., p. 283.
12. Op. cit., p. 203.
13. Op. cit., p. 417.
14. J.R.R. Tolkien, Christopher Tolkien, *The War of the Jewels*, "Part Four. Quendi and Eldar: Appendix D", 1959-60, p. 399.

Chapter 15: The Holy Mother, Elbereth, and Galadriel

Tolkien lost his mother, Mabel Tolkien, in 1904 when he was twelve. Having lost his father when he was four, his mother was the central parent in his life. From her he received his deep love of Catholicism. He wrote in one of his letters that in conceiving *The Lord of the Rings* he "should chiefly be grateful for having been brought up (since I was eight) in a Faith that has nourished me and taught me all the little that I know; and that I owe to my mother,..."[1] Further, she saw in him at a very young his gift for languages and nurtured it.[2] The sorrow of losing his mother never left him. Bradley Birzer speculates, accurately it would seem, that he transferred this love to the Holy Mother.[3]

Tolkien certainly revered Mary, the Virgin Mother, as is seen in his much-quoted admission that *LotR* is a Catholic work:

> I think I know exactly what you mean by the order of Grace; and of course by your references to Our Lady, upon which all my own small perception of beauty both in majesty and simplicity is founded. The Lord of the Rings is of course a fundamentally religious and Catholic work; unconsciously so at first, but consciously in the revision.[4]

Life, Death, Saints, and Intercessory Prayer

Mary is adored, not worshipped as some commonly think because many Christians pray to Mary. The difference between adoration and worship is simply that Mary is recognised for her achievement as a human being while worship is reserved for God.

The Churches teach that life in Christ is eternal. Saints and others in Christ who have died a physical death have just moved on beyond the physical

---

1. Humphrey Carpenter, *The Letters of J.R.R. Tolkien*, Houghton Mifflin, 2000, Letter 142, p. 172.
2. Michael D.C. Drought, Editor, *J.R.R. Tolkien Encyclopedia – Scholarship and Critical Assessment*, "Free Will" by Daniel Thomas, p. 141.
3. Op. cit., p. 87.
4. Op. cit. [1], Letter 142, p. 172.

senses. Jesus' message in the Gospel of Mark 12:18-27 is as follows:

> But concerning the dead, that they rise, have you not read in the book of Moses, in the burning bush passage, how God spoke to him, saying, 'I am the God of Abraham, the God of Isaac, and the God of Jacob?' He is not the God of the dead, but the God of the living.

Death is not the end of life. If saints have achieved a deeper union with God than other people, then their intercession on behalf of other Christians can be seen as more effective and yielding more immediate results. Mary can be counted among such intercessors, individuals with 'such a vital contact with God [that they are] like a live wire between the saving power of God and the sinful men who have been cut off from that power.'[5]

Likewise, Marian figures in *LotR* are invoked and revered as intercessors against the powers of Evil. Elbereth and Galadriel are of special note, as they provide a vital link between characters seeking grace and divine light.[6]

Elbereth as a Marian Figure

Elbereth is one of the Ainur who chooses to dwell in Arda and we do not encounter her directly in *LotR*. Elbereth is Varda, the second most powerful Vala after Manwë, and most beloved by the elves because she creates the stars. Elves awake under the starlight of the ancient past and live by their light for years uncounted, therefore they have a deep love for the stars. In Tolkien's Sindarin language, Elbereth means 'star lady'. The term Gilthoniel, often appended to the name Elbereth, means 'star-kindler'.

The first mention of Elbereth is when Frodo, Sam, and Pippin, who are being approached by a Black Rider, hear Gildor and his elves singing her name in the woods of the Shire and it drives the Nazgûl away.[7] Gildor's hymn to Elbereth, as identified by Stratford Caldecott, bears significant resemblance to a Marian hymn written by a Catholic priest named Father John Lingard (1771–1851).

> "Hail, Queen of Heaven, the ocean star,
> Guide of the wanderer here below,
> Thrown on life's surge, we claim thy care,
> Save us from peril and from woe.

---

5. Hannah Hurnard, God's Transmitters, Tyndale House, 1990, p. 12.
6. For further discussion of light and darkness metaphors in *LotR*, see Verlyn Flieger's *Splintered Light: Logos and Language in Tolkien's World*.
7. J R.R. Tolkien, *The Lord of the Rings*, Houghton Mifflin,1954-5, 1965-6, p. 78.

Mother of Christ, Star of the sea
Pray for the wanderer, pray for me.

O gentle, chaste, and spotless Maid,
We sinners make our prayers through thee;
Remind thy Son that He has paid the price of our iniquity

Virgin most pure, Star of the sea,
Pray for the sinner, pray for me."[8]

According to Tom Shippey, Tolkien indeed called Gildor's song to Elbereth a hymn.[9]

"Snow-white! Snow-white! O Lady clear!
O Queen beyond the Western Seas!
O Light to us that wander here
Amid the world of woven trees!

Gilthoniel! O Elbereth!
Clear are thy eyes and bright thy breath,
Snow-white! Snow-white! We sing to thee
In a far land beyond the Sea.

O stars that in the Sunless Year
With shining hand by her were sown,
In windy fields now bright and clear
We see your silver blossom blown!

O Elbereth! Gilthoniel!
We still remember, we who dwell
In this far land beneath the trees,
Thy starlight on the Western Seas."

Upon hearing the elves sing, Frodo is amazed by the name of Elbereth and immediately realizes these are "High Elves" that are set apart from most elves in Middle-earth. It also shows that Frodo somehow knows of the reverence to Elbereth, likely from Bilbo's tutelage over the years. It would also seem something touches Frodo's heart about Elbereth as he mentions her many times in need during his journey and struggles. From this point

---

8. Paul E. Kerry (Editor), *The Ring and the Cross*, Farleigh Dickinson, 2011, pp. 250-251, quoted from Marjorie Burns, "Saintly and Distant Mothers".
9. Tom Shippey, *The Road to Middle-earth*, Houghton Mifflin, 2002, p. 203.

forward in the story, both by Frodo and others, Elbereth is either invoked in an intercessory manner, or sung about in adoration. When Gildor and his company part from Frodo, he says, "May Elbereth protect you!"[10]

The Valar are the guardians of the world appointed by Ilúvatar and strive to do his will. Because they strive to do Eru's will, in this sense, they are continuous intercessors on behalf of him. Gildor petitions Elbereth to protect Frodo and because of who and what she is, it has an intercessory flavor since she is doing Eru's will. Gildor's statement is reminiscent of an aspect of Roman Catholic Mass: "…and I ask blessed Mary, ever virgin…to pray for me to the Lord, our God."

The next mention of Elbereth is again linked to the Nazgûl and the idea of light driving away darkness. Frodo is wounded by a Morgul blade on Weathertop. As he is being attacked he finds himself crying out *"O Elbereth! Gilthoniel!"* which, Aragorn tells him afterwards, caused the Nazgûl more harm than Frodo's sword.[11] Aragorn's comment speaks to the power of Frodo's prayer. Frodo invokes her name again as he tried to keep the Nazgûl from claiming him at the Ford of Bruinen.

In a more peaceful scene, Galadriel sings a hymn to Elbereth.[12] This is also the first of a few times where Galadriel and Elbereth, the two Marian figures of the story, appear in the text together. The reverence to Varda (Elbereth) is clear. It is also significant because in the hymn, she essentially prays that Frodo may receive a special grace to go in a purgatorial fashion to the Undying Lands to find healing.[13] This echoes the adoration given to Mary through hymns associated with Church services dedicated to her, such as the Orthodox "Salutations to the Theotokos", which takes place every Friday over five weeks leading up to Holy Week and concludes with a service called the "Akathist Hymn" to Mary. These hymns implore Mary's intercession much like Galadriel asks intercession of Elbereth.

The next mention of Elbereth is again in a prayerful way and it is the only time in *LotR* where someone other than a hobbit deliberately calls upon her in an intercessory way. All other elvish mentions of her are in songs of praise and adoration. Legolas invokes her name as he fires an arrow at some unknown winged creature that is "blotting out all light."[14] Although we do not learn this until much later, it is associated with driving off the Nazgûl and the language Tolkien uses once again has to do with light driving away darkness. As soon as Legolas fells the Nazgûl's mount Tolkien describes the sky as clean once more as light returns.

---

10. Op. cit. [7], p. 83.
11. Op. cit., p. 193.
12. Op. cit., p. 368.
13. Op. cit. [1], Letter 246, p. 386.
14. Op. cit. [7], p. 378.

Throughout the rest of *LotR*, it is the hobbits who invoke her name and the name of Galadriel, and in every instance, it is to empower them and to drive away the immediate threat of evil. For instance, Sam uses Galadriel's name when mustering up the strength to face Shelob. Interestingly, in this scene, it is through the mention of one Marian figure, Galadriel, that he is empowered by the other Marian figure, Elbereth, whose name is invoked next.[15] He receives grace through the power of the Phial. It suddenly flares up in his hand and drives off Shelob and her darkness with the light of Galadriel's "star-glass" and the fire of his spirit. Later, as Frodo and Sam prepare to escape from the Tower of Cirith Ungol, they agree to use the name *Elbereth* as their password to identify each other in the gloom. As they leave and are stopped by the Watchers and an invisible shield of malice, they use the Phial of Galadriel once more, call upon Elbereth, and the light and intercession destroy the dark Watchers and their evil will.

This is the last intercessory prayer to Elbereth in the story and her name is not mentioned again until the very end as Frodo and Sam are riding to the Grey Havens. In keeping with the cyclical nature of the narrative, the hobbits once more encounter Gildor's company, singing in elvish to their beloved Lady.[16] Thus, *LotR*, which begins, to an extent, with a hymn to the Marian figure of Elbereth, closes much in the same way.

Galadriel as a Marian Figure

Galadriel, a character Tolkien revisited and rewrote the most, comes closest to a Marian figure in his universe. Unlike Elbereth, we encounter Galadriel in the pages of *LotR*. From her first mention, her power is established as beyond that of ordinary elves akin to how Mary's word bears more intercessory weight than the words of other saints. We learn more about her when she invites Frodo and Sam to experience her Mirror. Her experience with the hobbits parallel's Mary's experience with the Archangel Gabriel as told in the opening chapter of the Gospel of St. Luke. After Frodo realizes she bears Nenya, one of the three Elven Rings, she explains what his quest truly means to her and her people. She says Frodo's coming is like the "footsteps of doom" and says if he fails Sauron wins and if he succeeds Lothlórien will fade away. When Frodo asks her what she ultimately wants she simply replies, "That what should be shall be."[17] Mary is troubled at the coming of Gabriel and reasonably inquires as to how what Gabriel says can happen. She then, in an obedient manner that serves as the highest model of obedience for all Christians, accepts God's will and her role within it saying

---

15. Op. cit. [7], p. 712.
16. Op. cit., p. 1005.
17. Op. cit., p. 356.

simply, "Let it be to me according to your word." Despite knowing the persecution she would face for bearing a child that was not her husband's, Mary accepts God's will anyway.

Similarly, Galadriel is troubled by her encounter with Frodo. She is troubled because of the temptation to take the Ring and troubled that by letting it go she is likely dooming her home if the Ring is destroyed or recaptured by Sauron. After a dialogue with Frodo her response is very Marian like. In saying 'what should be shall be' she is acknowledging a higher power at work, Ilúvatar, and accepting his will. She is subordinating a willful desire to take the Ring for the sake of God's will. Just as Mary received a special grace in being chosen to bring Christ into the world, and because she accepted this grace, she became the greatest saint in the Church. Galadriel, because of her obedience to God's will, is pardoned for her sin, ensures that the elves of Lothlórien do not suffer the fate of orcs, and allowed to return home to Aman in the West (this idea of her sin and her pardoning is a marked difference between her and Mary that I address later in this chapter).

Tolkien reiterates the importance of Galadriel's resilience:

> I think it is true that I owe much of this character to Christian and Catholic teaching and imagination about Mary, but actually Galadriel was a penitent: in her youth a leader in the rebellion against the Valar (the angelic guardians). At the end of the First Age she proudly refused forgiveness or permission to return. She was pardoned because of her resistance to the final and overwhelming temptation to take the Ring for herself.[18]

Furthermore, Galadriel receives Marian treatment similar to Elbereth as the story goes on and can be read as a tangible extension of Elbereth. Much like Mary is prayed to in an intercessory way and has at times physically appeared according to Catholic and Orthodox traditions, Galadriel can be seen as a physical manifestation of Elbereth. She sings to Elbereth herself and is eventually associated with Elbereth by Frodo and Sam, especially the latter, when they reach out in times of need. For example, when Sam uses the Phial to overcome Shelob he calls upon Galadriel and Elbereth.

> "Galadriel!" he said faintly, and then he heard voices far off but clear: the crying of the Elves as they walked under the stars in the beloved shadows of the Shire, and the music of the Elves as it came through his sleep in the Hall of Fire in the house of Elrond.
> *Gilthoniel A Elbereth!*

---

18. Op. cit. [1], Letter 320, p. 407.

And then his tongue was loosed and his voice cried in a language which he did not know:

A Elbereth Gilthoniel
o menel palan-diriel,
le nallon sí di'nguruthos!
A tiro nin, Fanuilos!"[19]

Prior to this, Sam has already called upon Galadriel. Though not as lofty as the prayers to Elbereth, Sam calls upon her in a prayerful way and his prayers are answered with the grace of strength, light, and water when he needs them most. In an emotional response, Sam's calls her name when he thinks he will not be able to retrieve the rope he received from her people in Lórien and to his delight the rope comes loose and falls at his feet.[20] Frodo, who does not hear Sam mutter Galadriel's name, chides Sam for making a loose knot. Sam, in a mildly prideful manner, reminds Frodo of his family's expertise with rope and knot making and insists it was essentially Galadriel.[21] This seems to depict a beginning of Sam's faith.

In Mordor, it seems his faith has grown from these experiences. He calls upon her in a very sacramental and mature way; not asking for deliverance from his trial, but simply wanting nothing more than two simple needs to be met to ensure them – "just clean water and plain daylight, better than any jewels, begging your pardon."[22] Upon finding them, Sam promises to thank Galadriel for the gift of light and water.[23]

The Complexity of Galadriel

From these examples, it seems very clear Galadriel's Marian likeness. If Tolkien wrote nothing else about her except what we read in *LotR*, this chapter would end here. But Tolkien did write more and, in many ways, was moving Galadriel away from being a penitent, who is like Mary in some respects, to resembling increasingly the post 1854 Roman Catholic Mary. Pope Pius IX proclaimed the Immaculate Conception as dogma in that year. This dogma states that the moment Mary was conceived by St. Anne (St. Anna in the Orthodox Church), by God's special decree, she was delivered from any stain of original sin. Being without sin, Mary is not a penitent in any respect. By contrast, we see Galadriel complete her penance within

---

19. Op. cit. [7], p. 712.
20. Op. cit., p. 597.
21. Ibid.
22. Op. cit., p. 897.
23. Op. cit., p. 899.

LotR and transcend from a penitent to a more saint-like character. She is a unique character in Tolkien's mythos to undergo such a transformation.

In her "penitent stage", before Tolkien reconsiders her background, there is a lack of consistency to her history. Depending on the source, Galadriel either left Beleriand sometime before The War of Wrath at the end of the First Age and migrated West with her husband Celeborn, who was one of the Sindar and a kinsman of Thingol; or she left and later met Celeborn who was a Nandorin elf.[24] She dwelt in Doriath and then seems to have gone to Lindon for a time before going to Eregion and then to Lothlórien.[25]

Regardless of the exact details of her personal history prior to and after her meeting Celeborn, Tolkien seems to think of her as a character whose motivation was to assert her independence and rule her own kingdom[26] which led her to make prideful choices and which required redemption. This was something Mary never did. Even though Galadriel did not participate in any bloodshed of other elves led by her cousin Fëanor, she did boldly and vaingloriously join his rebellion and leave Aman, making herself subject to the exile decreed by the Valar. Tolkien points out she was the only woman to "stand that day tall and valiant among the contending princes."[27] At the end of the First Age, she is the lone Noldo left alive who participated in the rebellion. Tolkien writes after Morgoth was defeated at the end of the First Age, the Valar banned her from returning to Aman and she proudly says she has no wish to do so.[28]

Despite her efforts against Morgoth and another six thousand plus

---

24. We learn in *LotR* that Galadriel has dwelt west of the Blue Mountains since sometime in the First Age. She states that she and Celeborn have dwelt in this same west since "the days of dawn." Putting this in the context of what we learn in *TSil*, this would make him one of the Teleri elves known as the Nandorin elves that never migrated west of the Misty Mountains. However, even without *TSil*, which was published twenty-two years after *LotR*, Tolkien wrote a contradictory statement in Appendix B where he writes, "In Lindon south of the Lune dwelt for a time Celeborn, kinsman of Thingol; his wife was Galadriel, greatest of Elven women."
25. In *The History of Galadriel and Celeborn* within *UT*, Christopher Tolkien states the likelihood of his father's early conception of Galadriel and Celeborn and provides a lengthy treatment of these character's conceptions and changes over his father's life. In brief, Galadriel's statement in *LotR*, contradicted in Appendix B, is further contradicted by what we learn of Celeborn in *TSil* which is more in keeping with the statement from Appendix B. Here, Celeborn is a Sindarin elf, the remnant of the Teleri elves that crossed the Misty Mountains and the Blue Mountains and dwelt in Beleriand. He is a kinsman of the King Thingol, Lord of the Sindarin elves and weds Galadriel in Thingol's Kingdom of Doriath. Yet another piece of evidence that is consistent with this portrayal is found in the book *The Road Goes Ever On*. This is a book of some of Tolkien's poems, mainly from *LotR*, set to music by Donald Swann and including written commentary from Tolkien, where he writes that she journeys over the Blue Mountains with Celeborn and goes to Eregion.
26. J.R.R. Tolkien, *The Silmarillion*, Houghton Mifflin, 1977, p. 84.
27. Op. cit., pp. 83-4.
28. J.R.R. Tolkien and Donald Swann, *The Road Goes Ever On*, Houghton Mifflin, 1978, p. 68.

years of toil against Sauron, we find her at the time of *LotR* still exiled but apparently much less prideful and in sad resignation that she will never return to Aman. As the Company approaches her and Celeborn to bid them farewell and continue their quest she sings a song that ends in a lament of whether there would ever be a ship that would take back across the sea.[29] In his letters, Tolkien comments on this in general and on Galadriel's hymn in Elvish that she sings a few pages later:

> "At the time of her lament in Lórien she believed this to be perennial, as long as Earth endured. Hence she concludes her lament with a wish or prayer that Frodo may as a special grace be granted a purgatorial (but not penal) sojourn in Eressëa, the Solitary Isle in sight of Aman, though for her the way is closed. (The Land of Aman after the downfall of Númenor was no longer in physical existence 'within the circles of the world'.) Her prayer was granted – but also her personal ban was lifted, in reward for her services against Sauron, and above all for her rejection of the temptation to take the Ring when offered to her. So at the end we see her taking ship."[30]

Galadriel, the bold and prideful penitent, whose pride melts over the years, receives grace due to her humility, sacrifice and goodness.

However, in the final years of his life, Tolkien drastically changed Galadriel's character. In a letter written in 1972, Galadriel does not partake in the rebellion with Fëanor and openly opposes and fights against him. Feeling confined in Aman, she longs to go to Middle-earth and eventually does so with the permission of the Valar even though this puts her under the Ban issued against Fëanor and other rebels. She arrives in Middle-earth and tries to persuade the other elves to abandon Beleriand and build up their defenses East of Ered Luin before Morgoth reaches those areas, however her counsel is not heeded and she moves east with Celeborn.

In this treatment, Galadriel commits no wrong and is more in keeping with Catholic thought on Mary in terms of her lack of sin. One month before he died, Tolkien wrote that "Galadriel was 'unstained': she had committed no evil deeds. She was an enemy of Fëanor. She did not reach Middle-earth with the other Noldor, but independently. Her reasons for desiring to go to Middle-earth were legitimate, and she would have been permitted to depart, but for the misfortune that before she set out the revolt of Fëanor broke out, and she became involved in the desperate measures of Manwë, and the ban on all emigration."[31]

Though I personally find it interesting how Tolkien continued to think of

---

29. Op. cit. [7], p. 363.
30. Op. cit. [1], Letter 297, p. 386.
31. Op. cit., Letter 353, p. 431.

Galadriel and the changes he considered, reading *LotR* and *TSil* in keeping with Galadriel's more saintly version versus her penitent version creates contradictions. If she was unstained and committed no evil, why would the Valar have enforced their ban for so long? Why would she lament about never returning across the sea? Why would she need to pass the redemptive test of being offered the Ring? Would a revised version of the scenes that fit the unstained version of Galadriel sacrificed the depth and complexity of her character? Regardless, Tolkien's devotion to his thoughts about Galadriel is a direct reflection of his devotion to the Blessed Mother and an undying love for his own mother long deceased. Galadriel, whether stained or unstained, is a wonderfully complex character and adds a richness to Tolkien's universe which the contradictions and changes only make richer.

Chapter 16: Other Biblical Types

Christ, the Holy Spirit, the Eucharist, and the Holy Mother are present typologically in *The Lord of the Rings* so strongly that they warranted detailed treatment. However, there are other aspects of Christianity in *LotR* which deserve mention and elaboration; they will be treated in this chapter. They all come from the book of Genesis which is very fitting because understanding the Genesis account of creation, paradise, sin, and "the fall of man" is critical to understanding Christ's purpose and mission, and other aspects of Christianity.

Lothlórien as a Type of Eden

Lórien can be read as a type of Eden, governed by Celeborn and Galadriel, a kind of Adam and Eve and, like 'a garden [planted] eastward in Eden' (Genesis 2:8), it lies in the east of Middle-earth. The Bible further details the four rivers of Eden:

> Now a river went out of Eden to water the garden, and from there it parted and became four riverheads. The name of the first is Pishon; it is the one which skirts the whole land of Havilah, where there is gold. And the gold of that land is good. Bdellium and the onyx stone are there. The name of the second river is Gihon; it is the one which goes around the whole land of Cush. The name of the third river is Hiddekel; it is the one which goes toward the east of Assyria. The fourth river is the Euphrates. (Genesis 2:10-14)

Rivers either border Lórien or flow through it. They are the Nimrodel, the Celebrant also referred to as the Silverlode, and the great river Anduin. The first Edenic river, Pishon, is said to skirt the land of Havilah which has gold. Similarly, Lórien is a land associated with gold in the form of the golden leaves of Mallorn trees. They fell to the ground during the spring covering the earth in a layer of gold. Eden at one point was not stained with sin and was holy in this regard. The word holy in New Testament Greek means "separate" or "to separate." The Company of the Ring palpably experiences a sense of separation from the world when they enter Lórien, both in terms of space and in terms of time, feeling as though they stepped into "a corner of the Elder Days."[1]

This is a direct result of the power and will of Galadriel and her Elven Ring. As can be seen in *The Tale of Aragorn and Arwen* after the departure of Galadriel, Lothlórien grows grey and inhospitable. Perhaps because he bears the Ruling Ring Frodo feels the power and Galadriel more deeply than the others and experiences its form of holiness. Perhaps this is why Tolkien chose to draw us into the experience of Lórien through Frodo.

> The others cast themselves down upon the fragrant grass, but Frodo stood awhile still lost in wonder. It seemed to him that he had stepped through a high window that looked on a vanished world. A light was upon it for which his language had no name. All that he saw was shapely, but the shapes seemed at once clear cut, as if they had been first conceived and drawn at the uncovering of his eyes, and ancient as if they had endured for ever. He saw no colour but those he knew, gold and white and blue and green, but they were fresh and poignant, as if he had at that moment first perceived them and made for them names new and wonderful. In winter here no heart could mourn for summer or for spring. No blemish or sickness or deformity could be seen in anything that grew upon the earth. On the land of Lórien there was no stain. (The Fellowship of the Ring, *Lothlórien*)[2]

The tone of the passage is distinctly Edenic, and yet Frodo's increased understanding of Lothlorien as he ventures deeper into it is also reminiscent of Peter, James, and John during Christ's transfiguration, when they experience God's uncreated light (Matthew 17:1-9). Frodo is like Adam both in his experience of a light which has no name and in his seeing reality for the first time and naming what he sees. When Adam is in the Garden alone, without sin, God brings the animals to Adam and allows him to name them (Genesis 2:19-20). Aligning with Tolkien's belief that all humans are subcreators who are able to reflect the power and love of God in their creations, God's love is so great for Adam that He allows him to participate in the creative process.

Although the Garden of Eden story is very brief, there is something in the writing of Genesis, when read slowly and deliberately, that evokes the feeling what it must have felt like to be in a fresh pure world, free from stain and all that comes with it. Through Frodo's experience we get an even more tangible glimpse of perhaps what Adam felt. He touches a tree and becomes aware of "the feel and texture of a tree's skin and of the life within it… the

---

1. J.R.R. Tolkien, *The Lord of the Rings*, Houghton Mifflin,1954-5, 1965-6, p. 340.
2. Op. cit., p. 341.

delight of the living tree itself."[3] Frodo experiences this "neither as forester nor as carpenter" but seems to have no utilitarian thought of how to use the tree for his own. He seems to be simply delighting in Ilúvatar's creation like Adam must have done in God's creation until he sinned by abandoning his vocation of worshipping and delighting in God and His creation and trying to live life on his own terms apart from God.

Just before Frodo has this experience of delighting in the tree, he has another subtle experience that foreshadows what will happen to him at the end of the book. He has climbed the hill of Cerin Amroth. On this hill within a circle of white trees, the wind blows through the branches (yet another experience of holiness as wind), and Frodo hears the oceans on long ago vanished beaches and the cries of seagulls.[4] He experiences the sea. He experiences the gulls that have long ago perished. Frodo will perish from Middle-earth via the sea himself. Further, he will do it by taking the place of Arwen who granted him her place on the ship that sailed with Elrond, Galadriel, Gandalf, and others.[5]

On his journey deeper into Lothlórien, Frodo brings evil into it by carrying the Ring. Adam and Eve bring sin into the Garden by allowing themselves to be beguiled by the serpent, and are cast out of the Garden as a result. Frodo, conversely, is not cast out and is treated with dignity and love.

However, this should not be viewed in juxtaposition to how Adam and Eve are treated. God's punishment of the first people should not be thought of as one of an angry parent who wants vengeance because he was not obeyed. Rather, it is simply the consequences of an abuse of freedom on Adam and Eve's part - a freedom given to them by a God who loved them enough in the first place to grant them this precious gift in hope that they would choose Him. God banishes Adam and Eve for their own good. To stay in the Garden in their immortality in a sinful state would be to doom them forever to this condition. Sending them out gives them an opportunity to "die." Since Christians view death in light of Christ's victory as a transformation rather than an ending to life, they believe they have the opportunity to grow back towards God in this life.[6] In contrast, though, Frodo is not sinning like Adam by succumbing to evil, but simply bears the evil of his own free will and with the intent of destroying it. However, it could be argued that Frodo does sin when he offers the Ring to Galadriel who wisely refuses. By doing so he intends to abandon the quest and give up his duty.

Much as Frodo's initial perception of Lórien felt like an experience

---

3. Op. cit. [1], p. 342.
4. Ibid.
5. Op. cit., pp. 952-953.
6. Michael C. Haldas, *Sacramental Living: Understanding Christianity as a Way of Life*, Eastern Christian Publications, 2013, p. 61.

of entering a paradise of sorts, when the Company departs, they all feel a palpable shift from safety to peril and a loss they are unable to prevent. As they watch, "Lórien [is] slipping backward, like a bright ship masted with enchanted trees, sailing on to forgotten shores, while they [sit] helpless upon the margin of the grey and leafless world."[7]

Grace also comes out of Lórien in another way as it did with Rivendell. Rivendell and Lothlórien represent the last remaining strongholds of the High Elves. These types of elves, more than any other, perceive the world, seen and unseen, as it really is and love it in a sacramental way. It is fitting that the Eucharistic aspects of *LotR* come from these two places that most closely resemble paradise and confer a holy type of sustenance and peace upon its visitors; *miruvor*, the blood, from Rivendell; and *lembas*, the body, from Lórien.

Sméagol and Déagol as a Type of Cain and Abel

Just as we are introduced to the story of Cain's murder of Abel early in the Bible, Genesis 4, we are also introduced to a similar murder early in *LotR*. Before delving into that murder, it is important to first explore the Cain and Abel story since the Bible, true to its manner, recounts the story in a brief way yet with so much meaning packed in so few words. Genesis 4:3-8 reads simply that both brothers brought their offering to God. Abel brought the firstborn of his flock and Cain an offering from the fruit of the ground. God accepts Abel's but rejects Cain's for what seems to be no apparent reason. He then asks Cain why face is fallen and warns him that sin desires Cain but that Cain needs to master it which he does not and kills his brother.

Why did God judge Cain's offerings to be insufficient and accept Abel's? Why does He warn Cain about sin? The word "priest" means "offeror" and, according to the Church, all human beings, clergy and laity, are supposed to be offerors in that we should offer our lives and all we have first to God because they belong to God. The story of Cain and Abel is a story of priesthood and stewardship. Abel offered that which was God's, the firstborn of his flock, back to God first. He did it instinctively without thinking. It flowed from him naturally because his heart was with God. He was a shepherd and as such had an understanding that which he tended was not his own. He was a steward of what was God's, not an owner, and this understanding kept his heart in a humble and worshipful state.

Cain was a farmer who worked the earth and selected what he determined should be offered to God. He did not do it maliciously nor is there evidence that he in fact did not offer God the best of his fruits or crops. However,

---

7. Op. cit. [1], p. 367.

the fact that he even thought about it means his heart was not with God as it should be. He acted as if he owned what he worked for by the very fact that he selected what should be offered. Abel put God first whereas Cain put himself first which is the essence of sin. Further, instead of humbling himself and ruling over sin as God warned him, he killed his brother out of jealously and pride. Instead of facing his own shortcomings and striving to overcome them, he directed his anger at his brother. God judges Cain and banishes him to the land of Nod as the story tells us. Nod means to "wander far from God" and that was how his heart had become. But in mercy and love, and to stop the cycle of murder, God forbids anyone to take vengeance on Cain.[8]

The story of Déagol and Sméagol, appearing in chapter two of *LotR*, greatly resembles this story. Though not brothers, they seem close as Sméagol calls Deagol "my love." In his letters, Tolkien indicates that Déagol is a relative of Sméagol's.[9] Déagol, the Abel figure, finds the Ring by chance and without any awareness of its properties. Sméagol, like Cain, immediately covets Déagol's "good fortune". He justifies his selfish desire by the occasion of his birthday and that it should be his birthday present. Déagol refuses since he already gave Sméagol a present and Sméagol then murders him for it. Like Cain, he craves something he does not have in possession of someone close to him.

There are some similarities and one marked difference between these stories. While Abel was innocent, Deagol, according to Tolkien's letters, was not devoid of character flaws. He is described as a "mean little soul".[10] According to Tolkien in this letter, Déagol is mean, though not as mean as Sméagol. Sméagol's justification that the Ring should be his because it is his birthday further accentuates the fact he is self-centered to begin with long before the Ring which simply magnified this flaw exponentially. Like Cain who went to the Land of Nod, wandering, Sméagol is doomed to exile and becomes Gollum. He does not receive a protective mark but does receive protection in the form of pity until he perishes by his own unyielding desire for the Ring.

Elendil as a Type of Noah

The Great Flood is strongly evoked by the destruction of Númenor. Caused by the wrath of the Valar against the corrupt king Ar-Pharazon, this cataclysmic event has Elendil, the leader of the faithful Numenoreans, at

---

8. Op. cit. [6], pp. 57-9.
9. Humphrey Carpenter, *The Letters of J.R.R. Tolkien*, Houghton Mifflin, 2000, Letter 214, p. 292.
10. Ibid.

its centre as a type of Noah. Elendil escapes the flood to play a key role in the first vanquishing of Sauron, and from him the line of Gondorian kings stems, culminating in Aragorn.

The similarities between the Biblical Noah and Tolkien's "Noachian figure"[11] are immediately apparent. Both escape a world changing, cataclysmic flood and destruction. In Noah's flood, all life is wiped out except that which is on the Ark. In Elendil's case, the island continent of Númenor and all of its life is destroyed, swallowed in a deep chasm that opens. The world goes from flat to round, and Aman is forever removed from the circles of the world. Noah escapes on the Ark with his wife, three sons - Shem, Ham, and Japheth – and their families. Elendil escapes the destruction of Númenor with his two sons, Isildur and Anárion, and their families though the minutiae vary.

Both destructive events are brought on by extreme wickedness and utter depravity. When God brings the flood, there is no one on earth that pleases Him, except for Noah. Wickedness and evil dominate. Tolkien provides a much more detailed treatment of decay and depravity in Númenor. The once bright kingdom grows wicked over time. Even though the Edain of Númenor are granted a life span many times that of normal man as a reward for their service against Morgoth, they become envious of the elves' immortality and begin to crave it. Being a seafaring nation, they move from good trade relations with the lesser men of Middle-earth to imperializing them and their relations with the remnant of the Noldor from the First Age grow cold. As described earlier, Sauron is able to corrupt them into offering human sacrifices and into rebellion against the Valar, ensuring their destruction.

Both the flood story in the Bible and events surrounding Númenor present "second falls." In the Bible, Adam and Eve represent the first fall of man as they allow sin to enter the world. Their descendants grow increasingly sinful, representing the second fall. In the case of Numenoreans, "the Downfall is partly the result of an inner weakness in Men – consequent, if you will, upon the first Fall (unrecorded in these tales), repented but not finally healed."[12]

Though hinted at in *TSil* when men are first discovered by the elf Finrod, who befriends a man named Bëor, we do not learn much else in that book. Tolkien only writes that Bëor told Finrod that a darkness lay behind him and his people and they left the east and came west to get away from it and find the light. Tolkien then as narrator explains that Morgoth left Sauron in command and left Angband when men awoke in the far east in Hildórien. He says the Eldar knew nothing of Morgoth's dealing with men but the implication is he caused something dark in them that Tolkien compares to Kinslaying that took place between the Noldor and Teleri when the Noldor

---

11. Op. cit. [9], Letter 131, p. 156 and Letter See Letter 156, p. 206.
12. Op. cit., Letter 131, p. 154.

fled Aman and killed their own kind to gain their ships.[13] It is clear that Morgoth was able to corrupt some men shortly after they awoke. Tolkien does provide a more detailed account of how men, in their beginning, fell. It is in *The History of Middle-earth* series, Volume X, *Morgoth's Ring*, with the *Athrabeth Finrod ah Andreth* (*The Debate of Finrod and Andreth*) the woman Andreth recounts a fascinating struggle of early man's perception of Ilúvatar in their hearts and the corrupting voice of Melkor who turns the "gift of death" from Eru into a corrupting fear of death.

Noah's flood and Númenor are also transition events to a new type of world. The pre-flood world is often referred to as the antediluvian period. The word antediluvian means "before the deluge," and it is the period between Adam and Eve's banishment from the Eden until the flood. The post flood world is very different. One of the marked differences is human beings declining life span. Where Adam and others lived into the nine-hundreds (some less), human's life spans decrease to the point where they do not live past one hundred and twenty. The events of Númenor also issues in a new world according to Tolkien.[14] Unlike our world where the Bible shows declining life spans after the flood, Númenorians began experiencing declining life spans prior to the cataclysmic event due to wickedness and mingling with lesser races of men.

Noah and his descendants found a new kingdom, being, according to the Christian doctrine, the progenitors of a new human race. But is it not without immediate strife. Noah settles into his new life as a husbandman and plants a vineyard. He drinks too much wine and passes out naked in his house. His son Ham sees his nakedness and mocks his father to his brothers, who respectfully cover their father while averting their eyes. When Noah awakens, and sobers up, he curses his younger son and indicates Ham, his son Canaan, and their descendants will serve Shem. From Shem come the Israelites and, eventually, Christ. The Israelites fight the Canaanites for possession of the Promised Land.

Tolkien parallels this type of family strife in the descendants of Elendil. Elendil, Isildur, and Anárion found the Kingdoms of Arnor and Gondor in Middle-earth. Elendil is the High-King who rules Arnor, the North Kingdom, and Isildur and Anárion jointly rule the South Kingdom. This divide into North and South Kingdoms loosely parallels Israel and Judah. We learn of the strife, both inner and outer, of these kings and kingdoms in the Biblical books of First and Second Kings (Kingdoms in the Septuagint) and First and Second Chronicles.

There is no record of strife between the two brothers, Isildur and Anárion. But by the time the Second Age ends with the defeat of Sauron, Elendil

---

13. J.R.R. Tolkien, *The Silmarillion*, Houghton Mifflin, 1977, p. 141.
14. Op. cit. [9], Letter 131, p. 154.

and Anárion are slain and Isildur is preparing to assume his father's seat in Arnor. He instructs Anárion's son, Meneldil, on the rule of the Gondor and leaves. Tolkien does gives us hints of the seeds of strife though it is not present in *LotR*. A note in *UT* reads that Meneldil was "well pleased" to see his Isildur and his sons leave Gondor and hoped that the affairs of the North Kingdom would keep them occupied for a long time.[15]

Meneldil being glad to see his uncle and cousins depart hints that had Isildur stayed, or installed one of his own sons to rule Gondor, it could have caused issues. Regardless, like Israel and Judah, from this point forward the kingdoms devolve into family strife, dissension from within and attacks from without. Arnor subdivides into three kingdoms before eventually disappearing. Gondor survives but goes into significant decline. It is not until the crowning of Aragorn, King Elessar, that Gondor is renewed, Arnor is reestablished, and two Kingdoms enjoy a period rivalling and surpassing briefly, their original glory. However, even this seems to have been short lived in Tolkien's mind. He began a *LotR* sequel, called *The New Shadow* that he abandoned. In a brief letter, he writes that about one hundred years after Sauron's downfall Gondor was already discontent with peace and falling into bad behavior.[16]

Tolkien's imagined history resembles our own ideologies. Aragorn, the messianic King and descendent of Elendil comes, renews, and re-establishes the Kingdoms, but people fall back into old sinful ways. Tolkien weaves into his world the myth of the end when Eru will heal the world.[17] Christ, descendent of Noah comes, ushers in the Kingdom of God, but it still struggles and though evil is ultimately defeated at the Cross, we live in the tension between His first and Second coming and final and permanent new Heaven and new earth free from sin and evil.

---

15. J.R.R. Tolkien, *Unfinished Tales of Númenor and Middle-earth*, Houghton Mifflin, 1980, p. 279.
16. Op. cit. [9], Letter 256, p. 344.
17. J.R.R. Tolkien, *Morgoth's Ring*, Houghton Mifflin, 1993, pp. 318-321.

Chapter 17: The Sacraments in The Lord of the Rings

There are already extant books that deal with this in-depth, such as Bernthal's *Tolkien's Sacramental Vision...* which takes a broader view of the entire Tolkien universe to include his others works beyond Middle-earth. For my part, I am going to touch upon the sacraments that I have not addressed, specific to *The Lord of the Rings* only, and the sacramental world view in general.

What is a Sacramental Worldview?

A sacramental worldview is, in the Christian tradition, seeing the world as God's altar, filled with holy matter not just physical matter.[1] Everything in the world and in the entire universe is perceived as a means to pointing an individual to God, to deepening their relationship with Him, to having communion with Him.[2] As Meister Eckhart writes,

> to live sacramentally we must become somebody who seeks and finds God in all things and at all times, in all places, in all company and in all ways. Then we shall always be able to grow and increase unceasingly and without end.[3]

Tolkien captures in his writing this feeling of "holy matter" that points to and conveys an understanding of deeper realities. For example, within the story itself Sam Gamgee experiences a type of sacramental perception while in Mordor when he sees the beautiful twinkling star, which he perceives to symbolize the temporality of evil and the endurance of goodness.

One of the blocks to not seeing the world sacramentally is the artificial understanding of spirit and matter that seems fairly embedded in western consciousness. This thinking typically posits spirit and matter as contending opposites. It treats matter as something evil or bad as opposed to something

---

1. Stephen Freeman, *Everywhere Present*, Conciliar Press, 2010, p. 52.
2. *Orthodox Study Bible*, Thomas Nelson, 2008, p. 2.
3. *Meister Eckhart: Selected Writings*, selected and translated by Oliver Davies, Penguin Books, 1994, pp. 44-5.

good and created by God as stated in the first chapter of Genesis. It stems from Plato and was perpetuated by the Gnostics early in the first millennium. The early church did not hold to this thinking and neither does the Catholic or Orthodox Churches to this day. Christian thinking has always held that God created spirit and matter and, as Genesis 1 says repeatedly, "It was (and is) good."

Further, traditional Christianity holds that human beings will not have eternal life apart from embodiment. A priest once told me that to say we have bodies is false and borders on heretical because it leads to false thinking. It is correct to say we *are* bodies and to understand that we believe that our bodies and souls are formed at the same time, not one before the other.[4] This comes from what The Bible states in Genesis 2:7 "And the Lord God formed man of the dust of the ground, and breathed into his nostrils the breath of life; and man became a living being." Two aspects of creation are occurring here simultaneously.[5] Christ demonstrates in His resurrection when He returns in a renewed state of body and soul but still retains His wounds (see John 20-21). Christians understand that "For the body is about the soul as a garment; and after laying aside for a time by means of death, we shall resume it again with more splendor."[6] Matter is good and remains inherently so even though it may be polluted and corrupted with sin. Sacraments are material means in which God imparts grace to His people.[7] They reflect the Christian understanding of unity of the spiritual and material and the body and soul. To Christians, matter used in the sacraments is purified and made holy.

The pattern in Tolkien's Middle-earth is clear in that the goodness of the elves, hobbits, dwarves, and men seems to be related to this understanding and reverence for the material world as something sacred and by which they receive and live within grace. For example, the elves create things infused with grace such as *lembas*, rope, and the cloaks which conceal the Company. They are not magic but created with deep love and understanding of the material world created by Ilúvatar. Tolkien reflected both this understanding of sacramental reality and lack thereof in a conversation between Frodo and Sam in Lothlórien. Sam notices a difference between the elves of Lothlórien and other elves. He tells Frodo he cannot tell if these elves made their land or the land made them and that if there is any magic, it is deep, beyond his touch, and Frodo acknowledges this, telling Sam he can "see and feel it

---

4. John Breck, *God With Us: Critical Issues in Christian Life and Faith*, SVS Press, 2003. p. 51.
5. Protopresbyter Michael Pomazansky, *Orthodox Dogmatic Theology*, St. Herman of Alaska Brotherhood, 2009 (Third Edition), p. 124.
6. Father Stanley Harakas, *The Orthodox Church: 455 Questions and Answers*, Light and Life, 1988, p. 99.
7. Op. cit. [2], p. 1786.

everywhere." Yet at the end of their conversation Sam still wants to see what he calls "Elf-magic."[8] This magic, in Tolkien's own words, is

> the artistic, aesthetic, and purely scientific aspects of the human nature raised to a higher level than is actually seen in Men. [Elves] have a devoted love of the physical world, and a desire to observe and understand it for its own sake and as 'other' – sc. as a reality derived from God in the same degree as themselves – not as a material for use or as a power-platform.[9]

Sam, though a gardener who loves created things and certainly is not one to try to exploit them, lacks a depth of sacramental understanding at this point to see the works of the elves properly and defaults to calling them magic. The elves themselves explain that this magic is the result of them putting "the thought of all [they] love into what [they] make."[10] To the elves, the cloaks simply function as they are designed and reflect the love and skill of their makers, but those without the same level of awareness perceive this level of skill as supernatural.

However, Sam seems to understand sacramental reality to a degree because he refers to the "magic" as something deep that he cannot touch. He feels this numinous aspect of sacramental reality though he cannot articulate it. Galadriel tries to help him deepen his understand when she asks if he wants to look into her Mirror. She tells him the Mirror represents what Sam would think of as magic though adds she does not understand what he means since he and his people use the word magic to refer to "the deceits of the Enemy."[11] Sam certainly gains a deeper understanding as the story goes on but this incident serves to also remind us of the sacramental reality Tolkien is conveying in his universe.

Both the Catholic and Orthodox churches hold to a sacramental worldview in general but within both churches they acknowledge seven sacraments that are considered special experiences in the corporate life of the Church, when the perception of God's presence and actions is heightened and celebrated. In these special seven events, God discloses Himself through the prayers and actions of His people.[12] These sacraments are baptism, chrismation of confirmation, the Eucharist or Holy Communion, confession or reconciliation, ordination or holy orders, marriage and unction or anointing the sick. A type of all seven of these sacraments is present in *LotR* in various

---

8. J.R.R. Tolkien, *The Lord of the Rings*, Houghton Mifflin, 1954-5, 1965-6, pp. 351-352.
9. Humphrey Carpenter, *The Letters of J.R.R. Tolkien*, Houghton Mifflin, 2000, Letter 181, p. 236.
10. Op. cit. [8], p. 361.
11. Op. cit., p. 353.
12. "The Sacraments," Rev. Thomas Fitzgerald, https://www.goarch.org/-/the-sacraments. [Accessed 07/06/2018].

ways.

The "Seven Sacraments" in *The Lord of the Rings*

Baptism is the second most prominent sacrament in *LotR*, after the Eucharist as described in Chapter 14. Arguably, unction or anointing the sick, is just as prevalent as baptism considering Gandalf's and Aragorn's Christ-like healing (see Chapters 10 and 11), not to mention Elrond's healing of Frodo. But these instances are more specific and succinct in their time and place. Baptism is more pervasive throughout the entire story.

Baptism, from a Catholic point of view, is the beginning of Christian life. No one is born a Christian. One initially becomes a Christian through the sacrament of baptism and if they embrace the faith, they then live life according to a sacramental worldview. Another function of baptism is that is cleanses a person of sin. It is this cleansing, and renewal, aspect of baptism that is present in *LotR* in many different scenes.

Cleaning and refreshing water dominate the encounter with Tom Bombadil. The hobbits, who have previously been under the spectre of fear, uncertainty and true danger from the Ringwraiths, the Old Forest and Old Man Willow, find renewal and refreshment in the house of Tom Bombadil. The spend an entire day indoors due to the rain, which "fall[s] gently" while Goldberry sings a "rain-song" that fills the hobbits with delight, particularly Frodo who experiences gladness in his heart.[13] Not long after, Frodo has his dream involving the "grey rain-curtain" that is his vision of the West, his final destiny.

The next vivid "baptismal scene" is at the Ford of Bruinen, the understanding of which requires an explanation of chrismation or confirmation. This sacrament is the seal of the Holy Spirit. Just as ordination, or holy orders, is the special sacrament to ordain clergy, the sacrament of Chrismation or Confirmation can be thought of as each Christian's personal ordination of sorts. Christians receive the Holy Spirit, just like the Disciples received the Holy Spirit at Pentecost. It is their personal Pentecost. After they are baptized and chrismated, they begin to understand and pursue their unique vocations in Christ's body, the Church. Also, since Chrismation, or Confirmation, is associated with ordination and calling, this sacrament is present in every page of *LotR* since the story is concerned with characters' callings, ordained events, and how they all work together for good. The formal sacrament of holy orders or ordination is not specifically present but because it functions the same as chrismation/confirmation in the significance of ordination, vocation and callings, it is evoked in that sense.

---

13. Op. cit. [8], p. 127.

The Holy Spirit is often associated with wind and fire, as previously described in Chapter 13. Bernthal points out in his book the blended imagery of water, fire, and wind in this scene of triumph over Sauron's servants. Bernthal notes the following:

> The flames that flicker on the crests of the horses are like the Pentecostal fire. The combination of roar and flame in this passage is so startlingly like the reading of Pentecost, Acts 2:1-11, that one is forced to speculate Tolkien used this Bible passage as a model. With this image, Tolkien directly connects what seem to be opposites, fire and water, which always go together in baptism: water becomes the vehicle for the infusion of spiritual fire, or in Tolkien's myth, the Flame Imperishable.[14]

Types of both sacraments are present though Bernthal only notes baptism. Tolkien is more overt about baptismal imagery in river Nimrodel as the Fellowship moves into Lothlórien. Frodo lets the flow of the river water wash over his feet and feels weariness leave his legs.[15] Here Tolkien focuses again on the cleansing and renewal aspects of baptism. He does the same at Isengard when Treebeard and the Ents use the river Isen to wash away Saruman's filth and evil.[16] When we see Isengard toward the end of the book, it is transformed into a green and growing place again. Tolkien returns to this cleansing motif of water many times before the book is done. After the Battle of the Pelennor Fields, a cleansing rain and wind quenches the fires burning on the battlefield.

Lastly, Bernthal offers the following analysis of the next example of both baptism and confirmation (and the Eucharist). It occurs as the Fellowship is breaking and Sam guesses Frodo is going off alone. He jumps into the river to follow him even though he cannot swim. Frodo rescues him from drowning by pulling him out of the water, in which Sam is fully immersed, and into the boat and tells Sam it is clear they are meant to go together. According to Bernthal, in this scene, "Sam is baptized and confirmed as Frodo's indispensable companion. They will make the final Eucharistic journey as virtually equal partners."[17]

Reconciliation, or confession, is a thread that runs through *LotR* and is the dividing line between positive and negative characters. The most notable confession is that of Boromir who, just before he dies, confesses to Aragorn about trying to take the Ring from Frodo. Though he dies, he is at peace and all indications are that he is reconciled to Ilúvatar. Pippin confesses to

---

14. Craig Bernthal, *Tolkien's Sacramental Vision*, Second Spring, 2014, pp. 153-154.
15. Op. cit. [8], p. 330.
16. Op. cit., p. 555.
17. Op. cit. [14], p. 192.

Gandalf about the palantír and is able to move forward past the incident. Théoden confesses to Gandalf about being in the grip of Wormtongue and he too is healed. Contrast this with prideful and ambitious Denethor and Saruman, who can neither repent nor admit to wrong, and therefore both perish. The narrative allows that had Denethor repented and had Saruman come down from Orthanc when Gandalf bade him to, both could have survived.

Marriage is also a prominent theme in *LotR* and it serves as an indicator of healing, wholeness and unity in the wake of the defeat of evil. Aragorn and Arwen's marriage is a subtle secondary plotline, but turns out to be a main motivator and driver of events and unites men and elves, along with the other two unions – that of Beren and Luthien and Tuor and Idril – between the two races. However, unlike Beren and Luthien and Tuor and Idril, it would seem that Aragorn and Arwen's story comes to a sad end on Cerin Amroth where Arwen dies in grief a year after Aragorn's death.[18] Her death in *The Tale of Aragorn and Arwen* is suffused with autumn fading and solitude. However, is she truly alone? After his own experience that foreshadows his end, Frodo finds Aragorn on Cerin Amroth and sees, as if in a vision, the Ranger dressed in white as a young man. Aragorn says "Arwen vanimelda, namárië" which translates into "Fair Arwen, farewell." He takes Frodo's hand and leaves and Tolkien writes, "he came there never again as living man."[19] The last phrase bears closer inspection. Craig Bernthal in his book *Tolkien's Sacramental Vision*, speculates that Aragorn comes back to Cerin Amroth so that they may leave Middle-earth together. This notion is somewhat not in keeping with the despair that surrounds Arwen's death in *The Tale of Aragorn and Arwen* but it is in keeping with Tolkien's choice on language here. Aragorn is saying farewell to Arwen in memory of leaving her temporarily after they pledge their troth here long ago. He is also saying farewell to her perhaps in some moment of foresight knowing her chosen mortal life will end on this hill and then they will journey united to what lies beyond.

Conclusion

Reading *The Lord of the Rings* through a Christian worldview, and in particular, a sacramental one, can be an enriching experience. Such a worldview engages with existence's best potential: freedom from death and decay, and reflects God's love, beauty, power, and glory. It presents people with the responsibility of good stewardship to the world and its goodness. Whether read through a Christian or a different lens, Tolkien's ability to

---

18. Op. cit. [8], p. 1038.
19. Op. cit., p. 343.

create a beautiful world that feels alive, and characters who fight to preserve that world through commitment, love, and sacrifice stirs many hearts and has been a lasting legacy that draws new generations to his work more than fifty years after its publication. A Christian understanding and reading adds an additional dimension to Tolkien's work because it connects his story to the Gospel which is a story of good news, the defeat of evil, and the promise of a better world. These are the hopes of many, no matter what their belief system. Hopefully, this book, written from a sacramental perspective as it explored the ethos and typology of *The Lord of the Rings*, has added to the rich body of Christian-based Tolkien works.

Author's Note

This book has been a labor of love and I was tempted to continue writing beyond the last chapter. I think of my favorite scene in *The Lord of the Rings*, when the cock crows and Pippin hears the horns of Rohan (getting chills even as I write this), and it reminds me of Peter hearing the cock crowing and weeping with bitter tears. I think of St. Paul writing about how we see through a glass darkly and Gildor's words to Frodo that he will take a dark road. What are the analogies here? There are many other examples I did not touch on. I could write on and on but I feel content that I have written what I have wanted to express in this book about the Christian faith as it comes through in Tolkien's work. My experience in writing it is that it further deepened my experience and a love for *The Lord of the Rings* and I know the next time I sit down to read, likely in Autumn as usual, it will be an even richer experience. My hope is that this book has also enriched your appreciation of Tolkien's work and the deep Christians aspects of it.

A collector's edition of *Echoes of Truth: Christianity in The Lord of the Rings*, illustrated by Elaina Olga, is also available.
Visit www.lunapresspublishing.com.

Acknowledgements

Thank you to my wife and daughter for giving me the time and space to write this book, which was truly a labor of love. I would also like to thank Elaina Olga for her wonderful illustrations and her suggestions for the text that made this a much better book. I would like to offer similar thanks to Francesca Barbini, Anna Milon, and Susan Douglas for their edits and revisions which also made this work superior to what it was in my initial draft. Thank you to the brilliant artist, Jay Johnstone, for connecting me with Luna Press Publishing. I would also like to offer a general thanks to all of the authors that have written on the Christian aspects of Tolkien's work for inspiring me to dare to offer my own contribution to this body of work. Lastly, I would like to thank J.R.R. Tolkien himself for creating such a profound work which has enriched me for more than forty years of my life, and to his son Christopher for continuing his father's great legacy.

Bibliography

Bernthal, Craig. *Tolkien's Sacramental Vision*, Second Spring, 2014.

Breck, John. *God With Us: Critical Issues in Christian Life and Faith*, SVS Press, 2003.

Brown, Devon. *The Christian World of The Hobbit*, Abingdon Press, 2012.

Brunner, Kurt and Ware, Jim. *Finding God in The Lord of the Rings*, Tyndale, 2001.

Caldecott, Stratford. *The Power of the Ring: Spiritual Vision Behind the Lord of the Rings and The Hobbit*, Crossroad Publishing Company, 2003.

Carpenter, Humphrey. *The Letters of J.R.R. Tolkien*, Houghton Mifflin, 2000.

Chance, Jane. *The Lord of the Rings: The Mythology of Power* (Revised Edition), The University Press of Kentucky, 2011.

Dickerson, Matthew. *A Hobbit Journey*, Brazos Press, 2012.

Dickerson, Matthew and O'Hara, David. *From Homer to Harry Potter*, Brazo Press, 2006.

Drought, Michael D.C. (Editor). *J.R.R. Tolkien Encyclopedia – Scholarship and Critical Assessment*, "Free Will" by Daniel Thomas.

Flieger, Verilyn. *Splintered Light: Logos and Language in Tolkien's World*, Kent State University Press, 2002.

Freeman, Stephen. *Everywhere Present*, Conciliar Press, 2010.

Guinness, Os. *The Call*, Word Publishing, 1998.

Haldas, Michael C. *Sacramental Living: Understanding Christianity as a Way of Life*, Eastern Christian Publications, 2013.

Hammond, Wayne G. and Scull, Christina. *The Lord of the Rings: A Reader's Companion*, Houghton Mifflin, 2005.

Harakas, Stanley, Father. *The Orthodox Church: 455 Questions and Answers, Light and Life*, 1988.

Hopko, Thomas. *Ecumenical Review 51 no 4*, 1999.

Hutton, Ronald. "The Pagan Tolkien", *The Ring and the Cross: Christianity in the Lord of the Rings*, Madison Teaneck Fairleigh Dickinson University Press, 2001.

Julian of Norwich, *The Revelations of Divine Love*, Wyatt North Publishing, 2014.

Kerry, Paul E. (Editor). *The Ring and the Cross*, Farleigh Dickinson, 2011.

Kilby, Clyde S. *Tolkien and the Silmarillion*, Harold Shaw Publishers, 1976.

Kreeft, Peter. *The Philosophy of Tolkien*, Ignatius, 2005.

Lewis, C.S. *Mere Christianity*, Macmillan, 1960.

Life Application Study Bible, Tyndale, 1996.

Manlove, Colin. *Modern Fantasy: Five Studies*, Cambridge University Press, 1978.

Markides, Kyriacos C. *Inner River*, Image Books, 2012.

Markos, Louis. *On the Shoulders of Hobbits,* Moody Publishers, 2012.

Meister Eckhart: Selected Writings, selected and translated by Oliver Davies, Penguin Books, 1994.

Muir, Edwin. "Strange Epic", *The Observer* [London], 22 August 1954.

Nelson, Thomas. *Orthodox Study Bible*, 2008.

Pearce, Joseph. *Bilbo's Journey: Discovering the Hidden Meaning in "The Hobbit"*, Saint Benedict Press, 2012.

Peck, M. Scott. *People of the Lie*, Simon and Schuster, 1983.

Pomazansky, Michael, Protopresbyter. *Orthodox Dogmatic Theology*, St. Herman of Alaska Brotherhood, 2009 (Third Edition).

Purtill, Richard. *J.R.R Tolkien: Myth, Morality and Religion*, Ignatius Press, 1984.

Reilly, R. J. *Romantic Religion*, Lindisfarne Books. 2006.

Schmemann, Alexander, Father. *For the Life of the World*, SVS Press, 1963.

Scott, Olof, Father. *Come Receive the Light,* Orthodox radio program, May 8, 2007.

Shippey, Tom. *J.R.R. Tolkien: Author of the Century*, Houghton Mifflin, 2000.

Shippey, Tom. *The Road to Middle-earth*, Houghton Mifflin, 2002.

Synder, Christopher. *The Making of Middle-earth*, Sterling Publishing, 2013.

Tolkien, J.R.R. *Morgoth's Ring*, Houghton Mifflin, 1993.

Tolkien, J.R.R. "On Fairy Stories", *Tales from the Perilous Realm*, HarperCollins, 2008.

Tolkien, J.R.R. *The Lord of the Rings*, Houghton Mifflin,1954-5, 1965-6.

Tolkien, J.R.R. *The Hobbit*, Houghton Mifflin,1937, 1966, 1994, 1996.

Tolkien, J.R.R. *The Silmarillion*, Houghton Mifflin, 1977.

Tolkien, J.R.R. *Unfinished Tales of Númenor and Middle-earth*, Houghton Mifflin,1980.

Tolkien, J.R.R. and Swann, Donald. *The Road Goes Ever On*, Houghton Mifflin, 1978.

Tolkien, J.R.R. and Tolkien, Christopher. *The War of the Jewels, "Part Four: Quendi and Eldar: Appendix D"*, 1959-60.

Ware, Jim. *Finding God in The Hobbit*, SaltRiver, 2006.

www.ingramcontent.com/pod-product-compliance
Lightning Source LLC
Chambersburg PA
CBHW071346080526
44587CB00017B/2988